Ken Hathaway comes from a family of clerics, with his father and two brothers also being ministers. Following his training for the ministry, he served for a number of years in a country parish before taking up a teaching post in a minor public school where he became head of the department, sixth form tutor and deputy head. He was also invited to act as an examiner at A levels by the Oxford Local Exam Board before developing his interests in business, whilst continuing his ministry. He also published a number of articles. This book is the product of his years in teaching and church ministry, in which he came to recognise the need for a more modern approach to reading the Bible.

In memory of my father, Rev W. G. Hathaway, to whom I owe so much.

In grateful thanks for the loving support of my wife, Julien.

Ken Hathaway

A New Introduction to the Bible

Austin Macauley Publishers™

LONDON • CAMBRIDGE • NEW YORK • SHARJAH

Scriptures quoted are from the *Good News Bible* published by the Bible Societies/Harper Collins Publishers Ltd UK © American Bible Society 1966, 1971, 1976, 1992.

A CIP catalogue record for this title is available from the British Library.

ISBN 9781398419421 (Paperback)
ISBN 9781398419438 (Hardback)
ISBN 9781398419445 (ePub e-book)

www.austinmacauley.com

First Published 2023
Austin Macauley Publishers Ltd®
1 Canada Square
Canary Wharf
London
E14 5AA

With grateful thanks to my colleague, Rev Tony Hearle, for his encouragement.

Introduction

Many people today, in the twenty-first century, want to dismiss the Bible as being out of date, irrelevant to modern society, relating to a small nation of deeply religious people but not reflecting modern society or the advances made in the understanding of man and his environment by modern scientific method. It is obvious that our knowledge of our history, the understanding of our genetic structure and the workings of the human brain have come about through the enormous advances made relatively recently by science, whilst the scientific advances in travel, communication and engineering are beyond the imagination of even fifty years ago. Equally, our knowledge of the universe acquired by space exploration is beyond anything which could have been envisaged one hundred years ago when mechanical flight was in its infancy.

Nevertheless, philosophically, to our knowledge, man has been exploring the meaning and purpose of life for at least some three thousand years. For example, we know that the Egyptians and, later, the Greeks and the Romans were doing this, as evidenced by our archaeological exploration and their writings. Archaeological studies of ancient civilisations have suggested that man's knowledge was possibly more extensive than had previously been realised. So we must not fall into the trap of thinking that the search for truth and understanding are confined to our current and recent centuries, whilst our reading of Greek and Latin literature discloses a vigorous search for the meaning of things, which is challenging to our minds today.

We also have to accept that what the Greeks explored some 3,000 years ago still has value for us today. In fact, many of our institutional ideas are based on theories first proposed by the Greeks, for example, the concept and practice of democracy. Their ability to reason and explore concepts means that their ideas still resonate with us today. The Greek poets like Aeschylus and Sophocles explored the purpose and meaning of life, often by re-enacting ideas dramatically on the stage, as they did with political ideas. The Latin poets, in exploring their legends, were seeking to understand the vicissitudes of human existence, often by dramatizing human emotional responses. Their ideas are still valid today because they were looking for a different 'truth' from scientific 'truth'. Even in those days, they had different approaches in their exploration, as for example Aristotle, who was a marine biologist, argued a priori from the observable fact to the principle, whereas Plato used Socratic dialogue to explore ideas intellectually, claiming that if even a novice were asked the right questions, he would be able to find the right answers.

In the same way, the Bible, written in many cases at a similar period in history to the Greeks, is exploring not scientific fact but ideas about man's character and his response to hardship, adversity and temptation and also his place in the universe. The difference is that in the Bible, the ultimate knowledge rests with God, and in that sense, to find Truth, one must first find God. So the Bible becomes a record of man's search for God as the ultimate truth and the ways in which progressively God has made Himself known through the events of history and the beliefs of certain men and women, culminating with the final revelation through Jesus Christ who stated, "He that hath seen Me hath seen the Father."

In this, there is no conflict between science and Christianity because they are completely different subjects. Science in its search for 'truth' mainly relies on observable evidence, and as Christians, we must not challenge that at all. Scientific fact is observed truth, and its unfolding revelation can bring us closer to the knowledge of the 'how' of creation so that now we have a much better idea of the way, the manner, in which what is has developed. The Bible is not concerned with that kind of knowledge; it is concerned with what science and academic study cannot define. It is concerned with that other dimension of humanity what has been described as the 'soul', that undefinable something which reaches out consciously or unconsciously to find the 'why' which has driven mankind from its earliest awakening of conscious thought to find an answer. It has given rise to various potential answers, often driven by limited knowledge. For example, the anthropological answers to human emotions, linking love, hate, envy, jealousy to gods; or the giving of names and personality to the forces of nature, the oceans, the wind, fire, the sun and moon and the planets and so on. The desire to placate unseen causes, to bring about fecundity, to regulate the seasons, to fulfil that untold hunger which exists in the human psyche. Even knowledge itself is an evidence of a something which cannot be explained by science. We cannot define what the emotion of 'love' is, or genius, but we know when we experience it and can observe its effect on others who experience it.

In the same way, much of the Bible concerns the observable effect on people who have had an experience of God. This was the basis of early Christian experience, when men and women who had met God in Jesus were prepared not only to die for their faith but whose lives were revolutionised by it. For example, the recorded changes in the lives and character of men like the disciples, Peter, James and John, Stephen and later the highly intelligent and educated Saul of Tarsus, the avid persecutor of Jesus, whose life and whose thinking were to provide the early Church with much of its theological doctrine.

The Bible, which is the source of our study, is a collection both of writings from a number of different authors written over a period of over 1,000 years and a verbally transmitted record of family history. Right at the start, one must state two things. First, that when we say that this is God's Word, what that really means is that the writings were written by human beings who felt that what they wrote was inspired by their experiences of God. "All scripture is inspired by God and is profitable for reproof, for instruction" (2 Timothy 3:16). Yet although inspired, the actual writers were subject to many of the human limitations of understanding and interpretation typical of their age. Later, the compilers recognised a certain defined spiritual connotation which marked the chosen scriptures from the many other extant writings which were not included. However, as the earliest-known writings date from the third century BC, in the main the older parts of their history were passed down verbally.

Then secondly, it is also important to realise that 'TRUTH' takes two forms: Literal Truth, that is what can be evidenced and verified by other sources, and Spiritual Truth, namely what the Holy Spirit can teach or we can discover from what may or may not be literal truth, such as an analogy, parable or metaphor. In other words, an account in scripture does not have to be literally true in order to contain spiritual truth. This is how God speaks to us through ordinary events and writings.

Jesus, for example, taught the ordinary people of his day by using parables which, in my young days, were defined as, "an earthly story with a heavenly meaning." Yet frequently, those people were unable to 'understand' the significance which lay behind the story. Even the disciples often required further explanation from Jesus.

An example of this in the Old Testament is the book of Job. Whether a man called Job actually existed is much less important than the truths which the book teaches. Note that this book was written at a time when the Greek writers were also exploring similar themes, notably the issue raised by several of their dramatists – why does the good man suffer? Aristotle, in his critical study, *The Poetics*, whilst relegating 'poetry' to the realm of unscientific knowledge, does admit that this method of searching for Truth can have benefits. For example, when an audience watches the portrayal of human frailty or tragedy, by observation, the persons watching can learn valuable lessons. Indeed, writing many hundreds of years later, Shakespeare in England takes up the same concepts in his own tragedy plays, like *King Lear*, *Hamlet* and *Romeo and Juliet*, where he also asks very similar questions of how and why.

Noteworthy in this book of Job is that the so-called friends of Job all use variations of the ideas which were common in their day as an explanation of what has happened to poor old Job, that is, that basically Job must have behaved very badly in order to bring this terrible judgement on himself or, as the |Greeks would have put it, he was the victim of 'fate'.

The Bible, as we know it, was formed by selecting from the many manuscripts which had been written presumably because the editors believed that they were faithful to the main thrust of scripture and were useful (2 Timothy 3:16) for teaching spiritual truth; but the canon of the Old Testament was not formally recognised until circa 314 AD even though it was in existence much earlier in the Hebrew language and later in Greek from about 250 BC. And the same is true of the New Testament which circulated from relatively soon after our Lord's resurrection as a series of letters and collections of recollections but was not assembled as a complete document until about 100 years later.

However, by this time, around 140 AD, there was a general consensus that the scriptures collected together as The Bible were worthy of inclusion and that the very many other manuscripts were not, comprising in many cases fanciful tales of Jesus' childhood and events which did not carry that sense of authenticity. The Bible was intended to be seen as a human record of the way in which God has revealed himself to mankind and one which showed, in human terms, the way in which God was achieving this – that He, God, is the ultimate creator of all things and that this is an unfolding revelation of man's growing knowledge of God, as in turn, man became increasingly capable of understanding and responding to that revelation.

Beginning, after an introduction, with the introduction of two representative people who are faced with a moral choice, that of obedience, which in itself introduces the concept of a superior moral being, we are led to the development of a God people. This was to continue through people like the descendants of Noah's son Shem, who became the ancestor of the Semitic people through one family, the children of Abraham, who himself had come to a personal knowledge of God in a remarkable manner. Here, the two Abrahamic Faiths find their source: the Jews through the miraculous birth of Isaac to parents who were far too old for childbearing and Islam through the natural son Ishmael, born to a concubine.

Through the miraculous birth of Isaac, the God line become more distinctive. It deals with the social and spiritual development of a people from wandering Bedouin tribespeople to a powerful nation which will be united into one by the king named David and brought to its height of power under his son Solomon, only to be divided into two by the poor behaviour of Solomon's son Rehoboam.

From that point on, the kingdom was seen as two nations, Israel to the North with its Capital Samaria and Judah to the South with its capital Jerusalem. These nations were then conquered progressively by the Assyrians and the Babylonians, who were in turn were replaced by the Persians who then, after some seventy years, allowed the Jews of the Southern kingdom to return to Jerusalem and rebuild the city and its Temple. Then followed a period of Jewish independence which led to their final conquest by the Romans.

At this point, we are introduced to the new 'prophet' whose coming had been foretold and who was expected but who, when he came, was completely misunderstood and rejected by the Jewish leaders but whose coming, life and remarkable ministry and whose death by crucifixion and resurrection to life, as recorded in the books of the New Testament, would become the instigator of a new revelation of God, leading to the foundation of a new worldwide order, based on the ideas first introduced in the Old Testament which would bypass the Jews, because of their failure to recognise their Messiah, but not exclude them from a future destiny, and which would reach out to the whole of the rest of the world.

We must remember, as we read the Bible, that the earliest records were not written records but verbal memories passed down and probably collected by certain 'elders' or priests. Therefore, one can expect variation in the records as different people record similar events. Equally when it comes to interpretation, different readers may well be struck or impressed by different aspects of the same passage.

The earliest written records probably began about 700 BC or earlier and were written by the scribes on parchment scrolls in Hebrew. These were subsequently incorporated into the collection we know as the Old Testament by around 200/150 BC. And it is this that our Lord would have studied as a child and his disciples would have taught from. This was later copied and translated into Greek by a committee of 70 Jewish scribes and became known as the Septuagint. From the European view, the next major version of Scripture was the one translated by Jerome into Latin, around 405 AD, which was a revised version using both Greek and Hebrew texts and produced as a handwritten copy during the fifth century. These were then copied over the centuries in Latin by the monks.

In Anglo-Saxon, the earliest-known versions were the translation of St John by Bede, eighth century, and the Psalms by Alfred, ninth century. The first English Bible was that produced by John Wycliffe in 1384. Then came two startling changes, first the discovery of printing by Gutenberg in Germany and the writings of Martin Luther in 1522 and then the rediscovery of classical Latin and Greek, in what became known in Europe as the Renaissance. These led to the first bibles printed in English, that of the New testament by William Tyndale in 1526 and then the first full English Bible, that of Miles Coverdale in 1535. Finally, in 1611, we had the Authorised Version, translated and printed under the authority of James 1st, and it was this version which was used in homes, churches and schools up until modern times, when the so-called modern translations appeared in the twentieth century.

It becomes quite obvious that the earliest compilers relied on several different manuscripts and verbal memories. For example, there are two different versions of Creation in the beginning of Genesis, Chapters 1 and 2. Whilst these are different, they are not contradictory; rather they are complimentary, i.e., two different views of what God did, written at different times by people who were not present when it happened. We also know that other similar versions of creation were written into the literature of other nations. The main difference being that the other versions referred to a variety of gods participating, whereas the Jewish version is totally monotheistic. In other words, where other nations believed in many gods, the Jews from day one believed in one God.

It is important to remember that from earliest times until the destruction of the Temple in Jerusalem under the Babylonian Invasion, the focal point of all

Jewish worship had been, first, the Tabernacle, the tent-like moveable structure constructed to a very precise detail, which the Israelite priests carried during their wanderings in the wilderness after their exodus from Egypt; and then, later, the Temple built by Solomon on Mount Moriah in Jerusalem.

When this temple was destroyed under the emperor Nebuchadnezzar in 586 BC and the Jews were carried away captive into Babylon, the scribes began to accumulate the ancient writings, and they in turn became their point of reference. And although the Temple was subsequently rebuilt by authority of the Persians some seventy years later, the priests resorted to putting their corporate memories into a written form, to maintain their traditional religious practice, and as a focus of their history, as a practical illustration of the way in which God had 'personally' formed and guided them as a nation. This nation was, therefore, to become a physical revelation of the power of God but also of his justice and of his love and, most of all, a way of showing how God was making himself known to mankind, all recorded through the events of their history.

Sadly, after the temple was destroyed, the sacrificial rituals were fragmentary and not listed until, under the authority of the Persian Dynasty and its Emperor Cyrus, the Jews were allowed, encouraged even, to return to their own land and given authority and funds to rebuild the temple (as recorded by Ezra and Nehemiah) and the city, and then, the written records having been read to them by the scholar Ezra, Temple worship was re-established, only to be destroyed twice more – the last under the Romans in AD 70.

It is most important to state at this point that modern scientific discoveries do nothing to undermine or challenge the spiritual statements of the Bible, and Christianity is NOT in conflict with modern science, as many modern scientists have declared. Rather, the more science discovers about the wonders of space and the intricate working of the human body, the more one marvels at the power, the compassion, the majesty, the absolute immensity of 'GOD' the Creator. We also know that this book has not only endured for over 2,000 years but its impact on those who followed it has been enormous. It has changed lives.

In the nineteenth century, the established order of society and the beliefs of the Church appeared to be undermined by the ideas advanced by scientific discovery, and 'faith' and belief were shaken from their orthodoxy by the publication of Charles Darwin's book on the evolution of the species. However, the idea that humanity may have taken a vast period of time to reach this level of sophistication, as we know it today, does not militate against the concept of God as the creator and His revelation of Himself as recorded in the Bible. Knowledge in the past century, for example, has increased at an exponential rate.

What we can say is that the Bible appears as an inspired record of the way in which God was revealing himself to a developing humanity and that man was himself making discoveries about God. But do not write Scripture off as totally unscientific, because modern archaeology has revealed that many things written there can be verified by external reference; rather see the Bible as the record of a journey of discovery so that, as we see evidenced, our God is a God of love who created the world as we know it for a personal and collective purpose of involving the people He had made, making sin the disobedience to His plans for us, redemption possible through the sacrificial life and death of His own Son, and the possibility of an eternal existence which, unknowable to us, He has planned.

Genesis

The Old Testament, which is comprised of 39 books, deals almost exclusively with the history of one nation, from Exodus to Malachi. The first book, Genesis, covers a period of some 1,000 years and serves as an introduction to the rest of the Old Testament by taking us up to the life of Abraham who is revered as the father of the tribes which will comprise the rest of the Old Testament.

It begins with two accounts of how this earth was formed and how it was populated. Do not be put off by the apparent contradiction between modern history, archaeology and geology and this book. Basically, the original writers had no idea of how, what or why the earth came into being and no means of finding out or understanding if they did. However, most religions of the same period had also devised an account of the beginning, for example, Hinduism, Sikhism, Buddhism and later Islam, to fill the gap in their knowledge.

When the writers of the Bible began, they used what was an accepted (in their time) account, but where the others saw creation as being the work of several gods, the Jewish writers, knowing by this time that there was only one God, made the creator one God, and then as an instrument for teaching, they added the origin of sin, as a story which was simply the act of disobedience. To this, under inspiration, they included in the Adam and Eve story, the promise of someone to come (seed of the woman) who would break the power of sin and deliver humanity from evil (crush the serpent).

So right from day one, we have the precognition of what would be fulfilled in the New Testament, in the coming of the Son of God as the redeemer of humanity, in the 'seed of the woman'. This is indicative of the unity of scripture as we have it. For in these opening chapters of the Book, we have clearly outlined for us a number of basic principles which will underline the whole Book. For example, right from the beginning, God is seen as a God of Covenant. His relationship with Adam and Eve, with Noah, with Abraham involved His promise of benefits and blessings but which required, in return, obedience and trust so that the people concerned were to believe and then to act upon that belief in order to activate the terms of the Covenant. In some cases, they had to act first, like Noah, and receive the fulfilment later. The same with Abraham to whom God gave a son in his old age and promised, amongst other things, that he, Abraham, would become the father of a great nation and that he would also be given a whole new country to call his own – and all this promised to a wandering Aramean, a Bedouin tribesman, who followed his flocks and herds.

This principle is well-illustrated in the case of Adam and Eve. The issue for them was not an apple or any metaphorical interpretation of that fruit. No, it is a clear example of God stipulating certain requirements as part of an agreement, which Adam and Eve lost by their disobedience. This can be seen as an example of the institution of a moral authority, of law and order and the recognition of a higher allegiance than to human laws.

It is John Milton, in his monumental seventeenth-century poem *Paradise Lost*, who puts his finger on the problem. He begins his opening statement: "Of man's first disobedience and the fruit of that forbidden tree whose mortal taste brought death into the world and all its woe, with loss of Eden, 'til one greater man restore us, sing heavenly muse that on the top of Horeb…" However, it is not until book 9 of that poem, that he introduces the human element when, after Eve has eaten and will face the consequences, he portrays Adam as torn between his love for Eve and obedience to God and, being human, he chooses in love to eat and face those consequences with his partner, rather than be isolated and continue a mystical relationship with God.

Once again, the book of Genesis is to set the theme of an awesome and feared deity of immense power, challenging human beings who are subject to human desires, which desires may be right in themselves but may be in conflict with one's relationship with God.

Later, as this relationship between God and man develops, one is introduced to the aspect of a God whose love for humanity will, in mercy, be demonstrated by his willingness to forgive and pardon. Yet like a responsible father, He knows that it is necessary to discipline as well as to help, in order to shape mankind. Ultimately, the enormity of the love of God will be revealed more fully in the New Testament through the sacrificial love of Jesus on the Cross: "For God so loved the world that He gave His only begotten Son." (John 3:16).

As we move on, it is quite clear from a studied reading of the early chapters that there were other people on earth at the time of Adam and Eve. For example, when Cain kills Abel, he is marked so that no one else will kill him, and he then goes out, marries a wife and builds a city. In other words, Genesis is the genealogical beginning of a race of people who would become the people of God, namely the Jews; it is not a history of the whole human race. It is evident that for this purpose, God chose certain individuals. Abel was accepted, Cain not. Out of Noah's three sons, it was Shem who became the ancestor of the Jewish nation. In the case of Abraham, Isaac the son born miraculously to parents way beyond childbearing age became the progenitor of the 'God line' through whom the nation of Israel, the Jews, would be created, whilst Ishmael the son born to the 'servant' Hagar becomes, ultimately, the progenitor of Islam. In other words, we see a race of people separated by their faith in God and obedience to his purpose from the rest of humanity.

What is so important about Genesis is that right from day one, there is a distinction between those who were acceptable to God and those who were not, with a clear statement as to why this was the case, most commonly, that reason being whether or not they believed in God and in faith obeyed him – as indeed both Noah and Abraham did. In each case, the choice was made on the basis of, what we later learn, was God's knowledge of these people, their character often being defined by their actions, which showed a confidence or trust in Jehovah together with the willingness to act upon that; in other words, the ability to respond to God.

After Adam and Eve, the next major event (Chapter 6) is illustrated in the life of Noah. As the population of the earth increased, wickedness became dominant. To reduce this prevalence of evil, God chose one man and his family and, by means of a massive flood, separated one good man and his family from the rest. Historically, we do not know the extent of this flood. Whether it was confined to the area of the rivers Euphrates and Tigris or more extensive, we do not know, but the principle was there – the separating and choice of the one line of heredity. What is remarkable is that as early in the Bible as this, there was evidence of supernatural events, whether it be in Noah's pre-knowledge of the coming flood as a result of which he built a huge boat on dry land or simply the ability to construct such a large vessel to a given design, at a time when boats were relatively small and of simple construction. The other interesting thing about the story of Noah is that it resulted in the introduction of another covenant between God and man. (Chapter 9:8).

In Chapter 11, we have the account of a tower built to reach the heavens and the reaction in the confusion of languages. What we now know is that such towers were a feature of that area and that time, known to us as ziggurats. Again, this might well be a later interpretation put on the two facts, the building of the towers and the fact that there was a diversity of languages. Once again, the writers put a religious interpretation on these events for teaching purposes.

Now, Chapter 12, we have the introduction of the person Abram whom the Jews would later describe as the 'father' of their nation. This was the beginning of God's choice of a whole nation of people through whom he could make himself known to the rapidly increasing population of the rest of the planet. Abram, later named Abraham, was to become the founding father of twelve tribes, whose history was intended to reveal the purpose of God in creation to the rest of the world and whose history would demonstrate to the rest of the world, the enormous love and power of this eternal creator God but also demonstrate quite clearly the consequences of obedience or disobedience to his will. But first, we need to know the character and life of the man whose progeny would, through history, right up to this present day, provide evidence of the love, the power and the purpose of God in creating the world in the first place. Their history and their relationship with their God would shape the history of the whole of the rest of the world.

This is a remarkable story because it recounts in some detail the life and actions of a 'chosen' man Abram, later called Abraham. It shows him as a man of trust and belief in his God who is so very different from the gods of his neighbours. However, the ancestral list of the previous chapter shows him also to be descended from one of Noah's sons, Shem. In other words, he has history, a Godly history which, even after so many intervening years, is emerging once again. He, Abram, is singled out by God and noted by the scribes, later, as a man with a purpose, a man chosen by God for a specific purpose.

In order that God might be able to reveal his purpose and his character through this man, he will have to be subjected to the most strenuous tests. The first being that, in order for him to fulfil his intended purpose, he must leave his family and kindred in Mesopotamia and move to a land far to the East, which would ultimately become, after many centuries, the land of inheritance. The importance of this action is highlighted many years later by St Paul in his Letter to the Hebrews 11:8 when he refers to Abraham in the words, "It was faith made Abraham obey when God called him to go out to a country which God promised to give him." Verse 10 then states, "For Abraham was waiting for the city which God had designed and built, the city with permanent foundations." In other words, Abraham was living on two levels, the purely physical, that of emigrating to a new country, and yet at the same time, he was looking for something which had a future purpose. This duality of intent, having a purpose other than the material one, will characterise the future generations.

Some years after they first settle in this new land, there is a severe famine, and the family move to Egypt where, unlike the mountainous Canaan, the country is sustained by the river Nile and watered by the annual flood. Here it is that Abram fails the next test, when instead of trusting God, he relies on deceit to save his wife Sarai who was very beautiful from the attentions of the king, stating that his wife is his sister. Actually, she was his half-sister. This also marks the beginning of the family's tempestuous relationship with one of the greatest nations of the time, Egypt, but it also shows just how fragile, how very human, the early God people were.

It is now (Chapter 15) that we have a few personal glimpses into Abram's life, leading to him having a vision in which he hears God promising to bless him and make him the father of a great nation. Now come a remarkable series of incidents. Abram complains to God that he has no heir, and God promises that, aged 90, his wife being about 80, they will have a son, and despite their incredulity, a son, Isaac, is born.

Then when this boy is about 16 and Abraham is well over 100 years of age, God challenges Abraham with the most serious test of his life. All of Abraham's hopes of this glorious future depend on the son, Isaac, but God now asks him to offer that son as a sacrifice, the ultimate test of his trust. Remarkably, Abraham obeys but does so believing that, when it comes to it, his God will provide – namely, replace his son with an alternative sacrifice. Note how in Chapter 22:5, the father says to his servants, "Wait here until WE return," both of them. Isaac, aged 16, also asks a similar question, "Here is the wood and the fire, but where is the sacrifice?" to which Abraham simply replies, "God will provide." And He does with the provision of a lamb.

Here again, we have a very early indication of what the New Testament will later reveal, simply that, as in the case of Abraham and Isaac, God in his love is willing to replace our sinful selves by the sacrifice of His only Son (John 3:16). In other words, through incidents like these, the integrity of Scripture is evidenced throughout, first Adam, then Noah and now Abraham, revealing by their actions that God has a plan for the world which they do not fully understand. It is only with hindsight, as we look back, that we can see how the plan unfolds, culminating in these hopes and promises being fulfilled in the life and work of God's Son, Jesus Christ. And that is why to understand the New Testament more fully, we need to look back at the Old Testament. They are not two separate books so much as two distinct phases in God's revealing of his purpose to us.

Another significant event is when Abraham, old and dying, makes his oldest servant swear that he will go and find a wife from Abraham's relatives and not from the neighbouring Godless tribes, which the servant does in another remarkable display of providential guidance. He asks God for certain signs so that the young woman will reveal herself as the right choice by performing certain duties. And the young woman, who turns out to be the daughter of one of Abraham's kinsmen, welcomes the servant, and her father finally agrees that his daughter Rebekah should return with the servant to marry his master's son, Isaac; the daughter also taking a step of trust, or belief, in consenting to marry someone whom she has never met. What a love story ending.

Following this love union, twins are born to Isaac and Rebekah, the eldest being the macho hunter Esau who soon won his father's heart. The younger twin Jacob was quieter, a meditative lad whose loving nature won his mother's heart. We are later to learn that Jacob was God's choice even though the father, Isaac, favoured the elder lad Esau. Here, once again, we see an element of choice rather than an arbitrary decision, as Esau sells his birth right to Jacob for a quick meal when he is starving with hunger from a long day out hunting, and the younger brother takes the birth right which he values. This in turn presents problems when their father is about to give his blessing and the inheritance to Esau, and Rebekah, his mother, realises that Isaac, their father, even though he is blind, will recognise the imposition of her favourite, Jacob, and so devises a simple deception by making the younger lad appear to be his brother by covering him with animal skin.

When their father dies, Jacob has to leave home in a hurry to avoid his brother's anger. However, having been warned by his father not to marry into the foreign tribes amongst whom they are living, Jacob sets off to find a bride from amongst his father's relatives. On the way, he has a remarkable dream of a ladder between earth and heaven, with angels of the Lord ascending and descending, with a vision of the Lord standing at the top, who revealed himself as the God of his ancestor Abraham and promised him that the great Covenant which he had made with Abraham would be renewed in him, Jacob. Jacob then vows that if God will protect and provide for him and enable him to return home in safety, he will worship God in that place and give him a tenth of everything that he will earn – again, a conditional agreement.

Then, a repeat of his father's experience. In answer to his prayer, Jacob meets the same branch of his father's family and falls for one of the daughters, the very beautiful Rachel. Jacob then contracts to work for his father-in-law, Laban, for seven years as a bride price. The story tells how Jacob's love for Rachel was so great that the seven years seemed only like days. Unfortunately for both Jacob and Rachel, on the wedding night, Laban substitutes the elder daughter Lear, and when daylight comes, Jacob is furious. Is this a recompense for his seven years of hard work?

However, the matter is resolved when Laban agrees that after the seven days of wedding celebration are over, he will give him Rachel as well. But all is not well, for whilst Lear produces several sons and daughters, Rachel is barren until, many years later, she gives birth to a son whom she names Joseph. And here again, it is Joseph who will become the one who will deliver the family, albeit having to suffer greatly as a direct result of his brothers' jealousy.

In the meantime, Jacob accuses Laban of cheating him of his wages. He had worked fourteen years for his two wives and then a further six years for his flocks. In this also, Laban tried to cheat him by not paying the agreed wage, so they devise a system by which Jacob's flocks and herds can be distinguished from Laban's. It is soon evident that God is prospering Jacob to the point where the two have to separate, and taking his two wives, their children and all his animals, Jacob leaves Mesopotamia (which is where his ancestors still lived and from which God had called Jacob's grandfather Abraham) to return home, which means having to face his brother Esau.

For all his fears, when the two brothers finally meet, Esau is very friendly, but when Esau returns to his home in Edom, Jacob goes on into the land of Canaan and settles there.

The narrative then continues to follow the chosen line through Jacob's sons, and we are introduced to the jealousy which arises between Joseph, the son born late to Rachel, and his brothers. The jealousy arose through two particular things. First, as the son of Jacob's favourite wife, his first love Rachel, their father had favoured Joseph, giving him as a mark of favour a coat of many colours, and secondly, Joseph had two strange dreams foretelling a future time when his family would be dependent upon him and subject to his authority.

The brothers, jealous of him, seize an opportunity when Joseph is alone with them to sell him to passing traders, and he ends up in Egypt as servant to Potiphar, the captain of the king's guard. Here he rises to prominence as a trusted servant, until Potiphar's wife attempts to seduce him and in frustration accuses him of attempted rape. Joseph ends up in prison where again he gains favour and is given a trusted role by the jailor. Here his unique status is shown by the fact that he is able to correctly interpret the dreams of Pharaoh's butler and baker who had also been imprisoned. Many years later, the butler is reminded of Joseph when Pharaoh has two dreams which none of his advisers can interpret. Telling Pharaoh the story of Joseph's ability to interpret, he suggests that Pharaoh send for Joseph from prison. Again, God gives Joseph the ability to correctly foretell that there will be seven years of famine in Egypt, and Joseph comes up with a plan to remediate the situation by storing corn during the years of plenty, to which Pharaoh responds by putting him in charge of the work, giving him a high rank next only to the Pharaoh himself.

In this role, he will later on be able to provide for his own family back in Canaan when they are reduced to starvation in the prolonged famine. Like his father and grandfather before him, Joseph is subjected to severe trials and testing to demonstrate to himself and to others the blessings which come from being true to oneself and to God. However, the writers or compilers of the narrative, obviously, had a further purpose in mind, for they were showing that the leaders of the bloodline from Abraham were being chosen for their fortitude, yes, but especially for their relationship with their God. However, what we can now see, with hindsight, is that in their way, they were illustrating, all these years early in history, that one day a child would emerge who in adult life would become the greatest deliverer of all mankind, that each of these events was foreshadowing the life and work of God's only begotten son, the Lord Jesus Christ.

The account of the way in which Joseph tests his brothers when they come to buy food, his emotional response to the fact that his father is still alive, and his deeply emotional reunion as he forgives his brothers, is well worth reading in detail in chapters 44 and 45. And the eventual journey of seventy of his relatives, all of his immediate family, to live in Egypt and their welcome by the Egyptians because of their respect for Joseph, is a remarkable account full of this sense of a purpose of there being a preordained plan of events and circumstances having a far-reaching purpose which we are able to recognise when we read the New Testament.

Undoubtedly, this was the purpose behind the recording of these remarkable events which distinguished the family of Abraham, events which would lead to the fulfilment of a covenant which God had made with Abraham all those years ago. The reward for Abraham's faith, trust and obedience to God were to serve as a lesson, as an illustration, a preparation for the founding of that nation called Israel, which is picked up so graphically later on in words by the prophet Hosea (Chapter 11) who uses the failure of his nation in their past history to rebuke the unbelief of his own day yet reminding them of God's love for those he called his children.

The book of Genesis ends with an account of the death of Jacob and the fear expressed by the brothers that after the death of their father, Joseph will somehow take revenge on them for their earlier treatment of him. Then Joseph himself dies, aged 110, after making his people vow and promise that when they return to their own homeland in Canaan, which will not happen for over 400 years, they will take his body with them and bury it there. Yet another example of the faith of a man of God who believed that God would keep His promise even after 400 years. Here, too, is a nation committed to the keeping of a covenant with God and looking to the future.

Exodus

Seventy people had gone down from Canaan at a time of drought and famine in their homeland, led by their father Jacob at the instigation of his beloved son Joseph as recorded in Genesis. Joseph had undergone immense hardship as a result of the extreme jealousy of his older brothers who had sold him into slavery but which, remarkably, as a result of his trust in and faithfulness to the God of his fathers, had enabled him to rise to a position of great authority in Egypt.

The book of Exodus, as its name implies, is a record of the way in which God delivered His people from a period of 470 years in Egypt, the large part of which saw them reduced to utter servitude following the death of Joseph and the Pharaoh who had promoted him. Above all else, it is a record of the way in which one man Moses, himself born into an Abrahamic family but brought up in the household of the ruler of Egypt, is used by God to bring about His purpose for that nation in spite of their disobedience and failure. It is the account of a God who uses His power to direct two nations in order to fulfil his supreme purpose in creation.

We do not know the exact number of people who came out of Egypt, but we are told that they had 600,000 men of military age, that is, between the ages of 20 and 50, plus all their dependents – probably close to 2,000,000 people. The account says that they became so numerous and strong that Egypt was filled with them, and as the years had passed, they now through their sheer numbers constituted a threat to the security of Egypt. In the event of a war, they could turn against their captors.

First, to prevent them escaping, they had been organised as a labour force under the control of Egyptian taskmasters and forced to build new cities for their captors and do menial work in the fields. But still, they increased in number until, finally, the Pharaoh issued an edict that all the baby boys should be killed at birth – which is where this book begins. Note also that here, again, we have a foreshadowing of the massacre which followed the birth of Jesus when Herod, in a jealous rage at having been deceived by the Wise Men, ordered a massive massacre of all baby boys.

Two of the Israelites in Egypt, Amram and Jochebed, both from the tribe of Levi, who already had two children, Miriam and Aaron, had another baby whom they hid for three months. But then, fearing that his cries would bring soldiers, they put him into a basket and hid him at the waters' edge, leaving Miriam his sister to keep guard. As they hoped, Pharaoh's daughter came down to bathe, heard his cries, felt sympathy for him and adopted him. Forty years later, having been brought up in luxury and privilege, Moses becomes aware of the horrendous circumstances under which his own people are living and is forced into making a decision when, having killed one of the guards who was beating an Israelite, he finds his own people reject him, no doubt convinced that he was 'one of them'.

Later on, the Apostle Paul is to refer to this when he comments that Moses, "chose rather to suffer affliction with the people of God than to endure the pleasures of sin for a season." An interesting point here is that so many years later, when Jesus came to deliver the nation of Israel, his own people rejected him, "He came unto His own but His own received Him not." "We will not have this man to rule over us." "Despised and rejected of men."

Unable to return to the palace, Moses flees and spends the next forty years living and working as a humble shepherd for a family who took him in. He, in turn, married one of the daughters. It is whilst he is out working in the fields as a shepherd that he has a remarkable encounter. He sees a bush which, apparently, was in flames but which, as he approached, turned out be irradiated with a brilliant light from which a voice addressed him. Remember that Moses is now eighty years of age, estranged from his family, living the humble life of a shepherd in the desert. Further, up until now, he had had no direct contact with the God of the Hebrews, as far as we know. In his childhood, he would have lived in the palatial splendour of an Egyptian city and he would have been seen as a potential successor to the king. He would also have been educated as a prince and no doubt forced to worship the Egyptian gods. Now, he is to have an experience which will transform his life, one for which his past eighty years will have provided both discipline and training, a life which would have broken a lesser man.

The voice, which speaks to him from the bush, introduces himself as the God of his ancestors, Abraham, Isaac and Jacob, and immediately, Moses realises that this is the God of all gods, the one whom his ancestors had worshipped and obeyed. His reaction is fear, created by the awesomeness of the encounter and the awareness of majesty and holiness, so much so that he covers his face, unable to look at God.

God now explains, telling Moses that He has seen the plight of his people and their suffering and that He is sending him back to the King of Egypt to bring the whole nation out. At which Moses is both appalled and made to feel totally inadequate. He then says in reply that the task is too great for him. But God insists, saying, "I will be with you… and as proof, when you come out, you will worship me on this mountain." Moses, remembering how he had been rejected by his own people forty years earlier, is most reluctant, raising several arguments including that he does not know who God is and that he is at best a very poor speaker.

What is so important is Moses' character and personality. Clearly a very humble man, in spite of his privileged upbringing, he is also very responsive to God, as his later life will illustrate. Important also is the way in which his previous life has singled him out. He was the second son of parents who were members of the priestly tribe Levi, who took the tremendous risk of exposing him on the riverbank to save his life. His upbringing, as the son of Pharaoh's daughter, would have ensured an education and enabled him to see the workings of the government at close quarters. He would have seen the enormous building projects and also the religious beliefs which were central to Egyptian life but also the suffering of his own people.

What had followed was a rigorous testing when attempting to help his own people who rejected that help, he was forced into isolation to the humble life of a common, simple man. An outcast from his own people as much as from his adopted family, he quietly makes a new life for himself as a very ordinary member of a Bedouin tribe, outside of his traditional roots as a descendant of Abraham or his childhood amongst the ruling classes of Egypt. Until now that is, when, after forty years, he responds to a 'call' which at the age of eighty years will involve him in so much hardship and enormous pressure, particularly, since he would also have to establish himself with his own people who had previously refused to accept him.

To every objection, God provides the answer. Moses is told to tell the people that "I am" has sent him, and he is allowed to use his brother Aaron as a mouthpiece. When the two of them go to Pharaoh to ask him to release the Israelites, the king is so incensed that he increases the burden on the poor

Hebrews. Even the Israelites themselves, so broken in spirit by their slavery, refuse to believe that Moses can or will help them.

Then comes that series of ten remarkable plagues visited by God upon the whole nation of Egypt by the hands of Moses and Aaron, which will ultimately demonstrate the power of Moses' God. The river turns to blood, frogs cover the ground, locusts eat the greenery and animals die. After each one, Pharaoh promises to let them go and then changes his mind, which culminates in the ultimate punishment when finally the firstborn of every animal and of each family dies, but miraculously, none of the Israelite families suffer because they are told to sacrifice a lamb and sprinkle its blood on the sides and over the top of their doorways so that the angel of death seeing the blood will 'pass over' their homes, thus preventing death from harming the children of the Israelites.

As this final disaster strikes, the king at last agrees to let the people go, an event which is still commemorated by the Jews to this day. BUT in Chapter 10, it is God who has the last word. He tells Moses that He has made the king stubborn in order that the Israelites shall realise, now and for all generations to come, that it is He, their God who has delivered them from slavery not Moses. And this is repeated in 13:17 when God states that they will not travel to the promised land by the shortest route but will have to cross the Red Sea.

As soon as the people departed from Egypt, God began to lead them by means of a pillar of cloud by day which turned into a pillar of fire at night, showing them where to go and when to stop. But this cloud, hiding them from the pursuing Egyptian army, had enabled them to avoid being engaged in battle until the whole nation had crossed the sea after God miraculously, again, had sent a strong wind to hold up the waters, after which the pursuing army were caught in the returning flood and were all drowned.

The purpose of this remarkable event, we are later told, was first to prevent them from returning when they discovered that they would have to fight their way into the new homeland and, secondly, to demonstrate, once and for all, to the Egyptians and the Hebrews, that their God was on their side and was powerful and able to work miracles to deliver them and to accomplish His purpose for them.

In fact, the news of their tremendous overwhelming victory over the armed forces of Egypt was not only a constant and oft repeated reminder to them of their dependence on their God but, as the news spread, the surrounding nations regarded them with fear, which in turn made their advance through enemy territory somewhat easier.

So this remarkable deliverance was to become the start of their relationship as a nation with the God whom they had not previously known, and even now was only known to them by his name "I am" and by the physical, tangible evidence of his awesome power over nature and events, and who demanded as a right that they worship him in a manner which will later be outlined to them in great and minute detail – a covenant relationship which will be enforced by death but which, when followed scrupulously, will bring enormous blessings and wealth.

Two things to note here. First, that they were told that on arrival in their new land, in the first month of the year, they were to commemorate their deliverance from the death of the firstborn and the day on which they finally left Egypt, with a special festival with specific sacrifices every year, and that henceforth, the firstborn male child should belong to God (Chapter 13).

Unfortunately for these Israelites, their path was not easy. Their courage would be tested in warfare and their faith in God by his ability to provide, literally, food and water in a desert country. Typically, of a people accustomed to relatively comfortable life in Egypt, apart from the hard labour, they soon began to complain that they were better off in slavery. Short memories. They soon forgot how they had cried out to God to deliver them from that forced labour and harsh regime. Now that God had heard and answered their prayer, they complained about the food, the lack of water, the hardship of travel and the threat from the surrounding nations who would, in some cases, oppose their passage.

During the whole of this period which will last for forty years, Moses is seen as a mediator, trying to argue the case for Israel with God who threatened to destroy them and to begin again with Moses' family as had happened with Noah. Moses argues very cogently that if God destroyed the people, then the other nations would believe that God was unable to deliver this nation, when in fact they were intended to see, in all this, a dramatic demonstration both of God's power and his love. Failure now would suggest that it was God who had failed. Anyway, God in mercy provided food in the form of manna, which was like a soft deposit on the ground overnight but, again to test them, only sufficient for one day could be gathered, except on Friday, when double the quantity was available to feed them on Saturday, their Sabbath of rest. On another occasion, when they complained of a lack of meat, God sent vast flocks of quails which fell to earth. Also, water came out from rocks or was made drinkable when Moses sought God's help for them, and even their clothes did not wear out.

The next major event was when, three months into their journey, they were camped by the mountain called Sinai in the southern part of what is to this day the Sinai Peninsula. Here, Moses was commanded to go up the mountain to speak with God who told him to inform the people that if they obeyed Him and kept His Laws, they would become a 'chosen' people dedicated to His service – no longer just individuals but a whole race. Moses then called all the people together and told them what God had said, to which they replied that they would do everything that God required. All of God's promises were conditional upon obedience, just as with Adam and Eve in Genesis.

The mountain was declared 'holy', a boundary was set about it, and the people were forbidden, on pain of death, to cross it. God would then descend to the mountain in a great cloud and Moses was to go up and listen to what God had to say. These commands, the Ten Commandments, were to form the basis of their relationship with God and with each other for all time and, indeed, in modern times were to become the basis of law in most European countries.

When God descended onto the mountain, the people heard a noise like a trumpet and saw lightning and smoke. The sounds were like a volcanic eruption, which in turn caused the people to back off in fear, complaining to Moses and saying, "… if you speak to us, we will listen, but we are afraid that if God speaks to us, we will die."

The commandments which God gave to Moses are very complex and very detailed, outlining both the various ways in which the people must worship God and the way they in which they must behave towards each other. It was to form the basis of the Covenant between God and this nation. It included precise details for the construction of a Covenant Box to contain the two tablets of stone on which the commandments were engraved and, in very fine elaborate detail, the design of what became known as the Tent of Presence where the various ritual sacrifices were to be made, and in which the High priest could offer, once a year, the ultimate sacrifice for sin, and where Moses and Aaron could commune with God.

This covenant (Chapter 24) was sealed when Moses and Aaron accompanied by his two sons and seventy of the leaders, went up the mountain, but only Moses was allowed to proceed into the presence of God.

Then after all this was complete, God called Moses up into the mountain again. There He told Moses that the people were to leave the mountain and proceed to the land which he had promised to give Abraham and his children all those years ago, promising to send an angel to guide them and that he would drive out the current inhabitants of the land BUT saying that because they were a stubborn people, He would not go with them Himself because He might get fed up with them and destroy them on the way.

When Moses told the people what God had said, they were very upset, especially when God told them to take off their jewellery. However, Moses once again intercedes for them, reminding God that He had said He was pleased with him and that He had chosen this nation to be His own. Moses actually said to God, "If you do not go with us, don't make us leave this place. How can anyone know that you are pleased with your people and with me if you do not go with us? Your presence with us will distinguish us from any other people on earth." The Lord then said to Moses, "I will do as you have asked because I know you very well and I am pleased with you." Moses then asked that, in confirmation, he might see the dazzling light of God's presence, and was allowed to see, not God's face but, hidden in a rock, he would be allowed to see God's back.

Earlier, whilst Moses had been up on the mountain for a very long time, the people had rebelled and 'forced' Aaron to make a golden image for them to worship. Moses was so angry that he threw down the stone tablets on which the commandments were written and broke them. Now, in response to Moses' fervent plea, God has rewritten the commandments and renewed his covenant with his people. "I now make a covenant with the people of Israel. In their presence, I will do great things such as have never been done anywhere on earth among any of the nations. All the people will see what great things I, the Lord, can do because I am going to do an awesome thing for you." What the people saw when he came down the mountain, was that Moses' face was irradiated, shining so much that he had to veil it.

The rest of this book is occupied with various instructions and regulations for worship and for the construction of the Tent of Presence and the vestments the High priest Aaron, and the other priests, the Levites, were to wear. After the deliverance of the firstborn at the Passover, God had claimed each firstborn male as his. Now God will take the whole tribe of Levi in lieu, their numbers almost corresponding, with the balance being redeemed with a redemption fee.

A census taken at this time tells us that there were 603,550 fit males between the ages of 20 and 50 – men of an age to fight.

The book ends with the completion of all the work of preparation and construction, so that the Tent of Presence was complete and dedicated two years after the people had left Egypt, and we are told that a cloud covered the tent wherever and whenever the people were to rest. When they were to stop, the cloud stopped, and when they were to move on, the cloud lifted and proceeded them, with a fire burning over it at night. And so this book, having begun with the Israelites leaving Egypt after 470 years, ends with them two years into their journey to Canaan.

Leviticus

Some will find this book somewhat tedious, with its elaborate and somewhat repetitive narrative, but please do not ignore it. It is there for us to read and reflect upon. To understand it, however, one has to understand why it is there and what it can teach us.

The fact is that this vast number of people, greatly increased over 470 years, had begun life in Egypt as a close-knit family of just seventy people and have now become a vast nation possibly numbering over two million, developing into twelve tribes named from the twelve sons of Jacob. In fact, after Joseph's death, God had separated out the tribe of Levi, assigning to them the work of carrying out all the religious duties which had been ordained by God. And then, to maintain the number at twelve, Joseph's two sons by Rachel, Ephraim and Benjamin, were classed as separate tribes, bringing the number of tribes back to twelve. Later, as we shall see, God had also separated out the tribe of Levi for a specific role and function which would keep them separate from the other tribes, to act as a holy priesthood and in fact replicating the work undertaken by Aaron for Moses. Remember that their father and mother were both from the tribe of Levi, as was their sister, Miriam.

So before we go further, we must look at the Israelites as a nation. They were rebellious, disorganised, lacking in respect for authority and, not least, accustomed in Egypt to the national worship of a multitude of gods represented by animals like the raven and the alligator or the river Nile or the sun; although, no doubt, some of them had retained the faith of their ancestor Abraham. They had also been introduced to a measure of philosophical thought from the Egyptians who were exploring the concept of life after death and studying the effect of the seasons, the role of the sun and the river as sources of life. Further, while the Egyptians were, by contrast, a highly organised society with a clearly defined social structure, the Israelites were, by tradition, Bedouin tribespeople. Out of these, God planned to create a nation, united under one God, who were capable of consolidated action which was to happen under two of their kings, namely David and his son Solomon. However, they would never lose their fragmented view of corporate life.

Above all, the Israelites needed, now, to learn respect for authority, to accept discipline and to accept that, as individuals, they were often subject to misplaced passions and desires lacking higher thought or ambition. Like the other nations round them, they were envious, jealous, warlike, greedy, sexually lascivious and lawless. God wanted to make these people a shining example to the rest of the nations, to use them to demonstrate to these other nations that he, God, their creator, was almighty, powerful but also scrupulously just and fair, with the added aspect that he was their father and they His children (Hosea) and that He loved them and wanted them to enjoy happiness and a long life.

So what we find in Leviticus is a very elaborate series of rituals designed to inculcate a sense of a higher authority, higher than their leaders like Moses, who was himself under the higher authority of one who could perform wonders and miracles – as in the crossing of the Red Sea and the provision of food in the desert – but also who would punish with great severity, any action or thought which indicated disrespect. In the colourful robes of the priests, they would see beauty and feel awe. In the elaborate ritual sacrifices, they would discover the concepts of punishment, of forgiveness and of sacrifice. They would be taught things like atonement, substitution, reconciliation, holiness and the dire consequences of disobedience, as the opposite to the rewards of love, happiness, peace and enlightenment for those who obeyed.

As we have already seen, the Bible is a record of the unfolding revelation of God by himself to a people who, over the centuries, were becoming more intelligent and capable of abstract thought, moving from the primitive to the more sophisticated. We shall later see how these things, elaborated in this book, would be seen as shadows thrown by a coming light, as harbingers of a greater and more enlightened understanding, of which these people were not yet capable, and which would culminate, in the New Testament, in the coming of God himself in the persona of His Son born as a man but possessing the absolute nature of God, one through whom God had created the universe.

It is also the record of the manner in which humankind became more and more responsive to God, beginning, as we shall shortly see, with the few 'chosen' ones and ending with the 'everyone'.

It is now two years since the Israelites left Egypt and, at the end of Exodus, we see that the Tent of Presence has now been set up, dedicated and has been filled with the shining glory of God. And so we come to the beginning of a new era, a fresh phase in their development and a new chapter in their understanding of God. Here, now God is no longer far, distant, whom Moses to converse with, had to climb the 7,500-foot mountain, to be overcome with the thunder and lightning of God's presence, with the people quaking with fear and forbidden to approach. No, now it is different. Here at last, God is with them, His presence known by the cloud over the tent by day and the fire by night. Here was guidance, when to stop and when to move. Here was one place, wherever they travelled, that God was permanently present. Here is the one place where the people, in the person of their high priest, could meet with God. Here was the place of forgiveness of sin. Here was the place where judgement would visit the guilty and worship would unite them.

It was also the place where the people could make their offerings, their sacrificial bulls, sheep and goats, whose blood sprinkled became the stern reminder that sin required a death, where their offerings of bread and wine, their sweet, savoured incense, could be acceptable to God. But the offerings must be perfect. The animal a male with no blemish, the bread unleavened and the wine or oil of the finest. The interesting point being, that even when they hungered for meat, the only animals slain were for God. The law of primacy. "Seek ye first the kingdom of God, and all these things shall be added unto you…" says the hymnist. And the bread must be there as a part of their offerings.

The laws which were given were precise, and the penalty, whether against God or against one's fellow man, were strictly enjoined and adhered to. Sins could be manifold. Sins of disobedience to God, sins of omission or commission, failure in civic duty like failing to give evidence in court or failure in some financial transaction were all seen ultimately as sins against God, hence the need for a sacrifice.

Interestingly, when food offerings or sacrificial offerings would be made, part of the offering became the property of the priest. The Levites were given no land, except city communities in which to live; their supply and sustenance was a specific part of the people's offerings.

They were also told which part of the animals could be eaten and which sacrificed, which parts must be burnt and which eaten. But before all this could happen, the priests themselves must be purified, made holy, and they must offer sacrifices to ensure that they are personally acceptable before they can act on behalf of the penitents. The priests themselves were bound by laws just as strict as any other person.

An example of this is given in Chapter 10 where two of Aaron's sons are killed when they made an offering which God had not ordained, a very heavy penalty because of their position, standing as they did between God and the ordinary people. What a very pertinent message for any person today who serves God as minister or priest; they must be scrupulously innocent of any sin; they must be above reproach for otherwise they defile the image of God. Even the High Priest may only enter the most holy inner sanctuary at the appropriate time, and then, only after he has made an offering for his own sins, can he enter with an offering for the people. Here the Day of Atonement is described in detail in Chapter 16.

The laws continue with laws of hygiene, personal and public, which must be strictly observed, foods which can or cannot be eaten, actions to be taken when disease is present in a person or even a building.

Great emphasis is made of the fact that blood, which represents life, is sacred. So much so that the blood of sacrificial animals may only be offered in the one place at the altar at the entrance to the tent. And this again marks a dramatic change. No longer may the people offer sacrifice anywhere else. There is only ONE place where the blood of sacrifice may be shed. Otherwise (Chapter 17), to transgress this meant instant dismissal from the family of God's people, as would be the case if anyone ate or drank blood, hence the Jewish laws for the killing of animals for food.

There were reasons for all this strictness. One must remember that these people were living in proximity to races who worshipped and sacrificed to the multitude of other gods, so frequently named in scripture.

Then, the laws of holiness and justice were reflections of God's holiness. It is at this point that we are reminded (19:18) of the words that Jesus would call the second greatest commandment, "Love your neighbour as you love yourself." Holiness had social obligations, as well as maintaining the uniqueness of God's own person.

We are then given lists of all the major Festivals which the nation must observe, in particular, Passover and Unleavened bread, Harvest, New Year, The Day of Atonement and the Festival of Shelters. More about these later.

Before you dismiss all these as being particular to one nation at a specific time in their history, let me state that these were also symbolic, pointing forward to the basis of our own Christian faith today, as we shall consider in detail later. The laws then finish with the Year of Restoration, the fiftieth year, when all people and lands are released, returned to their original owners or otherwise reinstated. The clear point being made that ultimately all persons and all property is in the ownership of God; therefore, land cannot be held freehold but only leasehold, with the 50th year of Jubilee being the term date, and in that year, all persons who may have fallen in debt or slavery shall be set free.

The book then ends with the reminder that all firstborn males, human or animal, belong to God and must either be sacrificed or bought back and one tenth of all produce of the land must be given to God.

Numbers

We are now at a critical period in the history of this nation Israel. The previous book, Leviticus, ends with the appointment of the rules of the Law of God as a contractual agreement between God and his chosen People, following the construction and dedication of the Tent of the Presence, as seen at the end of Exodus, two years from the time when they had been miraculously delivered from their 470 years in Egypt. We now know that God has appointed a place amongst them where he can be worshipped, where the people can be aware of his presence, and where Moses, in their midst, can meet with God. This Tent will also be a continual visible sign of God's presence with them, in the cloud and the fire over it, so that daily, morning and evening, they will be reminded of God' continual presence with them and of their obligations to him, represented by the daily sacrifice which had to be offered.

The book is named for the two accounts of the numbering of the people, first here at Sinai, and then repeated before they enter the promised land. The first chapters record the census, then various laws and instructions and end with the celebration of the second Passover.

Chapter 9. We are reminded again of the Cloud and the Fire as symbols of God's presence, and the signal to move or stop and the method of procedure. Two points of interest here. First, Moses' plea to his brother-in-law Hobab, son of Jethro, to act as their guide, and his refusal. He wishes to return home, obviously wanting a quiet life. Then, as the people leave Mt Sinai, we are told that the Covenant Box went ahead of them to find the place where they are to stop and camp.

Now comes the crucial issue. Why make them suffer and struggle for forty years when initially the journey from Egypt to Canaan could have been completed in some two weeks? The first answer to this question is the rebellious response of ten of the twelve spies sent out to prospect the land and who, on their return, emphasised the dangers of giants, heavily fortified cities and the fact that they would have to fight their way in. Joshua and Caleb, on the other hand, replied that with God's help, they could succeed. In consequence of this, God simply told the nation that all the adults would die on the journey and only their children would enter, apart from Joshua and Caleb. Even Moses and Aaron were not allowed to enter the Promised Land. God was so angry at their lack of confidence in his ability to do what he had said. Once again, the nation had failed the test.

We now recognise why crossing of the Red Sea and the significant defeat of the Egyptian army on their departure from Egypt was so important. Simply put, they could not go back. If they had, they would have been killed by the Egyptians. They now had no option but to continue, even though they would face a severe testing. And this testing of their courage, their learning to trust in God and their required obedience to his commands would in fact be the makings of them as a nation. For God had given Moses the task of turning twelve disunited and frequently quarrelsome tribes into a nation of warriors known for their remarkable success, whose exploits would create fear amongst all the other nations between the Euphrates and the Mediterranean – but only if they implicitly did what their God told them to do.

The lesson we learn from this is, that to become a true servant of God requires strict discipline and being prepared to face being tested and tried, to learn faith and confidence through the difficulties and problems of daily life – a major point made in the New Testament in 1 Peter 1.

Within a few days of their leaving Sinai, they began to complain. First it was the food, a lack of meat, and they spoke with regret of the luscious food they had enjoyed in that fertile valley of the Nile. Moses heard and was extremely angry, complaining bitterly to God in 11:11, "Why have you treated me so badly? Why are you so displeased with me? Why have you given me the responsibility for all these people? I didn't create them or bring them to birth. Why should you ask me to act like a nurse and carry them in my arms like babies, all the way to the land you promised to their ancestors?"

At this point, to reduce the stress on Moses, God tells him to appoint 70 elders to help him deal with these complaints, but Moses goes on and on. "Here I am, leading more than 600,000 people and you say that you will give them enough meat for a month? Could enough cattle and sheep be killed to satisfy them? Are all the fish in the sea enough for them?" "Is there a limit to my power?" the Lord answered. "You will soon see whether what I have said will happen." And of course, the result was the provision of manna daily and quails.

However, we can now see that it was not merely the people who were being tested. Moses also has to learn; his faith in God must be absolute because there will be another 38 years of this! And after Moses has died, even more problems. For then, of course, the conquest of Canaan had to be undertaken, which involved driving out the existing inhabitants, initially under the leadership of Moses' successor, Joshua.

Now follows the account of the next thirty-eight years, which will take them up to the borders of their new home but not to the Southern or Western boundaries, where they were denied access. They will eventually approach by the long circuitous route to enter from the East by crossing the river Jordan opposite the city of Jericho.

This record of the journey is a sad history of complaints, rebellion and jealousy even from Miriam and Aaron, who challenged Moses' authority and were punished for it. The people travelled South first to Sinai, then turned North towards the Southern borders of Canaan, and it was here at Kadesh Barnea that Moses sent out the twelve spies to reconnoitre the land. Sadly, the adverse report from ten of their number meant that (14:13) when the people heard the bad news, they rebelled, and in spite of the encouragement of Caleb and Joshua, the people all cried out in distress, repeating their plea, "Why have you brought us here to die in the wilderness? Let's choose new leaders and go back to Egypt" (verse 14). Moses cries out in deep distress to God who suggests to Moses that he will destroy all these ungrateful people and begin a new race from the family of Moses.

Moses' answer to God is an argument which he will use more than once. "The Egyptians have told everyone how powerfully you defeated them, and now all the nations are afraid of you. If you destroy these people, then everyone will say that their God had failed them, failed to bring them into the promised land because he could not do it, and they will simply destroy us. Whereas if you go with us and complete the enterprise, everyone will be amazed at your power." Then very humbly Moses pleads with God to forgive the people (verse 19), "And now Lord, according to the greatness of your unchanging love, forgive, I pray, the sin of these people just as you have forgiven them ever since they left Egypt."

God replies that he will forgive them in response to Moses' plea, but because they have disobeyed and tried his patience over and over again, none of those who have rejected him will ever enter the land (verse 23), the exception being Caleb and Joshua, the faithful spies. The punishment for the people that they will spend forty years wandering in the wilderness, one year for each of the forty days the spies spent in exploring the land.

At that point, the people repent and attempt to go ahead and invade the land there and then, but going out to battle as they did without God's blessing, their soldiers suffered a humiliating defeat. Then, after more rules and regulations comes the serious rebellion of three leaders of the nation, Korah, Dathan and Abiram, who challenge Moses' unique position as God's representative, saying that they are all equal in the sight of God. Result (Chapter 16), God responds by opening the earth under the men and all their families, possessions and their followers, and it swallows them (verse 32).

The next rebellion is the challenge to Aaron's position (Chapter 17), when in response, God tells Moses to write the name of all the Levite families on a stick, and overnight Aaron's rod budded into blossom. More problems of rebellion and disobedience, one of which was the provision of water from the rock in the wilderness of Zin after Miriam's death. Here Moses displeases God because, instead of speaking to the rock, Moses in anger struck it; a failure in God's eyes, a lack of faith and a failure to attribute the miracle to God, which would haunt him for the rest of his days, so that when it came to it, Moses was only allowed to see the promised land but not enter it. The leadership would pass to Joshua who had been Moses' helper and one of the faithful spies.

By now, marching through the nations which surrounded Canaan, they meet opposition from Moab, from Edom and the Amalekites. Then Aaron dies (20:28) and is mourned and buried on Mt Hor and his son Eleazar is appointed in his place. More encounters with opposing kings like Sihon of the Amorites and King Og of Bashan. However, now they are successful because they are acting under the authority of God. And it is at this point that Balak, king of the Amorites becomes so frightened that he sends for a prophet/priest named Balaam to curse them (Chapters 22–23), and there ensues a rather enchanting account of how God challenges him, speaking through his donkey, and when finally he does agree to meet the king, he can only (Chapter 24) do what God wants and issue a blessing and a prophetic statement which anticipates the future success of Israel in the years to come; but he cannot curse them.

Unfortunately, that is followed by an event which foreshadows the sin which will ultimately lead to the downfall of the nation. Some of the men, whilst they were in camp, met and had sexual relations with Moabite women who had invited them to a feast in honour of their god Baal. A similar incident was punished by Phinehas, son of Eleazar who killed the man concerned and the woman and thus averted the wrath of God. This intermarriage between Israelite men and women from the other nations who worshipped other gods would be one of the biggest problems to face the nation in the coming years. Yet another rebellion was met by a plague of snakes, and Moses was told that the cure was to put a bronze snake on a pole; anyone who looked at it was healed. Interestingly this was later referred to by Jesus as he likened himself, lifted up and made in the likeness of the curse, to this incident.

Now, after Joshua has been chosen to succeed Moses (27:12), we have a repeat of the festivals and ordained sacrifices (Chapter 28–30), which is a repetition of Exodus 29 and Leviticus 23. Then came war against Midian (Chapter 31), which was highly successful, producing so much loot that ultimately the tribes of Reuben Gad and part of Manasseh requested permission to settle in the very fertile lands which Israel had captured East of the river Jordan (Chapter 32). Moses was angry at their request, but the matter was finally settled when, under a serious obligation, those tribes were allowed to settle their families there but had to provide all their fighting men to lead the conquest of Canaan, otherwise their land would be forfeit, and to this they agreed. Now a second census of the fighting men was taken, then they set off to war.

Now, as Moses is about to die, God tells him to allocate the land West of the Jordan to the various tribes, with especial provision for the priestly tribe of Levi. The book here ends with Israel poised for their conquest of the promised land.

Deuteronomy

It is forty years since the children of Abraham, Isaac and Jacob, now numbering over 600,000 men of military service, plus all their dependents, livestock and possessions, had left the land of Egypt. After a very arduous journey and many problems, they were now at last in sight of the promised land. Moses has been told by God that he will never enter the country; that responsibility will devolve upon his helper Joshua.

However, before he dies, in this book, we have the record of Moses' very emotional final words to the people (1:9), in which he reminds them of all that God has done and of their failures and their successes. In other words, they are far from perfect, but God still loves them and regards them as his children, the chosen race.

Basically, this book comprises what Moses said to the nation of Israel as they were camped in the Jordan valley opposite the city of Jericho, which was a heavily fortified town with strong stone walls. He reminds them of their journey, the fact that 70 had been appointed as Judges to help him in maintaining justice and social welfare. And we have a repetition of the laws previously given.

Moses then refers them back to the time when, at Kadesh Barnea, they had agreed to send out 12 spies to survey the land, and it was their fearful response to the report and their refusal to obey God that resulted in them being sentenced to wander for 40 years in the wilderness, facing opposition from the surrounding nations, until all the fighting men of that generation had died. Then began their successful warfare against those nations which opposed them and friendship with those which allowed them to pass.

We are now reminded of the events at the end of the book of Numbers, when two and a half tribes were allowed to settle East of Jordan on the condition that they led the battles for the land to the West, but poor Moses, in spite of his earnest prayer, was only allowed to view the land from Mt Pisgah. And God was quite firm with Moses, "That's enough! Don't mention this again! Go to the Peak of

Mt Pisgah and look to the North and to the South, to the East and to the West. Look carefully at what you see because you will never cross the Jordan." Note here that the land included that area from the Mediterranean right up to the Euphrates.

Now Moses' final impassioned plea, Chapter 4 onwards, to obey the laws, not to add anything to them, to obey them faithfully and then, "the other nations will see how wise you are and that no other god is as great as our God. Tell your children and your grandchildren about the day when you heard His voice, you heard Him speaking through the clouds and fire but you did not see Him in any form at all." To emphasise this, Moses reminded them that they MUST not make any idol or image in any form at all. "If you do, you will be scattered among other nations and few of you will survive." The reason: God is and must remain unknowable.

"Search all of history from the beginning of the time when God created humanity on earth, has anything as great as this ever happened, has any other god done anything like it? The Lord has done all this to prove to you that He alone is God and there is no other god who is like Him. He has done this because He loved your ancestors and He chose you to demonstrate His power to the whole world. So remember today that the Lord is God in heaven and on earth and there is no other god. But remember that He did not choose you for your sakes but because of the faith of your ancestors."

Then to make the point, Moses promises that God will give them the land forever if they obey and warns that if they disobey, they will be dispossessed, and reminds them of the Ten Commandments.

This is followed by a series of warnings of trouble if they disobey and blessing if they obey, backing up what he says by reminding them of the enormous power which God has shown to them as a nation and how the difficulties they had faced over the forty years were a deliberate test of their response. "Remember how the Lord your God led you on this long journey through the desert these past forty years, sending hardships to test you so that He might know what you intended to do and whether you would obey his commands. He made you go hungry, and then he gave you manna to eat, food that you and your ancestors had never eaten before. He did this to teach you that human beings must not depend on bread alone to sustain them, but on everything the Lord says." (Chapter 8). During that time, their clothes did not wear out nor their feet swell. No wonder Jesus would quote this to Satan during his temptation in the wilderness. What a challenge for us today. God will provide for us if we trust Him and obey his commands.

Moses then goes on to tell what happened when he, Moses, went up the Mt Sinai to receive the Ten Commandments and all the other laws and instructions. He reminds them that whilst he was away for forty days, they, the people, rebelled and caused Aaron to make a golden calf to worship as their god and how in anger Moses broke the stone tablets which had to be remade. He reminds them of what God demands of them, how great God is, and what remarkable promises God has made for all who obey and love Him, that they will occupy their land in peace and safety, from the Euphrates to the Mediterranean. Moses then gives to the people a stark choice between blessing and a curse. The decision is theirs; they have the free will to obey or to disobey.

Now more reminders of laws concerning worship, justice, cleanliness and their social responsibilities, the administration of justice, the cities of refuge where innocent men could avoid summary punishment, as well as their duties towards God. All the various main Festivals are repeated, the Passover, Harvest and the Festival of Shelters.

Very significant here (18:14) is the promise of a prophet to come. When, at the foot of Sinai, they had recoiled in fear, they asked not to have to face God's fiery presence like that again. "They have made a wise request. I will send them a prophet like you from among their own people. I will tell him what to say, and he will tell the people everything I command. He will speak in my name, and I will punish anyone who refuses to obey him." Is this merely a foretelling of the great prophets like Elijah and Elisha or is it a long-term view of the time when God will send his own Son, Jesus, to declare the truth about God his father? Either way, it was certainly fulfilled.

What is so important here is the sense that running right through the Bible, from the Old Testament to the New, there is a unity, a common theme, linking the whole book which creates a sense that throughout the whole book, there is an order, a purpose and a single overriding author.

Here, now we have a series of further-expanded laws, covering a variety of potential problems which the nation will face as they begin a new phase of their journey. These laws are to be a permanent reminder of their duties before God, for all succeeding generations to come. Hence, (Chapter 27) they are told that when they cross the river Jordan to begin their occupation of the land, they are to set up plastered stones on which are to be written all the laws and teachings which they have received from God via Moses, on Mt Ebal, and there to set up an altar made of uncut stone on which to make their sacrifices and where they should eat their fellowship meals and be grateful in the presence of the Lord. However, this was also to be a renewal of their covenant relationship with their God and the confirmation that, despite all their failures, they had become "The children of God" (27:10). A remarkable promise which, for the Jews, is still in force today.

Inevitably, now follow a list of curses for disobedience and a list of blessings which will result from their obedience, "… keep all His commands that I am giving you today, He will make you greater than any other nation on earth" (28:1). And there is no question that this nation has survived all attempts to destroy it for over three thousand years. Part of this promise was that all people on earth would see this, that they were God's own people. To the extent, as history has shown, that they would become bankers to the rest of the world (28:10–13). Equally, they were warned that if they failed, God would scatter them among all the nations, from one end of the earth to the other (28:64) which has also happened. Then, in Chapter 29, Moses reminds the people of the terms of this covenant made in the land of Moab, which was to be in addition to the covenant which the Lord had made with them at Sinai. In other words, again, in spite of their failures en route, they had at least in part passed the test.

Then follows a remarkable statement, or series of statements in which we can see events foretold which will actually occur. In Chapter 30, God warns that in fact they WILL be scattered because they will fail, but if they then remember the Lord, He will bring them back from the nations where they are scattered (30:3), make them prosperous again and more numerous, and regain possession of this land where their descendants will be able to live. Again, a remarkable foretelling of what history has shown, in the fact of their return to their land in May 1948. Moses also tells them that the command that God is giving them is not difficult or beyond their reach, (30:11–14) "It is not up in the sky. You do not have to ask, 'Who will go up bring it down for us so that we can obey it?' No, it is here with you. You know it and can quote it, so now obey it!"

Here follow some personal comments from Moses, that he is now 120 years old, that he personally will not enter the land, that their leader will be Joshua. He tells both Joshua and the people to be determined and confident. At this, Moses hands over the law to the priests and reminds them that the law must be read to the people every seven years.

Now God calls Moses to enter the Tent of Presence with Joshua, and in a most remarkable statement, God simply tells Moses that after his death, the people will be unfaithful, that they will be driven from the land and be destroyed as a nation. Many terrible things will happen to them because God will abandon them. They will turn away from him and break the covenant which had been made between them and God. (31:14–21).

Moses is then given a song, which he teaches to the people, in which are a record of God's dealings with them, past, present and future. Then (Chapter 33) the blessings which Moses the man of God pronounces on the people and, in Chapter 34, the account of his death on Mt Nebo, at the top of Mt Pisgah East of Jericho. God buried him in a valley in Moab, opposite the town of Bethpeor, but no one knows where. To the time of his death, aged 120 years, Moses was strong as ever and his eyesight good.

All one can say is that Moses was one of the most remarkable people ever to live, one who demonstrated in his life a most remarkable faith in God. Beginning, as he did, in the household of the Pharaohs of Egypt, he was also a very humble man, obedient and loving, full of the knowledge of God, who spoke personally to him. Yet he was capable of anger and frustration, exhibiting some very human characteristics and failures, but at all times true to the God whom he loved and served. Small wonder then that over a thousand years later, he would appear in the New Testament with Jesus and Elijah, another stalwart, on the Mt of Transfiguration, talking with Jesus. And we can guess what they were talking about.

Joshua

This book effectively takes over the story of the nation of Israel from the time of Moses' death at the end of Deuteronomy and through the conquest of their new homeland in Canaan – an almighty task for the new leader of a nation of people who had been so difficult during their forty-year journey, which had been prolonged because of their unruly and rebellious behaviour which had very sorely tested Moses. Now, they have to fight their way in and drive out the resident nations, whose appalling behaviour had brought the judgement of God upon them and whose idolatrous ways would ultimately undermine the relationship of Israel with their God.

We have seen, in the previous book, that the man God had chosen to take over the leadership of this nation was Joshua the son of Nun. So first, we need to have a look at what we know of this man. We know that he had been with Moses for many years, starting as a young lad probably of about fifteen years of age. We are first introduced to him as a leader of soldiers fighting the Amalekites (Exodus 17:9), then, importantly, he accompanies Moses up Mt Sinai to receive the stone tablets with the Ten Commandments (Exodus 24:13) and so shared in Moses' powerful experience. We also find him a vocal supporter of Moses (Numbers 11:28), where he apparently queried a possible challenge to Moses' authority.

As a supporter of Moses, Joshua had clearly proved himself as a capable and trustworthy leader because later he had been chosen as one of the twelve spies sent out from Kadesh Barnea to survey the land, before the nation began their conquest, and it was he who, along with Caleb, had stood firm in their confidence in God's ability to deliver the land to them, in spite of the problems raised by the many fortified cities and the presence of giants in the land. Hence, he and Caleb were the only two adult males who had been through the long wilderness journey and were now allowed to enter the promised land, which even Moses was not allowed to do. So a strong man whose faith in God would enable him to lead these vacillating people forward and one who had been with Moses for many years.

Right at the beginning of this book, we read of God instructing Joshua, giving him details of the borders of this vast new territory and commanding him to be determined, to obey the law and to study it, and promising success in reward for the unstinting obedience of his people.

The first major task now facing the nation, encamped as they were on the East side of the river Jordan, was how to cross the river. This was an echo of the crossing of the Red Sea forty years earlier, which had both delivered the nation from the anger of the Egyptians and committed them to their future. There could be no going back. Here too, under Joshua's leadership, God would provide a miracle which would convince the people of his almighty power and bring fear to their enemies. Note how the tribes of Reuben, Gad and half Manasseh had been allowed to settle their families in the fertile valley East of the river but only on the condition that their fighting men remained with the main army until the conquest of the land was complete.

At this point, Joshua again sends out spies. Two men are told to survey the approaches and, in particular, the city of Jericho which blocked their passage. This, the story of how Rahab conceals the spies and wins a reprieve for herself and her family, is a wonderful account illustrating as it does the fear of the inhabitants of the land in the face of this multitude of people. And this even before they had crossed the river. When the spies returned, they reported this, saying, "All the people there are terrified of us" (2:24).

The river crossing was another remarkable miracle. As soon as the priests carrying the Covenant Box entered the river, the waters parted, piling up for some miles upstream, and completely cutting off the flow downstream to the Dead Sea, enabling the whole nation to cross dry shod. This remarkable event was then to be commemorated by two piles of stones, one in the river and the other on dry land, so that future generations would be reminded of what God had done (Chapter 3). Result, all the nations through the land and right up to the Mediterranean, when they heard of this, lost their courage.

For the Israelites, this was the time to renew their covenant with God, which was done by circumcising all the males who had been born on the journey (Chapter 5). They also now were able to eat fresh produce from the country and the supply of manna stopped. It was also an occasion for God to reveal himself again to Joshua. Joshua saw a 'man' standing with a drawn sword and went to

50

challenge him, only to be told that he was there "as the commander of the Lord's army" (5:14), at which Joshua prostrated himself and was told to remove his sandals because the ground he was standing on was holy. An echo again of Moses' initial contact with God at the age of eighty years when he was commissioned to deliver his people from the Egyptians.

Then follow a number of incidents which reveal the character of many individuals. Like Achan, whose theft of goods from Jericho led to a defeat at the siege of Ai, which in turn undermined the status of the Israelites – an incident which showed how one individual's disobedience can cause havoc and bring trouble to the whole community. Just as later even Joshua himself is deceived by the treachery of the Gibeonites (Chapter 9) into making peace with them and subsequently going to their rescue.

However, despite these human failings, God was with the nation, and their military success was remarkable as they defeated so many kings and seized their territories. Even the united confederation of Canaanites, the Amorites, the Hittites, the Perizzites, the Jebusites and the Hivites, armies from the hills as well as the plains, were unable to resist their onslaught. Until by the end of Chapter 11, we are told that Joshua had captured the whole land and divided it amongst the tribes as Moses had instructed, with Ephraim, Gad and half Manasseh remaining to the East of the river Jordan. Chapter 21:44, "Not one of their enemies had been able to stand against them because the Lord gave the Israelites the victory over their enemies."

However, by the time that Joshua dies at a very old age (Chapter 23), it was quite clear that the land was far from clear of all its original inhabitants. As we shall see later, it was the that fact, that they failed to have captured or destroyed all the major fortified cities as they advanced, which caused those sinful nations, ultimately, to be the downfall of the Israelite nation. Simply because the Israelites disobeyed the strict commands given by God, and which were repeated in his dying words by Joshua (Chapter 24), that is, not to intermarry with alien tribes and to destroy all their false gods together with their images, altars and priests. In not destroying those gods which they themselves and their ancestors had previously worshipped in Mesopotamia, they had laid a trap for themselves. It was from the worship of these very gods, that their ancestor Abraham had been called out and told to leave home. Their presence within the boundaries of their nation would cause Israel endless problems and cause them, ultimately, to fall back into error.

Nothing could be more clear than that, above all other things, for Israel to develop as God wanted and to serve and obey him meant being separate from all of the other false gods and the people who worshipped them. As we shall see later, it was that failure by Israel which destroyed their integrity and finally led to the destruction of the nation and their exile from the land. Now, aged 110 years, Joshua dies and is buried in the hill country of the Ephraim tribal lands.

But the book of Joshua does not end without a very solemn warning, (24:31), "As long as Joshua lived, the people of Israel served the Lord, and after his death, they continued to do so as long as those leaders were alive who had seen for themselves everything that the Lord had done for Israel."

Why is it, we may well ask, that so many people need to see physical evidence in order to believe? Whereas the original belief in God had come down through their ancestors whose faith had been sufficient for them to take God at his word and act on it, even when it meant personal suffering and rejection in order to do so. The nation was now settled within the borders of the promised land, land promised all those years ago to Abraham. But as we shall see in the next book, they have a great deal to learn about themselves and about God, and they will face some five hundred years before the answer comes. The next book tells what happens after Joshua's death.

Judges

This book follows the death of Joshua and describes the deeply troubled period when the twelve tribes, scattered as they are over a vast area of land and just as quarrelsome and rebellious as ever, try to establish themselves as farmers and shepherds and herders amongst a hostile and unfriendly group of different nations with very different backgrounds and cultures and who specifically worship very strange gods and engage in the most horrendous practices. God's intention for Israel was to keep them separate, a nation chosen by him for a specific purpose.

What the book of Judges describes is a period in which the tribes are separated and lack a unifying leader. There are examples of internal conflict as well as continual problems from serious attacks by the local tribes and petty kingdoms, as well as by the major nations which they were told to destroy.

To make matter worse, with both Moses and Joshua dead and the priests themselves lacking true leadership, they begin to show that lack of unity which will put them at a serious disadvantage especially when facing nations which previously had been afraid of them because of the previous success of Israel under Moses and Joshua. Now, leaderless and disorganised, the Israelites are at the mercy of their predators – and predators who are very determined to get rid of them. This, partly because with a predominantly westward migration of people who were looking for fertile pastures and land for cultivation which required secure enclosures as opposed to free ranging grazing, there was an increasing pressure to seize and secure the best lands. And equally there was the need by those already there to protect their land and animals from invaders with the inevitable conflict.

However, the fact remains that whilst the Israelites suffered because of their failure to adhere to God's law and ignored the prophetic voices warning them of the dire consequences of their disobedience, some of the responsibility for their failure to occupy the land was due to other factors. For example, geographically, the land was divided in two by a North/South rift valley in which the river Jordan flowed. On either side were mountain ranges with, particularly on the West, steep mountains riven by steep-sided valleys. Here various people had established themselves, hill tribes and valley people, all under various 'kings' who, in general, were military leaders.

Further, as the Egyptian dominance of the area declined, more and more peoples, in addition to the Israelites, were trying to establish themselves here. In this, the arbitrary division of the land under Moses left many of the Israelite tribes quite isolated, forced to act for themselves. Even their appointed place of worship at Shiloh meant travelling some distance. The nation was now faced with aggressive defenders, fortified cities and the problems associated with establishing themselves. For the Israelites were, by heritage, a nation of nomadic tribesmen now trying to re-establish themselves as farmers, at a time when to farm implied defending your land. Previously, as with Abraham and his nephew Lot, when the place was too crowded, one party moved elsewhere. Even in Egypt, Joseph had warned his brothers to tell the king that they were sheep herders, a job which the Egyptians hated and, therefore, there was in general no conflict of interest.

This sense of isolation is emphasised when we look at the 'judges', local heroes who were used by God to rescue the people. For example, Deborah and Barak operated to the North and West of Lake Galilee, Gideon further South along the river, whilst Samson, who was used by God to incite the Philistines, operated West of the Dead Sea in the area dominated by the Philistines. These people, previously thought to have come from Crete, are now believed to have migrated from Anatolia and established themselves along the coast.

The opening words of the book of Judges begin with Israel seeking God's help in getting rid of their opponents, but at the same time, we are reminded that the various tribes had NOT driven out or destroyed their enemies. And by Chapter 2, an angel of God is sent to tell them point blank (2:1), "I took you out of Egypt and brought you to the land I promised your ancestors... you must not make any covenant with the people who live in this land. You must tear down their altars. But you have not done what I told you. You have done just the opposite. So I tell you now, that I will not drive out these people as you advance. They will be your enemies, and you will be trapped by the worship of their gods." At this, the people began to cry. To be honest, without God's help, they were in a predicament.

Then follows the repetition of the warning of the previous chapter: "That whole generation died, and the next generation forgot the Lord and what he had done for Israel." And that is followed by the damning words, "Then the people of Israel sinned against the Lord and began to serve the Baals (False gods), the gods of the peoples round them. And so the Lord became furious with Israel and let its raiders attack and rob them He let enemies all around overpower them, and the Israelites could no longer protect themselves." Chapter 2:22 actually states that God allowed this to happen, as a way of testing the nation, to see whether they would remain true to him.

The lesson! That Israel was only powerful because of God's presence with them, and when they sinned so terribly in their blatant disobedience, two things: first, God could not be with them, and second, they would reap the result of that disobedience. In other words, God's laws were there for a specific and valid reason. To disobey was to see the consequences. And that is true for individuals and nations today.

But, thank God for the God still loved them! As today, God loves everyone and longs to be able to bless them. So, what did God do? He gave them leaders, and while those leaders lived, the people obeyed, but when the leaders died, they went back to their old ways. Like weeds in a garden which can overpower the precious plants, their sinful nature was stronger than their good intentions. So God did not drive out all those nations after Joshua's death, but (3:1) He left some nations in the land, "to test the Israelites who had not been through the wars in Canaan." These other nations were to be a test for the Israelites to find out whether or not these succeeding generations would obey the Lord as their ancestors had done. No wonder one man remarked, "God has no grandchildren."

Then follows a list of the leaders God sent, called Judges, and a list of some of their exploits – men like Othniel, Ehud, Shamgar and then Deborah and Barak. After many years, the situation had become so desperate that when God called a man named Gideon (Chapter 6), we find him threshing the wheat in a wine press for fear that the Midianites would seize the grain and they would starve. The people had cried out to God in deep distress, and the Lord had sent a prophet to tell them exactly why they were suffering, that they had fallen from the faith of their ancestors and through disobedience had lost the presence and blessing of God. "I told you that I am the Lord your God and that you should not worship these other gods, but you did not listen to Me."

Now God is going to perform several miracles to deliver the people because Gideon, His chosen man, is a good man, one who is able to believe in God and obey him. In chapters 6, 7 and 8, we see how God reduces Gideon's army of 32,000 men to just 300 deliberately to prove that the victory comes from God's help not from any human resources. Gideon is inspired by a dream, and by following instructions, he leads his men to the top of a hill surrounding the enemy, and at Gideon's command, they blow their trumpets, break the jars concealing their flaming torches and shout out, "The sword of the Lord and Gideon." At this, the whole Midianite army is made to panic, and believing that they are surrounded by a vastly superior army, they panic and, in the confusion, they fight each other. Gideon then follows this up by calling on the other tribes to help, and between them, they then route another army of over 135,000 men, desert tribesmen.

Such was his success that the Israelites wanted to make him their king, but he refused and went home. However, one of his sons, Abimelech, offered himself as a king and to promote himself, he murdered his 70 brothers (Chapter 8). But in spite of some success, he was finally killed whilst making an attack on a fortified tower when a woman threw a millstone down on his head which fractured his skull, and then, to avoid the shame of having been killed by a woman, one of his own men at his request drew his sword and finished him off.

Then follow several more leaders such as Tola, Jair and Jephthah who had a measure of success in rallying the nation. But the one who stands out here is a man named Samson who was born miraculously to a childless couple, Manoah and his wife, who were told by an angel that the child must be consecrated to God from birth. This angel, who said that his name was "a name of wonder", caused fire to consume the sacrifice which Manoah had offered, and then he ascended to heaven in the flames. It is suggested that this might be one of the several appearances of our Lord himself prior to his coming as Mary's son. (Chapter 13). Certainly, the story describes Samson's miraculous birth and how God gave Samson extreme power and strength.

When Samson comes on the scene, the Israelites are suffering badly from the Philistines who, moving into the semi-power vacuum left by the declining Egyptian power, were themselves seeking to enlarge their territories. The fascinating story of Samson is the tale of a local hero who manages to so annoy the Philistines that he is able to seriously challenge their authority. Then, weakened by his love for a Philistine woman who deceives him into revealing the secret of his strength, he is finally captured, blinded and made the butt of their jokes. However, he turns the tables when blinded and bound, he is being exhibited in celebration of their god Dagon in Gaza. Having regained his strength, his hair having grown, he pulls down the hall in which the five Philistine kings and many thousands of people had gathered, by calling upon God to help him and enable him to pull down the supporting pillars, killing more in his death had he had during his life. (Chapters 13–16).

An exception to this localised conflict occurs (Chapter 18) when the tribe of Dan, who as yet had not managed to occupy their land, were scouting for more and met the prophet Micah who was fostering a young Levite as his priest and they persuaded him to join them. They then met another Levite. He tells a sad story (Chapter 19) of how his concubine was raped and killed by sexual perverts. This so incensed the Levite that he cut the body into twelve pieces and sent a portion to each of the twelve tribes. The resulting horror, something not seen by them since they left Egypt, resulted in the tribes coming together. When the other tribes heard that this had happened in the territory of Benjamin, they massed an army of over 400,000 men and fought Benjamin, killing over 25,000 of their soldiers and decimating the tribe. To make matters worse, they decreed that none of the remaining Benjamite men should be allowed to marry any of their daughters. However, not wanting to lose the whole tribe, they allowed the young men to take a wife by force at a festival, thus ensuring that the tribe kept its place in the nation.

The book ends with Chapter 21:25, "There was no king in Israel at that time. Everyone did just what he pleased." There is no attempt here to portray the nation of Israel as some kind of super race. It is a sober reflection on the appalling state of the nation over a period of some two hundred years, as they sought to establish themselves on the land of promise. However, it not merely illustrates the consequences of disobedience. They only turned to God briefly when in trouble. It also shows the weakness of this nation, both militarily and spiritually, when they lacked unity and a just and righteous leadership. At the same time, it reinforces two things. God's measureless love for his people and also the fact, as will be revealed later, that God had a plan in which they would finally accept him and be restored to favour. But there is a long way to go before that plan will be revealed.

Ruth

This short book is a dramatic picture of life amongst the ordinary people; it is not concerned with kings or prophets, but it does show how love and faithfulness, arising out of tragedy, can lead to remarkable blessing. Set during the troubled times of the previous book, it tells the story, no doubt recorded for posterity to marvel, of how God can intervene and bless, how out of tragedy can come unselfish love. And out of that unselfish devotion, came a strategic place in the nation's history. It also serves as a contrast to the faithlessness of the nation, showing how a foreigner, a woman from the tribe of Moab could, by her love and faithfulness to Israel's God, become a living part of that nation and one of the ancestors of that great King David and indeed of Jesus himself.

Very simply, we have a family, the wife and two sons of an Ephraimite, Elimelech, living in Bethlehem who, in a time of famine moved to the land of Moab. There the sons married local women. Then, first, Naomi's husband Elimelech dies, then, ten years later, her two sons Mahlon and Chilion also die.

Hearing that there has been a good harvest back home, Naomi decides to return to Bethlehem. Having no other children, sons for the girls to marry, she urges them to go back to their own kindred. Tearfully and reluctantly at last Orpah agrees, but Ruth, in a remarkable display of commitment, says no. "Your people shall be my people, and your God shall be my God. Wherever you die, I will die and that is where I will be buried. May the Lord's worst punishment come upon me if I let anything but death separate me from you."

Then follows the account of how Naomi is welcomed home and tells of the disaster which has befallen her, but Ruth's actions bring her credit, especially as she takes on the burden of providing for her mother-in-law.

Out gleaning for the stray wheat from the harvest, Ruth is working in the field of a man named Boaz, who is both a wealthy and influential man but also, it appears, a relative of Naomi's deceased husband Elimelech. He befriends her and helps her, no doubt understanding fully the details of the tragic death of his relative and the remarkable faithfulness of the daughter-in-law.

The story then unfolds, with guidance from her mother-in-law, as Ruth risks her reputation and her future by throwing herself on the mercy of Boaz, by spending the night close to him. He could have destroyed her reputation, but instead he opts to give her security and status.

Realising that the deceased Elimelech had owned land, Boaz calls on a closer relative to buy in the land to keep it in the family. The relative agrees, only to be told that as part of the deal he must marry Ruth, the heir to her husband's property. This he refuses to do because it would dilute his own estate descending to his children. Boaz then buys the land, marries Ruth and thereby makes her a part of his own family, and she in turn presents her husband with a son. Naomi is comforted; she has a grandson. Ruth names her son Obed, who becomes the father of Jesse who was the father of David, the shepherd boy who becomes Israel's greatest king.

What a remarkable story, illustrating as it does, the way in which God rewards the faithfulness of individuals, and no doubt, it was also included as a contrast to the behaviour of the nation at that time, showing that even when whole nations are disobedient and faithless, there are also some individuals who will remain faithful and loyal to God and love Him.

1 Samuel

Sadly, this book outlines a story which is echoed down through the ages of human existence. Here a whole nation commits acts of folly, either deliberately or through the mismanagement of ordinary human passions. Then, when everything goes pear-shaped, tragically wrong, they cry out to God for help. Often this is true of people who otherwise would not recognise the existence of God. Sometimes it is believers themselves, sometimes individuals and sadly often whole communities or nations. That is what is unfolding here.

After two hundred years of the chaos of Israel's occupation of the land, the most urgent need had been for military leadership because the Israelite tribes were attempting to wrest the land from the various local tribal kingdoms ruled over by kings. These often-joined forces to face the increasing challenge from the invading Israelite tribes who, it must be said, were largely autonomous, disorganised and without a central unifying command.

Here it was, in the central highlands, that the Philistines were attempting to cut off the Northern tribes from those in the South, and much of their attack was directed at Shiloh, which is where the Ark of the Covenant was kept, watched over by the elderly and ineffectual Priest Eli whose sons, Hophni and Phinehas, were not only dissolute but irreligious, in the sense that they treated the holy things with complete disregard; which was not merely a dereliction of duty but an affront to the holiness of God. The national problems arose out of a situation which was caused by a lack of spiritual leadership after the death of Moses and Joshua, and the death of those who had previously witnessed the miraculous power of God in action. Now, the focus has to be on the situation amongst the Priests and Levites rather than simply on military expedience.

So we find the Lord sending a prophet to Eli (Chapter 2) to lay the blame firmly on the old man's shoulders, both his own failure and his inordinate failure to discipline his sons. God reminds him of his ancestor Aaron and the enormous responsibility handed down to him to maintain the honour and holy righteousness of the God whom he served. The warning was simply that he and his sons will die and the rest of the family will be extinguished, yet God will preserve one branch who will faithfully serve Him.

Samuel is the focus of this book, and it begins with yet another unexpected birth as a very devout but childless woman pleads with God for a child and, in return, offers to dedicate him body and soul to the service of God. Is this what God was waiting for? The child was Samuel. As soon as he was old enough to live away from his mother, she took him to Shiloh to serve as an assistant to Eli.

Samuel's first encounter with God came one night as he heard what he thought was Eli calling him, but Eli, realising that it was God, told the lad to respond, "Speak Lord for your servant is listening" (Chapter 3). What God told Samuel that night was that he was going to do something terrible to the nation which would stagger them, and that he was going to punish the family of Eli forever because of the horrendous things they had done.

After this, the Philistines made a bold foray right into the heartlands of the Israelite nation, camping at Aphek. The Israelites opposed them at Ebenezer, but in the ensuing battle, the Philistines won. However, the Israelites were not driven from their hilltop position, so in desperation they sent for the Ark of the Covenant in the hope that by so doing God would intervene on their behalf. However, when the enemy heard the shouting that resulted, they redoubled their efforts, with the result that Israel were soundly defeated, some 30,000 of their soldiers were killed including Eli's two sons, and the Ark of the covenant was captured. (Chapter 4). When the news reached Eli, he was sitting on a gate waiting, he fell off backwards, broke his neck and died, and when the news of this reached the widow of Phinehas who was pregnant, she died in childbirth, naming her son Ichabod, meaning the glory has gone.

Meantime, the Ark of the Covenant was taken by the Philistines and put in the temple of their god Dagon in Ashdod. In the morning, they found that the image of Dagon had fallen face down in front of the Ark. They set it up again, but the following morning the same thing happened, however, this time both its arms and it head were broken off. In horror, the people of the town and the five Philistine kings sent The Ark to the town of Gath, but there the Lord sent a plague of tumours, so they sent it to another town Ekron where the people cried out in panic.

After seven months, they decided to send it back to Israel, but to prove that the Ark was the cause of the trouble, the priests advised that they put it on a cart drawn by two cows whose calves had been separated from them. If the cows went to their calves then it was not the God of Israel causing the problem, but if it headed to the territory of Israel, they would know that indeed it was God. They also sent with the Ark a present and an offering – gold models of five mice and five tumours. And of course, the cows set off straight to Beth Shemesh, mooing as they went and without turning off the road.

Now begins a remarkable story, as the Israelite Levites lift the Ark from the cart and sacrifice the cows as a burnt offering, using the cart as fuel. Yet the men of the town incurred God's anger, because they looked inside the Ark, and seventy of them died. So they sent a message to the men of Kiriath Jearim who came and collected it and put it in the house of Abinadab, where they consecrated his son to act as a priest to care for it. And there it stayed for twenty years, whilst Israel cried to the Lord for help. (Chapter 7).

Samuel, now the priest of the Lord after Eli's death, warned the people that unless they repented, God would not help them and, as evidence of their repentance, they must get rid of all their foreign gods and their images and dedicate themselves to the worship and service of God alone. He gathered them at Mizpah where they did indeed confess and offered themselves to God whilst Samuel prayed for them. Result, the Philistines, hearing that the tribes were gathered at Mizpah, went to attack them yet again, but while Samuel was offering a sacrifice, God sent a mighty thunderstorm on the Philistines who panicked and fled, enabling Israel to pursue and kill them. For the rest of Samuel's life, there was peace. The Philistines no longer attacked.

As Samuel grows old, he appoints his sons as judges, but they were totally dishonest and so the nation turns to Samuel to demand that they have a king to lead them like the other nations. He was bitterly disappointed, feeling betrayed, and he warns them of what a king would exact from the people. God responded by telling Samuel to appoint a handsome young man from the small tribe of Benjamin named Saul and to anoint him as king. This after quite an interesting account of how Saul himself became involved. (Chapter 9) Saul is anointed with olive oil and acclaimed by the people at Mizpah. However, not all the people liked this choice. However, Saul's moment to establish himself came about a month later when King Nahash of Ammon laid siege to Jabesh in Gilead and demanded the right eye of each of its men in order to avert a destruction of the town. They sent out messengers seeking help and Saul heard. In response, a furious Saul and Samuel called out the nation to respond, Saul by killing two oxen and cutting them in pieces which he sent throughout the land, saying that if they did not follow them into battle, this would be done to their oxen.

The ensuing battle, as Saul rapidly crossed the Jordan and made a sudden attack on the Philistine camp, was swiftly over. The Israelites were so delighted that they proclaimed Saul as their king on the spot, as their own choice. Encouraged by this striking victory, Saul looked to confront a far more serious threat. With his son Jonathan, he advanced on the Philistine garrison at Michmash where they were threatening to cut the nation into two at a vital mountain pass. With an army of just two thousand men, leaving his son in reserve with another one thousand, they inflicted a crushing defeat on the enemy who retired to gather strength. Saul then watched his army slowly wither away and seek refuge in caves and cisterns, even in the tombs, frightened, as the Philistines gathered their resources. Finally, Saul was faced with a mighty army, as numerous as the sand on the shore, comprising chariots, cavalry and infantry. Waiting in vain for Samuel to come to his aid and invoke the presence of God, he made the mistake of making an unauthorised burnt offering himself. Samuel was bitterly displeased at this flagrant breach of religious ceremony and warned Saul that God would punish him for it.

In the meantime, Saul took his remaining 600 men and advanced to face the enemy but held off. Jonathan, a remarkably able and courageous young man, together with his armour bearer, crawled up a rocky defile and challenged the Philistines, killing some twenty of them. This threw the enemy into a panic and, as they fled, Saul called out his own men from their refuges where they were skulking and completely routed the whole Philistine army, who fled, leaving their corpses behind all the way to their own homeland.

Encouraged by his success, Saul proceeded to clear the enemy from the vital heartlands and fought a number of battles with great success, but already pride was beginning to destroy him as we note that at Carmel, Saul had built a monument to himself. But he then made a second dreadful mistake. Told to destroy all the enemy and their possessions, when victorious over the Amalekite King Agag, he spared the king's life and failed to destroy the goods, chattels and livestock. (Chapter 15). "Because you have rejected the word of the Lord, He has also rejected you," said Samuel, and in spite of Saul's admission of guilt and attempt to make recompense, God told him that He would reject him. "I did obey the Lord," says Saul. "Why then to I hear cattle mooing and sheep bleating?"

replies Samuel (verse 14). And at the command of God, Samuel then set off to anoint with oil, a man after God's own heart, the young David.

Samuel's problem (Chapter 16) was how to anoint a new king whilst the old one was still alive, and this led to a subterfuge, a sacrifice at Bethlehem, to which Jesse and his sons were invited; at least most of the sons, but not God's choice, the youngest son David who was out in the fields keeping the sheep. When finally, he was summoned, in front of his brothers, Samuel anoints him with oil. "Immediately the spirit of the Lord took control of David and was with him from that day on." Which meant that the spirit left Saul who was tormented by an evil spirit which manifested itself as an insane jealousy and hatred of David.

God establishes David in a remarkable way. On a visit to his brothers who were in the army, David noted that the whole Israelite army is paralysed by their fear of a Philistine champion named Goliath (Chapter 17) who was defying them to personal combat. Armed only with a stone and staff, David takes him on. "You are coming at me armed with sword spear and javelin, but I come against you in the name of the Lord Almighty, the God of the Israelite armies which you have defied." A stone from a sling and God's help and Goliath was senseless on the ground where David decapitated him with his own sword. And this was the beginning of David's incredible achievements which would result in his uniting the whole of the twelve tribes into a kingdom which would excel all others of the day.

But first, David has to establish himself. Taken to the king by the army chief, Abner, still carrying Goliath's head as a token of his exploit, Saul keeps David at court where Saul's son Jonathan and David form a bond which will help him to survive Saul's jealousy. Marriage to Saul's elder daughter Merab was the reward for David's bravery, but a younger daughter, Michal falls head over heels in love with David, and Saul sees in her an opportunity to trap David and kill him. Saul had made no secret of his hatred for David because his success was undermining his declining popularity and, inevitably, threatened the succession of Jonathan to the throne. However, Jonathan, because of his very strong attachment, conspires to alert David, who is able to escape and then follows a period when Saul actively and openly searches for David to kill him, and David has to flee to the wilderness of the mountainous highlands.

David flees with a few followers and goes to Ahimelech the priest (Chapter 21) who gives him the sacred bread to feed the men with him, and he also gives the unarmed David Goliath's sword which had been placed in the holy place.

From there, David and the few men loyal to him go to one of the Philistine kings who welcomes him, but David is afraid because his own reputation makes him a threat to this traditional enemy of Israel. From there to a cave where he is joined by his own brothers and disgruntled citizens, creating a band of 400 men.

Now the hunt for David intensifies as Ahimelech's help to David is reported to Saul, who slaughters 85 of the priests and their families, but one escapes to tell David who blames himself for the tragedy.

Then follow a series of incidents: David rescues a town from a Philistine attack; he repeatedly has Saul in striking distance but spares his life because Saul had been anointed by God; Samuel the guiding light of the nation dies; David marries Abigail, the widow of a man who had refused to help him but who dies of apoplexy. He meets Saul, having again refused to kill the king when in a position to do so, and then in despair, David goes over to the Philistines, to Achish king of Gath (Chapter 27), where he and his now 600 men settle with their wives and families.

When subsequently, the Philistines again go to war with Israel, Achish assumes that David will support them, and David agrees, but when their army regroups, the other kings reject David's men as potentially a threat. David and his men return to Ziklag their home, only to find that in their absence, the Amalekites had raided and burnt the town, taking as loot all the men's belongings, flocks and herds and most importantly their wives and children. David then pursues the attackers, and at dawn the next day surprises them, inflicting a massive defeat on them and recovers all the loot plus all the families of his men.

So great was the loot taken by the Amalekites in their raids on Philistia and Judah that David is able to restore their possessions to the cities of Bethel Ramah, Jattir, Aroer, Siphmoth, Eshtemoa, Racal, and to the Kenites and to the towns of Hormah, Borashan, Athach, and to Hebron, the raided cities and some of the towns where the people had helped him during his time in the mountainous wilderness (Chapter 30).

The book ends with the Philistines again defeating the Israeli troops on Mt Gilboa, at which battle, Saul and his three sons were killed. This man who was chosen by God via Samuel to lead the people, had all the qualities of leadership. Physically outstanding, a good leader and a courageous fighter, he won the respect of the nation by his actions in facing the enemy. However, human weakness, a certain arrogance and pride, undermined by his obsessive jealousy of the man who would become his successor, ultimately destroyed him.

Working in conjunction with David, the two men could have achieved so much. However, what we see is that the Spirit of God, which came on Saul after his anointing as king, left him at this point, the moment when David was chosen as his successor. Was this because of his inordinate jealousy of David or solely because he disobeyed God? What we do know from the past is that without God's help, human effort does not bring the results that God wants, which is that He, God, receives the honour, and that people are made aware that it is only through God's help that the underlying purpose of God can be achieved. However, with the death of his son Jonathan and his other sons, Saul's mantle would fall on another as we shall now see.

2 Samuel

This book continues from where the first book of Samuel finishes, to trace the actions and achievements of King David, the second man chosen by God to lead the nation of Israel. Surprisingly, after the more heroic status of his predecessor, the one chosen by God for the momentous task of establishing this dissolute and widely dispersed group of tribespeople was the youngest of his family. Bypassing the elder boys, the choice fell on a youngster who was out in the fields looking after the family's flocks, not considered important enough to be invited to meet Samuel.

However, working with the help of God's spirit, by the time this book opens, David had already made a name for himself, both as a warrior and as a compassionate and fair-minded person. And this was amply demonstrated by his respect for the dead Saul who had been God's chosen man. For example, he put to death the messenger who admitted, or boasted, that he had administered the final death blow to Saul, something questioned in other accounts, and the wonderful song of lament which he, David, composed in memory of the late King.

Now, straightway, David asks for God's guidance. "Shall I go and take control of one of the towns of Judah?" "Yes," the Lord answered. "Which one?" "Hebron." Then, when this modest move is accomplished, as David moves his family and his men into the town and its surrounds, the men of Judah came to Hebron and they anoint David as King of Judah. So far so good, as they say, however, the commander of Saul's army, Abner, had fled over the Jordan to Mahanaim with the one remaining of Saul's sons, Ishbosheth, and they had anointed him as king over that area, and indeed, of all of the North, thus creating a serious division which had the potential to destroy the monarchy and send the nation back into anarchy.

However, things soon came to a head and Abner, the leader of soldiers still true to the family of Saul, and David's men under the leadership of Joab, faced one another at Gibeon. The two commanders suggested a contest between twelve men from each side, but this degenerated into a bloody battle in which Joab's men overcame the others, and in the conflict, Joab's brother was killed. Peace was agreed, but for a long time there was bitter conflict between the supporters of the dead Saul and David's men, with David's men gaining strength and position to the point where Abner went to meet David at Hebron and offered to bring the Northern tribes over to David. An agreement was made, and Abner left. When Joab returned from a raid, he was incensed to hear of the treaty and went after Abner and slew him because Abner had killed his brother Asahel.

David's reaction was deep sorrow at the unnecessary bloodshed, and to show that he was not a party to the death, he declared a day of mourning and walked behind Abner's coffin. The rebellion of the Northern tribes under Abner and Ishbosheth lasted some seven years and was finally brought to an end when two of his own men killed Ishbosheth in his own bed whilst asleep. The murderers brought the head to present to David at Hebron as evidence, and his reaction was the same to them as for the messenger who brought the news of Saul's death because this was simply murder, not death in battle. This left as the only living relative of Saul, his grandson, Jonathan's child, Mephibosheth, to whom David would show compassion and respect because of his own deep love for his father.

Now the tribes of Israel came to David at his residence in Hebron to make him their king, pointing out as they did so, that even during Saul's reign, it was David whose skills in battle had given the Nation the upper hand over their enemies, and they reminded David, God had promised that he, David, would be their leader and their ruler.

The first exploit following this settlement was David's capture of the city of Jebus, later called Jerusalem. The inhabitants had baited David, saying that their fortress was impregnable, but entry was made via a water tunnel and the city soon capitulated. This city was then reconstructed by the king who enlarged it by filling in the valley to the East and making it his capital, and Hiram of Tyre provided him with cedar logs and skilled masons to build a palace. Now, David, blessed abundantly by God, is firmly establishing the nation and bringing security, where before the individual tribes had struggled to retain their foothold in the mountainous territory.

As soon as their main opposition, the Philistines, heard that David was now king, they redoubled their efforts to dislodge him, setting up their forces in the valley of Rephaim. In answer to prayer and encouraged by the Lord, David twice inflicted a defeat on the enemy. In the second battle, he routed their forces so severely that they retreated to their own country leaving Israel reasonably secure. So secure was the king with his united kingdom, that he now does something to undo some of the more serious depredations which had haunted him for years.

As a prime example, The Ark of the Covenant, lost to the Philistines since the days of Eli the priest and left at the house of Abinadab, needed to be restored if the Lord was to be their God. But tragedy struck because David, in his great enthusiasm, neglected the basic rules that only the priests should handle The Ark. When the oxen drawing the cart with the Ark stumbled in the ruts, Uzzah, Abinadab's son, in whose house the Ark had rested for so many years, put out his hand to prevent the ark from falling and was immediately struck dead. Familiarity, they say, breeds contempt. David, afraid now of the holiness of the Lord, turned aside and left the Ark at the house of Obed Edom in Gath. The awesome holiness of God had been breached, but David, whose intentions were above reproach, was both angry with God and afraid. So long had the Ark been left out of their recognisance that David, in his righteous desire to accord it the prominence which it should have, overstepped the mark.

The irony of the situation was that Gath was a Philistine city, and Obed Edom had been a citizen. The Ark will now remain for a further three months, during which time God blessed the house of Obed Edom. Soon the news reached David, and he then set out again to restore the Ark in the proper manner and with due respect, but in doing so, dancing in front of it in a holy dance, David incurs the scorn and the mockery of his wife, Saul's daughter Michal, who thought her husband was humiliating himself in public by his display of devotion.

The kingdom now being relatively secure, David's thoughts turn again to ways of pleasing and honouring his Lord, the one whose blessing had made both him and the nation what it had now become. Ah, thought David, I have a beautiful palace, but God still dwells in a wooden box whose resting place, at best, is the Tent of the Presence. Therefore, I will build my Lord and my God a place worthy of his glory – a palace, a temple, a dwelling fit for the King of kings.

Calling for the prophet Nathan, he describes his proposal. Nathan agrees, an excellent idea, but that night, God speaking to Nathan says "No!" Reminding Nathan of their national history, God says that he had never sought anything other than to be with them, and in any case, David cannot build it; he is a man of war, of bloodshed. Tell him that I will establish his kingdom, make him as famous as the greatest leaders of the world. I have chosen this land for them and settled the people here. Ever since they entered, they have been overset by violent people, but no more. I will give peace and establish the family of David forever, but it is his son who must build the temple, not David.

On hearing this, David enters the Tent of the Presence, and in deep humility, he worships and praises the God of Israel. In thanksgiving, he calls to mind the greatness, the glory of God, and gives thanks for all that He, the God of all Gods, has done for his people and for himself, the shepherd boy. "I am not worthy," he says, "and yet you are doing even more because you are looking ahead to the future, to my descendants in the years to come. What you have done, Lord, has spread your fame throughout the whole world." For God had promised to establish David's dynasty forever. Ultimately, this will come about through the one who, in later years, will be called 'great David's greater Son."

Now back to business, and (Chapter 8) we are given a list of King David's victories. He had defeated the Philistines and ended their control over the land. He had defeated the Moabites and went on to defeat Hadadezer who was on his way to assert his authority over the region of upper Euphrates, capturing horses and foot soldiers and then continuing to defeat the Syrians of Damascus when they, in turn, went to the aid of Hadadezer; with the result that all these territories became subject to King David, paying him taxes and tribute. All in all, David made Israel both totally victorious and very wealthy as he also defeated the Ammonites and the Syrians, seizing their treasures and making the people subservient to his rule.

Two things now. First we see David's great kindness to Jonathan's son Mephibosheth, in memory of the great affection which had been between Saul's son and the persecuted David running away from Saul's jealousy – a deep friendship, even though Jonathan knew that David would become king on his father, Saul's, death. And then, what is really the most shameful and sinful event in King David's life – his adultery with the wife of one of his bravest soldiers.

At home in his palace when his army went out to war one spring, David sees a beautiful woman bathing in the river, sends for her and then, when he later hears that she has become pregnant, tries make her husband, Uriah, responsible by bringing him back from the battle. When that fails, he orders his army commander, Joab, to ensure that Uriah is killed in the siege of the city. On hearing of this, Nathan the prophet rebukes David very seriously in a parable. However, when Uriah the husband is dead, David marries Bathsheba, but her firstborn son, born in adultery, dies. David's actions here indicate his awareness of his great guilt – adultery and murder.

Later, Bathsheba will give birth to another son, Solomon, who will succeed David, but much is to happen before that – particularly, trouble within his own family, from Absalom in particular. First, Absalom has a very beautiful sister Tamar who is seduced by her half-brother Amnon. Absalom takes his revenge for this by having his half-brother killed, and then, to avoid the king's anger, he flees and remains out of sight for three years. David recovers from his grief over Amnon and then grieves over Absalom's absence.

Joab, knowing how fond the king was of his son Absalom, engineers his return, and they are reconciled. However, some years later, Absalom plans a rebellion against his own father, and to curry popularity, he intercepts people who are coming to the king with a complaint or a grudge and offers them benefits.

After four years of such scheming, he asks permission from the king to perform a vow in Hebron, the Holy place. Once there, he sends messengers to all the tribes who accept him as his father's successor and crown him, Absalom, as their king. David is warned of what has happened, and on advice, he leaves the city with his immediate family and some loyal soldiers, weeping bitterly as they leave.

Then comes a time when the kingdom is divided in its loyalty. Some express their loyalty to David, whilst others effectively curse him. Absalom then enters Jerusalem and occupies the palace. Then follow some very bitter battles, between followers loyal to David and those who support Absalom, civil war, until finally the two armies confront each other. In the ensuing battle, David's men, mostly from his own tribe, defeat Absalom's forces, mainly from the North, which division, recurring repeatedly will ultimately lead to the two separating as independent nations. But not in the lifetime of David or his son Solomon.

But now, Absalom fleeing from the battle, as his side is losing, is caught by his hair in an oak tree. Joab, ignoring David's plea to spare his son, kills him as he hangs there. David, told of his son's death, mourns bitterly and deeply until Joab reprimands him by saying that if he continues to put his love for his son before the national interest of unity, he will lose all the support of the nation who have witnessed Absalom's treachery.

David now returns to his capital, Jerusalem, and a kind of sanity returns to the nation which, having been deceived by Absalom, now on his death remember that David is their rightful king and return to him. Once again, it is Judah who first assert their loyalty and then the Northern tribes equal their vows of loyalty, and the kingdom appears to be reunited once again.

However, there are still rebellious elements and a further tragic division is threatened by a man named Sheba who rallied a measure of support from the Northern tribes, which the king and his advisors saw as more dangerous that Absalom's rebellion. Calling his own loyal men together, he sent Amasa to rally them. When he did not return, David sent the loyal Abishai and his brother Joab, together with the royal bodyguard. Challenging Amasa, the left-handed Joab surprises him by thrusting his sword with his left hand whilst greeting him with his right hand. Leaving the corpse, they find that Sheba and his men were sheltering in a fortified town, to which they laid siege, until a wise woman reports that the town is loyal to David and the people deliver up the renegade, allowing the troops to return to David in Jerusalem.

Saul's remaining descendants are put to death, and David fights a last battle against the Philistine giants, but in doing so, almost loses his life as his strength is now failing. Now follows a repeat of David's song of victory, (Psalm 18) and, for the record, the words, "David son of Jesse was the man whom God made great, whom the God of Jacob chose to be king and who was the composer of beautiful songs for Israel." "These are David's last words: 'The spirit of the Lord speaks through me; his message is on my lips.'" And he gives honour to God for all that had been promised was now in him fulfilled. Referring to the Eternal Covenant which God had made with Abraham and his descendant, singular, that would never end.

What now follows is a list of the king's famous soldiers, and yet another act of pride as he commissions another census, listing a total of one million three hundred thousand men of military age. This is wrong because it lays the emphasis on human endeavour rather than the true source of his success which is the demonstrable power of the living God. Punishment? Yes! A choice of three things, of which David chooses to fall into the hands of God's angel, rather than suffer by human means. Repentance, humility and sacrifice follow. God's anger is stayed, as the prophet Gad orders him to go to the threshing floor of Araunah to offer sacrifice. The oxen and threshing instruments are offered freely by Araunah as a gift, but David, famously and in character says, "No, I will pay you for it. I will not offer to the Lord my God sacrifices that have cost me nothing." And he bought both the place and the oxen and built an altar where he offered burnt offerings and fellowship offerings. The Lord then answered his prayer and the epidemic of disease ceased.

1 Kings

One could dismiss the next two books as merely anecdotal ancient Jewish history, but to do so would be to ignore the reason why they were included in the canon of sacred scripture, for they paint a tragic picture of a nation with enormous potential, supported by the promises made to their godly ancestors and backed by a Covenant agreement with God, the God of their fathers, which could only be undermined or broken by the failure of the people and their rulers. A nation which time and time again would be warned by God-appointed men who at the risk of their lives would declare, point out, illustrate the utter folly of disobedience. The sin which broke the unity between Adam and God at the start of this narrative would prove to be their ultimate downfall – disobedience. And that in spite of God's offer of forgiveness, His compassion and His willingness to help them, all supported by continuing evidence of his divine, miraculous power and His presence with them. Because, even in their signal failure over a period of many hundreds of years, God still loved them, as His prophets would repeatedly tell them.

For us today, it is a salutary reminder of the folly which results from our inability to learn from our mistakes, to benefit from past failure, whether it be as individuals or as nations. In many ways, history can teach us so much, about human character, as well as in the repetition of events. As has been said, 'there is nothing new under the sun.'

As this book commences, we see the Nation of Israel transformed by the remarkable success of their king, who had been both a military strategist and a man of outstanding faith, who endeavoured to honour God in all that he did but was still a man with human passions, just like us – a man who loved God but who fell short of the glory of God on a number of occasions; which reminds us, that in the sight of God 'all have sinned and come short of the glory of God'. But also that in spite of it all, God looks not on the outward but sees the inward heart, the thoughts, ambitions and desires as we were reminded so succinctly at the time of God's choice of both Saul and David.

Now the king is an old man being kept warm by a pretty young girl, and the burning issue is that of the succession. As the eldest of David's sons after the death of Absalom, Adonijah appeared to have the prior claim, and in this, he was supported by both Joab, head of the military forces, and Abiathar the priest. But against him were some notables including Zadoc the priest and Nathan the prophet, plus David's own bodyguard. To strengthen his cause, Adonijah invited the nobles of Judah and the other king's other sons but not his half-brother Solomon, to a feast and a sacrifice to be held at the spring of Enrogel.

When Nathan heard this news, he went directly to Bathsheba, Solomon's mother, to remind her that unless she acted quickly, it would be a fait accompli. She was told to go straight to the king himself and remind him of his promise to her and what Nathan the prophet had told him of the Lord's promise. She was then backed up by Nathan himself, who came in and reported that already they were proclaiming Adonijah king.

David acted swiftly, telling Nathan and Zadoc the priest to take Solomon with them, anoint him as the king chosen by David, put him on the king's mule and proclaim the accession very publicly, making enough noise to disturb Adonijah's feast, as the people in the city joyously responded to the news. In fear, Adonijah clung to the horns of the altar in the tent of the Lord's Presence, but Solomon assured him that provided he accepted the situation, his life would be spared.

David now gave his final blessing to Solomon. "Be confident and determined and do what the Lord your God orders you to do," and then he died.

Meanwhile Adonijah was to make a terrible mistake which would cost him his life. He went to Bathsheba and asked for the Shunemite woman, who had nourished the king in his old age, in marriage. When Solomon heard this, he saw the threat to his throne and ordered that Adonijah pay the price. In order to prevent any further threat, he also banished the priest Abiathar, thus confirming what had been prophesied about the family of the dissolute priest Eli. Joab, hearing all this, also fled to the horns of the altar where he was killed because he refused to come out. Shimei was allowed to live under strict rules which he broke and also paid the price. There had been too many rebellions in the past.

Now as the focus is back on Solomon, we see the early stages of his laying the foundations of a gross error which would ultimately undermine the religious purity of the nation. For perfectly valid political reasons, he married the daughter of the king of Egypt, and he will later marry a number of other 'foreign' wives. And it is their sons who will turn the nation away from the worship of the God of Abraham because Solomon allowed his many foreign wives to continue to practice their vile worship of their gods whom Israel had been told to destroy in order to establish the worship of the one true God.

Then follow examples of Solomon's wisdom, notably the most famous ruling over whose child it was, between two prostitutes. And evidence of the increasing prosperity of the nation under his rule which had become a kingdom which spread West from the river Euphrates right to the borders of the Mediterranean, with Kings and princes paying tribute to him but living at peace with Israel. His wisdom, given to him by God, made Solomon wiser than any other of the wise men of the East or of Egypt, and that was saying something.

It is now time for the overriding task, to build the Temple as the dwelling place of Jehovah, which David had wanted to do but was not allowed because he had been a 'man of blood', yet for which he had made abundant provision during his lifetime. Aided by King Hiram of Tyre who provided quantities of cedars from Lebanon, the Temple took seven years to construct and employed 30,000 men as builders, plus 80,000 in the quarry and 70,000 to transport the cut stone to site. The finished building was magnificent, rivalling in splendour the great temples of Egypt. Solomon now spent a further thirteen years building himself a palace which also was stupendous. Then came the construction of all the exterior accoutrements for the Temple, massive in size, constructed mainly of bronze, a mixture of tin and copper, in a blast furnace built in one of the valleys. The total weight of the bronze used was too great to weigh. Inside, the most costly ornamentation was in gold, and finely woven linen made the Temple a place to honour the majesty of God and create a sense of wonder, awe and amazement in anyone who looked at it.

Then came the ceremony of bringing the Ark of the Covenant to the Temple, its resting place, and such was the holy emotion that as the priests left the temple, the glory of God descended as "a cloud shining with the dazzling light of the Lord's presence," so that the priests were unable to return to perform their duties. Solomon now addressed the people, praising the God of their ancestors who had brought all this to pass, and he followed it with a dedicatory prayer in which he praises the majesty of God and invokes God's continued presence with them.

Then followed the enormous dedication ceremonies of massive sacrifices, 22,000 head of cattle and 120,000 sheep being slaughtered.

The Lord now appears to Solomon again, to remind him of the covenant responsibilities of the nation and the ensuing blessings for those people who remained faithful.

Following his successful enterprise with Hiram, the king now proceeds to enlarge and fortify the city and, still using his army of forced labour, he rebuilt and fortified a number of cities also. This army of forced labour was comprised of the citizens of nations he had conquered and enslaved rather than killing them, but not from citizens of Israel. It is at this point that the reign of Solomon reaches its apogee with the visit of the Queen of Sheba, who came to wonder at the absolute splendour of this kingdom, saying, "The half had not been told me," and to test him with hard questions and then to depart, marvelling at what she had seen. "King Solomon was richer and wiser than any other king, and the whole world wanted to come and listen to the wisdom that God had given him" (10:23).

The subsequent fall of Solomon, like the descent of a man from a cliff, was not the result of pride. No, Chapter 11 graphically confirms what we had been told. "He was not faithful to the Lord his God as his father David had been." And the cause? He had married women, 700 princesses and 300 concubines from the enemy countries, that is, those which worshipped the awful gods of sun, moon and stars and to whom children were sacrificed. And the evil gods, their worship and the altars to them which he built, are listed in Chapter 11. Solomon had built places of worship where his wives could burn incense and offer sacrifices to their own gods, even though God had twice appeared to Solomon and warned him NOT to do so. Result, God was extremely angry with him and simply stated that because he had flagrantly and deliberately broken his covenant, God would take part of the kingdom away from him and give it to one of his officials.

To accomplish this, God allowed neighbouring kings to remember past grudges and turn against Solomon, and one of his own officials Jeroboam, son of Nebat, who by his skill had been promoted, was told by the prophet Ahijah that, because of the king's rejection of the Lord God, he would succeed him and become king of ten tribes, however two tribes, Judah and Benjamin would remain faithful to the memory and ideals of David. Jeroboam then fled to Egypt to avoid Solomon's anger.

Solomon reigned for forty years, and his exploits and achievements are on record in a book, The History of Solomon, which we do not have. He died and was buried in David's city, and his son Rehoboam succeeded him as king. However, when the new king travelled to Shechem where the Northern tribes had gathered to make him king, he greatly angered them by threatening, on the advice of his younger advisors, that his rule would be far harsher than his father's rule. Result, when Solomon returned to receive their answer, the ten tribes rebelled, leaving Rehoboam king only of the Southern two tribes and Jeroboam, who had returned from his exile in Egypt on the news of the king's death, as King of the North, the larger and in fact more prosperous part. This dramatic event would now colour the whole of the future of these peoples for all time to come, indeed, it is believed, right up to this our own day.

However, from here on, we have recorded for us, the separate histories of two nations, not of one united country. The original purpose of God having been frustrated by the disobedience of one man, the king.

Rehoboam's initial response was to gather an army, 180,000 of his best men, to go to war to re-establish his control over the North, but he was warned by the prophet Shemaiah not to do so. "Do not attack your own brothers, the people of Israel; go home, all of you. What has happened is my will." Interesting, is it not, that in this history, God is seen to be in control of every circumstance, turning apparent disasters, even flagrant disobedience, into something which would demonstrate his overriding purpose for humanity. Truly, "God is not mocked."

So we shall now trace the events of these two nations and, to begin, we see that in the North, Jeroboam turns away from God and, to prevent his people from travelling South to Jerusalem to worship the God of their fathers, he made two bull calves of gold and placed one in Bethel and the other in Dan, so the people sinned by worshipping other gods in another place, not one God in the one place, Jerusalem, where the Temple was. And there at those shrines which he had erected, Jeroboam instituted a new festival for worship, one which he had decreed.

The response from God? He sent a prophet from Judah to Bethel who denounced the altar and proclaimed that a child, Josiah, would be born to the family of David, and that he would punish the people and the altar would be destroyed, and that would be a sign that the Lord had spoken. Jeroboam responded by ordering the prophet's death but, even as he spoke, the king's arm was paralysed and the altar fell apart. The king asked for prayer, and God did heal him, but his continued evil ways brought about the ruin of his dynasty. The details of what would happen to the family were made clear to Jeroboam's wife by Ahijah the prophet, and we will later see the literal fulfilment of that.

In the meantime, in the Southern kingdom of Judah, Rehoboam also led his people astray to a greater degree than any of his ancestors, with the result that Shishak, king of Egypt, attacked Jerusalem and took away all the valuables from the Temple. Rehoboam was succeeded by his son Abijah who, whilst not as bad as his father, did not stop the sin and continued also the war with the North. However, to maintain the covenant with David and continue a God-fearing line, Abijah's son Asa followed the ideals of David and did much to undo the damage.

Now follows, for the Northern kingdom, a period of some one hundred and twenty years in which that original prophecy to Jeroboam is fulfilled in the death of Ahab and his evil wife Jezebel. All of these kings at this time were disobedient to God and disloyal to the covenant. God's voice was made known through various prophets, ordinary men imbued with the spirit of God who, at considerable risk to themselves, declared the word of God.

Most notable of these was Elijah, whose challenge to the prophets of Baal in the time of King Ahab is quite dramatic. Elijah had called down fire from heaven on an altar soaked with water, after the prophets of Baal had tried in vain to rouse their god. But in turn, Elijah is persecuted by Jezebel. Three years of drought had seen Elijah fed, first by ravens and then by a widow in Zarephath, whose son Elijah subsequently restored to life. Then came this dramatic confrontation on Mt Carmel, as Elijah challenged the 450 prophets of Baal to persuade their god to send fire on the altar. When they spectacularly fail, Elijah builds an altar and soaks the wood with water, and then prays, "O Lord, the God of Abraham, Isaac and Jacob, prove now that you are the God of Israel and that I am your servant... Answer me, Lord, answer me, so that this people will know that you, the Lord, are God." In answer to this prayer, fire fell from heaven and consumed the offering, the water-soaked wood and even the stones.

We now have further details of Ahab's misdeeds and those of his wife Jezebel. It also covers the reaction of Elijah to all these events, as he sits in despair under a juniper tree, and then a most remarkable account of his forty-day journey to Mt Sinai and his subsequent meeting with God who hid him in a cave. Then with a strong wind, followed by an earthquake and a fire, God declared himself, before then speaking to Elijah, whose face was covered, in a still small voice. He told Elijah to anoint his successor, Elisha. Then follow two more particulars of Ahab's reign. His encounter with Ben-Hadad king of Syria in which God intervenes and gives him the victory in two battles, but Ahab fails to destroy the king and is rebuked by the prophet for this, and also for his, or rather his wife Jezebel's, murder of Naboth who had refused to give the king his vineyard.

In a final encounter with Elijah, the prophet tells Ahab, "You have devoted yourself completely to doing what is wrong in the Lord's sight. So the Lord says 'I will bring disaster on you. I will do away with you and get rid of every male in your family.' And concerning Jezebel, the Lord says that the dogs will eat her body in the city of Jezreel." In response, Ahab did humble himself, and it was not until his son came to the throne that these disasters occurred. It then follows that after two years of peace, Ahab conspires with King Jehoshaphat of Judah to retake the city of Ramoth in Gilead. The kings agreed that Ahab should go in disguise, but by chance, a Syrian soldier's arrow struck him and he died. The army was sent home and Ahab's body was buried in Samaria; his chariot was washed in a pool where dogs licked up his blood and prostitutes washed themselves, thus fulfilling God's prophecy.

The book ends, at this point, with the brief account of Jehoshaphat in Judah who, having become king on the death of his father Asa, did what was right in the sight of the Lord but in a limited measure. He made peace with Israel, failed in an attempt to sail a fleet of ships to Ophir for the gold, and died, being succeeded by his son Jehoram. Ahaziah, Ahab's son, succeeded him as king of Israel and continued the sinful conduct of his parents and aroused the anger of God.

2 Kings

What we need to recognise, as we look at this record of the histories of the kings of Israel and Judah is, simply, that the success or failure of the nation depends almost entirely on the relationship of the king, and to a lesser extent the people, with God. It is God who holds the nations in his hand, and He is the creator who is ultimately in control. Man proposes but God disposes. The kings must bear the main responsibility because, especially at this time, they did not have a democracy. This is absolute monarchy in which the king has ultimate power and, therefore, must accept ultimate responsibility. Whether or not things would have been better as they had been prior to the establishment of a royal line, is speculation, and what we can only do is judge by what it there. However, all the events in this book must be seen in their true light, which is the bearing they ultimately have on that relationship with God. Because these are a chosen people who, from the time of their ancestors, have had a covenant with God. Obey the covenant, keep his laws, love and serve him, and within bounds all will be well. Disobey or turn to other false gods, and the bond is broken, just as it was in the case of Adam and Eve at the beginning of the Bible narrative, when they disobeyed.

However, even when the priests were corrupt, as was often the case, God's voice was clear through the prophets, men like Samuel and later both Elijah and Elisha. At no time is God without a witness and a standard of right behaviour, against which the others could be measured. And do not forget that even in the worst of times, as Elijah was told when he claimed that he was the only one left who was true to God, "I have reserved seven thousand who have not bowed the knee to Baal," there were always the ordinary people who had remained faithful. Even though Saul, and particularly David, had established the unity and stability of the kingdom, the real enemy was not military obsession but the pernicious evil of disobedience, the worship of other gods – which is why God was adamant they must be eradicated, otherwise these gods will destroy the uniqueness of

God's image as the only God. The nation of Israel had been chosen by God for the specific purpose of making himself known to the rest of the world. The purity of that standard must be maintained throughout all generations.

In this book, we see first the fate of the Northern Kingdom up to the reign of Hoshea in 723 BC, when the Assyrians invaded Samaria and conquered the Northern tribes, taking them into captivity. Then we follow the affairs of the two Southern tribes, until they too are overcome, this time by the Babylonians under Nebuchadnezzar in 587/6 BC. Therefore, the period of the Kings is as follows: as a united kingdom 1030 to 931 BC, then as two kingdoms 931 to 722 BC and finally the kingdom of Judah alone, 722 until 587/6 BC.

To continue, Ahaziah is now king of Israel, but he falls off the roof of his palace and is badly injured. However, instead of consulting the prophet Elijah, he sends messengers to consult Baalzebub, the god of the Philistines, in Ekron. Elijah meets the messengers and warns them that, as a consequence, the king will die and his brother Jorum succeed him. Elijah is now succeeded as prophet by Elisha in another demonstration of the awesome power of God, Elijah being taken up in a chariot of fire in front of Elisha. Miracles then follow as Elisha is established as the true servant of God. Mesha of Moab having rebelled against Israel, Jorum enlists the aid of the kings of Judah and Edom. They appeal to Elisha for help, and the Lord provides water for them and gives them victory over Moab.

We are now given a number of examples of the miraculous power of God through Elisha. A poor widow of one of the sons of the prophets is in debt. She is told to gather as many pots and jars from her neighbours as possible and to pour her little pot of olive oil into them to fill them. The oil did not cease flowing until all the jars were full. She then sold the oil and had enough money to live on. A rich woman from Shunem had invited the prophet to her house, fed him, and then she and her husband built a room on the roof which he could use whenever he was in the district. The woman would take no reward, but being childless, Elisha promised her a son. Later the son died, but Elisha was able to restore him to life.

However, the most remarkable miracle occurred when Naaman, who was the commander of the Syrian army, was found to have been smitten with leprosy. (Chapter 5). On the advice of a little captive Israelite girl who told her mistress of Elisha, Naaman went to Elisha loaded with gifts and was simply told to wash seven times in the river Jordan. Naaman felt humiliated and refused. However, on the advice of one of his servants, he did as the prophet had said and was immediately cured. The same account tells of the perfidy of Elisha's servant Gehazzi who, when Elisha refused to receive any recompense, went after Naaman and asked for some of the gifts for himself. Elisha knew what was happening, and as a result, Gehazzi was himself struck with Naaman's leprosy.

During the wars with Syria, Elisha was remarkably used by God to help the nation of Israel but, inevitably as their sin progressed, the time had come to replace Jorum, Ahab's son, (8:16) and the person chosen was Jehu, who set out to meet Jorum at Jezreel where he was recovering from wounds gained in the battle with Hazael of Syria. Ahaziah king of Judah, was also there visiting. When the watchmen saw Jehu's chariot approaching, the two kings set out to meet him at Naboth's field. "Is it peace?" asked Jorum. "There cannot be peace whilst we still have all the witchcraft and idolatry that your mother Jezebel started," he replied. "Treason Ahaziah," cried Jorum as he fled, but he died when Jehu's arrow caught him in his chariot and they flung his body in Naboth's field, and thus another prophecy came to pass. Ahaziah was also killed and, most importantly, Jezebel also died, (9:30) being flung from the window by one of her officials, and the dogs ate her body as had been foretold. Following this, Jehu, who had become king of Israel, killed the remaining relatives of Ahab and then the relatives also of Ahaziah. (Chapter 10) Finally Jehu himself dies because although he had largely eliminated the worship of Baal, he had introduced the worship of the gold bull calves which he set up in Bethel and Dan.

This saga ends as we see the Lord reducing the size of Israel's territory by allowing King Hazael of Syria to capture all the lands East of the Jordan, land which had been occupied by the tribes of Reuben, Gad and half Manasseh. (Chapter 10).

Further turmoil now in Judah as Ahaziah's mother, Athaliah, kills off all the remaining members of the royal family with the exception of one of Ahaziah's sons, a child of around twelve months, hidden by his nurse. It is the priest Jehoiada who, six years later, in a remarkable coup, declares him king, and Athaliah is then killed. Joash, this young king guided by the priest, is an ardent reformer reigning for forty years in Judah, during which time much-needed repairs are made to the temple, but sadly, he was betrayed and killed by his court officials, and his son Amaziah became king of Judah. He too was a reformer, but he challenged Jehoahaz of Israel, another evil king, and was defeated by him; and he was later assassinated by his own people to be succeeded by his sixteen-year-old son. Uzziah became reasonably good king, but although Judah was proving to be more true to the commands of God than the larger and more powerful Northern kingdom, none of these kings was wholly committed to the service of God.

In the North, the sin of the nation had exhausted God's patience, and finally in 723 BC under the reign of Hoshea, the Assyrians subdued the kingdom and forced them to pay tribute. One year later, Hoshea rebelled, refused to pay the tribute and turned to Egypt for help. Shalmaneser of Assyria, then invaded, captured the Northern capital Samaria and took the inhabitants captive, settling them in various towns. Chapter 17:7 tells us that Samaria fell because the people sinned against God who had delivered them from Egypt, by worshipping the foreign gods of the people, setting up shrines and places of worship to those false gods, and disobeying the strict injunction from God not to worship idols. This, in spite of the fact that God had sent prophets and messengers to warn them. And in sinning, they broke the Covenant that God had made with them. The Southern tribes of Judah and Benjamin also disobeyed the Lord, but they were more righteous and made some attempt to reform. However, after the separation of the two kingdoms, the Israelites had made Jeroboam, son of Nebat, their king, and it was he who more than any other had led the people astray. The Assyrians now settle in Israel. However, strangely, because these people failed to worship the Lord, he sent wild beasts to attack them and, in desperation, they sent for one of the Israelite priests to re-introduce the worship of Israel's God. But to no avail. They still made their own idols in each city. Even those who did follow the true God were half-hearted about it and greatly displeased the Lord because they were not committed to the Covenant laws.

In the South, Hezekiah had now become king, and he was totally committed to the service of the Lord. "Judah never had a king like him who trusted the Lord and kept all the commands of Moses" (18:5). "So the Lord was with him and he was successful in everything he did" (verse 7). However, fourteen years into his reign, the Assyrian emperor Sennacherib began to attack Judah with a very large army, who besieged the capital Jerusalem. To frighten the people, he sent one of his officials to harangue Hezekiah (verse 22), and by speaking in the local dialogue, they ensured that the townspeople would hear their sneering remarks about the king's trust in the Lord.

However, Hezekiah turns to the prophet Isaiah who tells him not to be afraid, God will deliver them, and that was the king's response to the Assyrian official who in turn went to the Emperor and told him. Then the prophet Isaiah sends a message to Sennacherib, "The city of Jerusalem laughs at you, Sennacherib, and despises you. Whom do you think you have been insulting and ridiculing? You have been disrespectful to me, the holy God of Israel" (19:22). God tells the Emperor that what he had achieved in war had been what he had allowed. God knew everything about Sennacherib and how he raged against the Lord, and Isaiah told Hezekiah that although they would face hardship for twelve months, by this time next year, they would be flourishing. God had determined to save the city for the sake of his servant David.

That night, the angel of the Lord slew 185,000 of Sennacherib's army. The Emperor withdrew and was later killed by two of his own sons. Whereas Hezekiah, who had fallen ill, turned in humility to the Lord who, through the prophet Isaiah, promised him that he would live for a further fifteen years, confirming this with a remarkable miracle, the sun going back on the sundial by ten degrees. (Chapter 20)

The kingdom continues, although from 605 BC some of the Jews, including Jeremiah, are taken into exile, but it is not until 587/6 BC that Jerusalem is captured and the temple destroyed. After Hezekiah's death, some kings are bad, like Manasseh and Amon, whilst some like Josiah are good. It was in his reign that the Book of the Law was discovered in the Temple, having been lost. It was Josiah who restored the true worship and destroyed the pagan altars and idols and re-established the old festivals, like the Passover, some of which had not been celebrated correctly since the time of the Judges.

Josiah, who was facing an increasing threat from both Egypt and Assyria, went out to stop the Egyptians and was killed in battle. He was succeeded by Joahaz his son for three months, before he too was taken captive by King Neco of Egypt, who put Josiah's son Eliakim on the throne and changed his name to Jehoiakim. God however could not overlook the terrible sin of Manasseh, and it was during Jehoiakim's reign that Nebuchadnezzar of Babylon invaded Judah. Egypt had lost power in the region, being succeeded by the Babylonians who, when Zedekiah rebelled against their authority, finally invaded under Nebuchadnezzar, and in 587/6 BC, they captured Jerusalem, burnt down the Temple and the palaces, pulled down the walls and took the most important of the inhabitants to Babylon, leaving just the poorest behind and making Gedaliah the governor of Judah.

1 Chronicles

Although these books of Chronicles are in part a rehash of the history of Israel as a nation, they present to us the data from a different standpoint, and therefore, they shed a different light on events.

The book opens with a resume of the ancestry of their nation. It begins with the genealogy from Adam to Abraham. But we are then given the descendants of Abraham's other son by a concubine, Ishmael, who had been cast out by his father because of the jealousy of Sarai, but yet who was still a son. Then we are told of Isaac's other son, a twin to Jacob, Esau. The progeny of these were to become the heads of nations, some of which would oppose the God line through Isaac and Jacob such as Midian and Amalek. We are then given the dynastic precedents of the inhabitants of Edom and a list of their kings. This, in contrast to the previous narrative, which was largely concerned with the God line, demonstrates that the world at that time was increasingly being populated and new nations created.

Now follows the family tree of Judah, one of Jacob's twelve sons, because it leads us to the antecedents of King David, traced through Judah's son Perez who in turn had sons named Hezron and Hamul and, although the royal line continued through Hezron to David, we note that many of the other children would subsequently crop up, some in positions quite crucial, like Joab and Jair. We then are given a list of David's sons and the ancestral line through Solomon, which takes us right up to the point at which the Southern kingdom of Judah was overwhelmed by the Babylonians in the reign of Jehoiachin. But that did not end the royal line, for we have a list of further descendants, which serves to remind us that, very many generations later, a son would be born into that royal line who would bear the title 'great David's greater son'.

We can pass over the lists of the other of Jacob's children, the lists of which include details of their exploits, their battles and their prosperity, including the fact that, despite God having reduced the nation of Israel East of Jordan, many of the inhabitants were still living there at the time of the Assyrian exile. We also have lists of the families of the priestly tribe of Levi and of Aaron's children. These lists would have been passed down verbally at first, but later, written down, they became the equivalent of legal documents, giving title of ownership to the succeeding generations, especially on their return from exile, when the families needed to claim their inheritance. We must remember that all the land apportioned in the distribution at the conquest was owned by families in perpetuity. Any land lost through debt or other failure had to be restored to the original owners at the fiftieth year of Jubilee.

Following these pages of family history, we now (Chapter 10) return to some of the important events such as King Saul's death and David's accession to the throne, together with a list of those who had loyally supported him on his long and painful journey to fulfil God's promise to make him king of all Israel.

The following chapters are descriptions of some of the more important events like the return of the Ark of the Covenant, but written by a different scribe and, therefore, including details which we had not previously seen. For example, we are told when David moves the Ark, that during Saul's reign, it had been ignored since its capture, and we read of its subsequent return to the land of Israel. We also have a recapitulation of the celebration which followed the return of the Ark.

David's desire to build a Temple for the worship of God is outlined and Nathan's confirmation that this would not take place until the reign of Solomon. There is also a clear indication that David not only had made the initial proposal to build the Temple, but he made a number of important preparations, including choosing the site, implying that although he was not allowed to build it, David was the real instigator of the project. At the same time, the narrative here ignores some of David's errors or sins, such as his adultery with Bathsheba and the subsequent murder of Uriah her husband.

Above all, even more important than tracing David's ancestry, is the way in which David, in all humility, worships and praises the God of Abraham, whose vision, some one thousand years earlier, had brought the nation into being from a family numbering just seventy people to an enormous nation which, now numbering several millions, would become a nation under his, David's, rule.

2 Chronicles

Following on from the previous book, here we have the account of King Solomon's reign as David's son, and confining itself mainly to the Southern kingdom of Judah, we have a record of events, right from the Nation at its peak of prosperity and international importance, through the separation into two parts under Solomon's son Rehoboam, to the fall of Jerusalem to the Babylonians under Nebuchadnezzar in 587/6 BC, with a final note of the fact that some seventy years later, they would return under the Persian emperor Cyrus, whose rule extended to all the territory known as West Euphrates as the Persians replaced the Egyptians as the dominant power in the region.

We start then with the account of Solomon's construction of the Temple in Jerusalem on the site chosen by King David, which was the threshing floor of Araunah the Jebusite on Mount Moriah, which David had bought from Araunah in order to make a sacrifice to God to stop the plague which had resulted from David's sin in taking a census of the people, namely numbering them. Interestingly, we find that of the vast number employed in the construction, the majority of the workers were foreign slaves.

The construction of the Temple being complete, we then see the Ark being brought and placed inside and then Solomon's dedication and prayer. Far less detail here than in the book of Kings. Then follow in outline, the visit of the Queen of Sheba, a summary of Solomon's reign, the revolt of the Northern tribes under his son Rehoboam, and the notable fact that after the revolt, the priests and Levites from the whole of Israel came South to Jerusalem because Jeroboam, their new king, refused to allow them to serve as priests of the living God. This was the first sign of the decline of the North, which would lead to their being conquered by the Assyrians in 722 BC and, notably, not returning when the Southern tribes returned to Jerusalem under Cyrus.

Now follows a list of the kings of Judah and their wars and their failures. Some kings were good and some evil, beginning with Rehoboam who did evil,

"... because he did not try to find the Lord's will." Abijah his son, by contrast, obeyed the Lord and challenged Jeroboam, reminding him of his ejection of the priests from their role, and in whose place he had made two golden calves and chose unauthorised priests to serve them. Abijah warned Jeroboam that he was challenging the authority of God himself. Then, with 400,000 men and God's help, he defeated the Northern army which was twice the size. Later his son Asa, who succeeded him, defeated an Ethiopian army of a million men with 300 chariots. Asa carried out many reforms, especially when inspired by the prophet Azariah who, when the spirit of the Lord came upon him, inspired the king to remove all the idols which were cropping up, and such was the inspiration that members of the tribes of Ephraim, Manasseh and Simeon came over to join him. Such is the effect of religious revival – it encourages people when they witness and acknowledge the power of God.

However, the influence of the North was also strong, and whilst Ahab was king of Israel, he persuaded Jehoshaphat, for example, to join him in an ill-fated expedition, in which Ahab was killed. However, Jehoshaphat also carried out reforms, including reminding the judges that they were not acting on human authority but on the authority of God. All of these things were recorded in order to make two points. First that for a nation to succeed, it must obey God's laws and, secondly, that even a God-fearing nation needs to be reminded constantly of their obligation to the God who had given them so much. We also discover that in spite of human failure, God loved his people and was willing not to overlook their sin but to forgive it. And this is a constant theme all through the Old Testament. God may be exacting in his demand for obedience, but he punished out of love and remained true to His covenant even when the people failed.

This was a time of bloody wars and merciless killing. Jehoshaphat's son succeeded him on the throne and then had all his brothers killed, and himself followed the idolatrous ideals of Ahab of Israel, building pagan places of worship in the mountains. He was so determinedly evil that he was severely reprimanded by the prophet Elijah and warned of the consequences. In other words, God was never without a witness. The nation was always being held to account and warned of the consequences of sin, as well as being reminded of the goodness of God to them in the past.

Ahab's influence crops up again through his daughter Athaliah, whose son Ahaziah, who became king on the death of King Jehoram, followed his grandfather's evil ways because his mother gave him advice that led him into evil. (Chapter 22) Fortunately the priest Jehoiadah was able to circumvent this by plotting her rather spectacular downfall and promoting Joash the seven-year-old son of the king to succeed his father. This lad had been nurtured by the priest, and his reign, inspired by Jehoiadah's reforms, did what was right in the eyes of the Lord, but only for as long as the priest was alive. When Jehoiadah died aged 130 years, the leaders of Judah persuaded the king to listen to them, and all the reforms were abolished even though Jehoiadah's son Zechariah, inspired by the spirit of God, stood out and denounced the people. But they stoned him, with the king joining them, and Zechariah died calling out, "May the Lord see what you are doing and punish you." Joash himself was punished, killed by his own officials after being wounded in a foolish battle against a small Syrian army. (Chapter 24).

The succession passed to the son of Joash, Amaziah, who did what was right but 'reluctantly'. An example of his attitude is seen in his hiring of 100,000 soldiers from Israel to fight an Edomite army. He was reproved by the Lord because it demonstrated his lack of faith in God, believing that success relied on human effort, and even though he sent them back, they were angry and retaliated by launching an attack on some unfortified cities, capturing quantities of loot which was the reason for going to war. Amaziah further angered God by bringing back the Edomite idols he had captured, setting them up for worship. Reproved by God's prophet he responded, "Since when have we made you an advisor to the king? Stop talking or I will have you killed" (25:16). The prophet stopped talking but not before commenting, "Now I know that God has decided to destroy you because you have done all this and have ignored my advice." Result, Amaziah foolishly challenged the Israelites but was defeated by them and was finally killed in Lachish, his body being carried back to Jerusalem on a horse.

Amaziah was succeeded by his sixteen-year-old son Uzziah who "did what was right in the sight of the Lord," as long as his spiritual advisor Zechariah was alive. When he died, Uzziah became full of pride at his achievements, became arrogant and defied the Lord his God. He was challenged by the priest Azariah in the temple, "Leave this holy place. You have offended the Lord God and no longer have His blessing" (26:18). Uzziah was smitten with leprosy and became ritually unclean, was confined to his house, and his son Jotham became regent, ruling in place of his father until his father died. Ironically, Jotham was obedient to God but the people ignored him and went on sinning. Ahaz his successor was unfaithful, following the sacrilegious practices of Israel, and was defeated both by the Syrians and the Israelites.

Incredibly, with all these dramatic examples of human folly and their disastrous consequences, nations and kings failed to learn from history even though God, in his loving mercy, spoke so clearly through both prophets and priests to tell the people to alter their ways. The indictment is illustrated in the written words, "When his troubles were at their worst, that man Ahaz sinned against the Lord more than ever. He offered sacrifices to the gods of the Syrians who had defeated him. He said, 'The Syrian gods helped the kings of Syria, so if I sacrifice to them, they may help me too.' This brought disaster on him and on his nation" (28:23).

It was not until Hezekiah came to the throne that things improved. He followed the ways of King David by purifying the Temple, by declaring to the people that their disastrous situation was a direct result of their disobedience to God, and he renewed the Covenant as a means of restoring God's favour. The nation also celebrated the festival of Passover, though a month late because not enough priests were ready to act. In a remarkable statement, he called on those Israelites who had survived the Assyrian invasion to come South and join them, "If you return to the Lord… The Lord your God is kind and merciful, and if you return to Him, He will accept you" (30:9). And he sent messengers to all the tribes, "but people laughed at them and ridiculed them." But there were some who listened and came to Jerusalem, which act in itself was a confirmation of their belief. "God was also at work in Judah and united the people in their determination to obey His will" (verse 12).

A clear demonstration of God's blessing on those who were faithful to him now occurs. Sennacherib of Assyria invaded Judah and was repulsed in a most miraculous way (Chapter 32). The poet Lord Byron dramatically describes the event, "The Assyrian came down like a wolf on the fold, his cohorts were gleaming in purple and gold, and the sheen of their spears was like stars on the sea, when the blue wave rolls nightly o'r deep Galilee." However, despite all this, Hezekiah's life ends in pride and illness, and even though his life is spared for a while, ultimately he falls foul of human folly. God allowed him to be tested only in order to test his character, we are told. Of his successors, Manasseh has to be brought to book for idolatry, although he did repent. Amon sinned, did not humble himself like his father, and was assassinated. Josiah followed as king aged eight years, and he, in the eighth year of his reign was 'converted' and began a thorough purge of evil, promoted by the discovery of the Book of the Law some ten years later. Jeremiah, we are told, composed a lament for the king at his death.

The people of Judah chose Joahaz the son of Josiah as king, and he ruled for only three months before being captured by King Neco of Egypt who made his brother Eliakim king in his place, changing his name to Jehoiakim. This man also sinned against God with 'disgusting practices' and he was captured and carried off by Nebuchadnezzar of Babylonia. His son, Jehoiachin, succeeded him, sinned, and in turn was carried off by Nebuchadnezzar, who appointed his uncle Zedekiah as king of Judah and Jerusalem. Zedekiah sinned against the Lord, refused to listen to the prophet Jeremiah and rebelled against Nebuchadnezzar, who had forced him to swear allegiance. We are told clearly here that it was not only the king at fault, the officials and the priests as well as the ordinary people followed the example of the nations around them and worshipped idols, defiling the Temple made holy by God himself, in spite of all the dire warnings. They laughed at the prophets until God's anger at his people was so great that He brought the king of Babylonia to attack them. He burnt down the Temple, the palaces and the city walls and took the survivors to Babylonia to serve as slaves until the rise of the Persian empire.

Thus were the words of the prophet Jeremiah brought to pass, that the land should lie desolate for seventy years to make up for the neglect of the Sabbath rest.

The book ends with the new Emperor of Persia, Cyrus, who, in the first year of his reign, was prompted by God to issue the decree which would enable the Jews to return to their city Jerusalem and their country.

Ezra

This book follows on from the previous chapters of Chronicles, taking us on to a future period, beginning with the fulfilment of Jeremiah's prophecy concerning the return of Judah from exile under the decree of the Persian emperor, Cyrus. We almost feel that this book and its companion Nehemiah, should follow the prophetic books which deal with the actual exile. The book is a companion to the next book, Nehemiah, in that they both record the detail of the events leading up to and following on from the return of the Jews from exile. But they were written from a different standpoint.

Note that now, the inhabitants of the Southern kingdom are referred to as Jews, from the title of their tribe Judah, to distinguish them from the rest of the nation, the Northern tribes who have not returned. It is interesting to note that part of the book is written in Aramaic (4:8 to 6:18), the official language of the Persian empire, and not in Hebrew. What is important to recognise is that during those seventy years of exile, the world had changed, empires had fallen, old foes had been destroyed and new rulers had emerged.

Basically, the overthrow of the Northern tribes had been a result of the long-planned conquest of Syria by the Assyrians under Tiglath-Pileser, who had begun his assault by striking far down the Western border of Israel to block the Egyptians' access via the way of the Sea through Philistia, to prevent them from interfering. Then, in his campaign to subdue Syria, it was necessary for him to secure the Southern approaches through the territory of Israel, during the three campaigns of 734, 733 and 732 BC. Then finally, he swallowed the rest of Israel, who under their king Hoshea, had foolishly sought the help of the Egyptians, by his assault on the capital Damascus, which, being a highly fortified city, only fell in 721 BC after a prolonged siege lasting three years, and thus was ended two hundred years of nationhood for Israel.

The book then starts by reminding us that what is about to transpire had been foretold by God through the prophet Jeremiah, which implies, yet again, that there is a preordained order about events on this planet and, that in the case of the Jewish nation, there is evidence of a Covenant relationship, which even their failure did not break. It also implies that in his loving mercy, God is willing to forgive, when he sees that there is hope. He has a future for them.

Now come several lists. Lists of the goods taken by Nebuchadnezzar and which are now returned. Lists of the people who returned to Jerusalem and its surrounding district, with a record of their trades or offices. Finally, we are told that by the seventh month, they were all settled and the altar to the living God was rebuilt, and offerings were being made in accordance with the instructions given to Moses, even though no move had as yet been made to reconstruct the Temple itself.

But, yes always a problem, the people who had been moved into the land during the seventy years of Jewish exile did not approve. In fact, they vigorously obstructed the work of reconstruction and the returning exiles were afraid of them. When building work began, the priests and Levites praised God with music and song. Later they would work armed, sword in hand. The enemy very cleverly tried to disrupt the work, first, by offering to help, which was rejected, and then by bribing Persian officials to work against them, and then, many years later, to lay charges of rebellion against them in the reign of Xerxes. This is recorded here, probably to account for the fact that work on the Temple had been stopped, and it was not until a search was made in the Royal records under Darius, that confirmation was found that, indeed, Cyrus had issued an edict (which could not be altered) that work should not only be sanctioned but that materials and provisions should be supplied as and when necessary to enable the work to proceed. Darius then issued a further order that the work should proceed.

Finally, the work was completed, and the Temple was dedicated. Fine, the temple was operating, and the festivals were observed with much rejoicing that the emperor had been supportive. Now, many years later, when Artaxerxes was emperor of Persia, there was an exile, a man named Ezra who could trace his ancestry (how important these records were) back to Aaron, Moses' brother, and to the high priest. He was a scholar with a thorough knowledge of the Law that God had given to Moses, a man who had devoted his whole life to the study of the word of God and its practice. Because he was known to be a man blessed by God, the emperor gave him everything that he asked for. So in the seventh year of Artaxerxes, Ezra set out on a four-month journey to Jerusalem, taking with him a document from Artaxerxes that gave Ezra specific instruction to re-establish the worship of the God of the Hebrews, to collect money from exiled Hebrews in Babylonia and any others who wished to donate and, with the money, to purchase materials and goods to re-establish the Law, the sacrifices and the service of worship to the Lord God. He was also instructed, using the wisdom which God had given him, to teach the law to anyone who did not know it and punish severely anyone who failed to obey it, and to appoint legislators, judges, to govern the people who were there in the province of West Euphrates.

This must be one of the most remarkable events in Hebrew history, that a non-Hebraic emperor of a mighty empire should wish a distant department of his kingdom to worship the Hebraic God and to establish rules and sacrifices which would re-establish the Covenant relationship with their God. By God's grace, Ezra had won a mighty victory for his people through his own vital relationship with the Lord. What a challenge to us. What one man can do when obedient to God. And Ezra gives the praise for all this to God (7:27).

Now we have a list of the exiles who returned, and we see Ezra finding Levites to serve in the Temple as he leads the people in humbling themselves in fasting and in prayer.

However, one major problem occurs. Many of the men had, during the exile and possibly before, intermarried with the women of their sinful neighbouring tribes and nations, and these women (remember Solomon) were undermining the sanctity and holiness of their nation. A very difficult and painful decision followed. They must end these mixed marriages. Bitter weeping and much pain ensued, but the men agreed and their names are recorded. They divorced their wives and sent their children away. And there the book ends.

Nehemiah

What precedes the events of this book is the record of a remarkable conquest. The Northern Israelite nation of ten tribes, with their capital in Damascus, had been overrun by the Assyrians during their conquest of Syria, which had initially involved simply encroaching on the Israelite territory. Shortly after the Assyrian ruler Sargon II had captured Northern Israel, he was faced with problems from the rising power of a newly independent Babylon, which in turn was arising from the remnants of the Chaldean empire. And it was his son Sennacherib who was to become a threat to the Southern kingdom of Judah, this, despite an untimely alliance and then rebellion under Hezekiah. Sennacherib was to be a serious threat to Judah for some twenty years, during which time Hezekiah sought help from other nations who had cause to resent the power of the Assyrians, and even paid tribute to them.

However, ultimately, the Babylonians reduced the power of Assyria, kept Egypt at bay and assumed power over an increasing area of what became known as West Euphrates. Finally, they attacked and captured the Southern kingdom of Israel and destroyed its capital, Jerusalem, at the end of 587 BC, in spite of Jeremiah's plea to King Zedekiah to surrender the city and save the Temple. Then, by the time of this book, the Babylonians in their turn have been replaced by the Persians as the ruling power in that region.

Now, in this book, we have a further account of the remarkable return of the Southern tribes, now referred to as Jews, to their homeland. Written from an entirely different prospect, we see the same events through the eyes of another mighty man of God, who also won the ruling Persian emperor's favour but at a different time and for a different purpose. It acts, therefore, as yet another view on how this all happened. It is believed that, in fact, Nehemiah, who became governor of the nation of Judah, returned prior to the return of Ezra, but they were different people and with different tasks – Nehemiah as a political figure,

Ezra the scribe as a religious reformer, both equally necessary to re-establish the kingdom.

This is now the twentieth year of the reign of Artaxerxes the emperor of Persia, and living in the capital Susa is Nehemiah, the Emperor's wine steward, an important position in the household. He has just received bad news from one of his brothers who has returned from the province of Judah with another group. He asked them for news about the exiles who had returned. The news was bad. (This takes us back to the interlude in the previous book, which occurred about one hundred years later than the rest of the narrative when work had stopped.)

What he heard was that the exiles were in great difficulty, that the foreigners who were now living there had impeded their work, that the walls of the city were still broken down and the gates, burnt during the siege, were still not replaced. In other words, the Temple itself was at risk.

Nehemiah was so upset that he mourned, could not eat and wept in humility before God. He confessed freely that he and his ancestors had sinned, failed God so seriously that they had incurred His wrath, just as God had foretold through the prophets but which the people had ignored. However, he reminded God of what the prophet Jeremiah had said, that even though they were scattered to the ends of the earth, he, God, would bring them back.

Four months later, while taking wine to the Emperor, Artaxerxes noticed his sadness and asked why. Startled at the Emperor's sensitivity, he explained why he was so upset. How can I help it when the city of my ancestors lies in ruins? Equally startling to Nehemiah and to us, the Emperor asks him what he wants. Prayerfully, he simply states what is lying so deeply on his heart, permission to go back to Jerusalem and rebuild the city, which now was a part of the empire. God answered his prayer, because the Emperor and his wife approve his request and simply ask how long he would be away. The Emperor then issues orders and authority for Nehemiah to travel and gives him a letter which will enable him to acquire all the building materials he would need for the walls of the city and even for his own house.

On his return, Nehemiah keeps silent about the reason for his return, but he enlists the co-operation of his fellow exiles, pointing out that the perilous state of the city is an affront to God and a danger. Then follows a schedule of the work and workers participating in the reconstruction of the city walls, and the serious opposition they face from other Persian officials like Sanballat and Tobiah who imply that the Jews are doing this in order to rebel against the Emperor.

Rapidly, however, the work is completed in fifty-two days, and now a further large group of exiles return to an otherwise sparsely inhabited city, and they set to rebuild their own houses and occupy the city. We are given a list of the names of the exiles who returned.

At this point, we join Ezra of the previous book, as he comes to read the law of the God of Moses and to re-establish the worship of the sovereign Lord, the God of Abraham, Isaac and Jacob, as laid down by God in his Covenant agreement with his people. We now have a very much more detailed account of the prayers of the people as they confess their sins and humble themselves before their God. The prayer is a detailed re-enactment of what God had done for their ancestors and how in the past God had been merciful to them, a reiteration of their sins, and an acknowledgement of God's greatness and their humiliating position now, because of their sins. At the conclusion, they sign a written agreement, signed and sealed by the leading citizens beginning with Nehemiah, that outlines how they will become obedient and what they will do to observe the laws of God.

Then follows another list of the citizens who have returned, with details, particularly, of the priestly and Levitical tribes, with the evidence of their ancestry and their assignment to their various duties.

The temple having been dedicated previously by Ezra, we now see the completed city walls being dedicated, with the Levites leading the march round the walls with songs and music of rejoicing. Then comes a repetition of some of the reforms of Ezra, such as the divorce of the foreign wives, and then the reforms instituted by Nehemiah, which included the reinstatement of customs and duties in the temple and its purification from foreign influence, as illustrated by the removal of Tobiah, a non-Jew, from his possession of a space in the temple storerooms. The book then ends with a repetition of orders for the separation and purification of people as well as the temple.

This may all seem very simple, but it is not. These two books are vital elements in the history of the nation of Israel, for they describe in painful detail the enormous consequences of disobedience to God and of their breaking of a Covenant, which carried a very clear and detailed account of what those consequences would be for individuals and for the nation. Even to the fact that whilst we know that some of the Northern tribes did return on their own, in our Lord's day, they were known and despised as Samaritans. The bulk of the returnees were from Persian Babylon not from Assyria, and the Hebrews were henceforth to become known as the Jews. In fact, we do not know, to this day, the actual whereabouts of the rest of the Northern tribes.

The events of this book are also a clear declaration of God's mercy and his love for his people, and as we shall later see, it is an example of the way in which God will demonstrate to future generations, the power of his love and his commitment, both to the people of the Covenant and to the rest of the world.

Esther

The wonderful story of Esther, like that of Ruth, is set during the period in which the Jews were in exile in Persia, in the years following the capture of the Southern kingdom in around 587/6 BC, and it highlights a number of important factors. First is the fact that many of the exiled Jews had achieved quite high status in the hierarchy of the empire, and such a one was Mordecai, a fact which enabled him to be able to act as he did. Again, the emphasis has to be on his strict adherence to the practices and beliefs of their worship of the God of their fathers, even though they were in a foreign land, Just as in turn, Joseph, so many years earlier, had proved by his faith in God that he was a 'better' man than his fellows, following in the footsteps of his ancestor Abraham who had stood out amongst the others of his day, thereby assuring him of a place as an antecedent of Jesus, yes, but also politically and economically, it placed him head and shoulders above his contemporaries, which is what the followers of Jesus were later commanded to do – to demonstrate their belief through their actions, the conduct of their lives.

The second factor here, which underlies the whole drama, is the fact that the Jews were hated, whether this was because of their success and wealth or simply because the 'enemy' were attempting to destroy God's people as a race, not satisfied with destroying them as a nation. Here the enmity is focused on Mordecai's refusal to bow to Haman, and the fact that he did not do so because he was a Jew. Certainly, right from the beginnings of man's early attempts to 'understand' God, there had been something or someone doing his best to prevent it.

God, in His infinite wisdom, had enabled Mordecai to perform a vital service to the Emperor by uncovering a plot against his life, an action which had hitherto been unrecognised. And this became a secret weapon.

Now the scene is set. The drunken Emperor, showing off before his officials and leaders, ordered his very beautiful wife, Vashti, who was also enjoying social success amongst her friends with a banquet, to leave them and come to his drunken group. In other words, to obey, to please her husband, which was a very demeaning position for her to be placed in – effectively to be treated by her husband as a mere servant, a toy, a plaything. No 'please', no loving words, just a sudden order, and she knew exactly what could possibly follow her refusal. Yet confident in her hold over the Emperor, she maintains her status amongst her peers by refusing! One can understand her objection to this demeaning order, even before the days of women's lib.

Now, what is the Emperor Xerxes going to do. If he allows her flagrant disobedience, he will have been humiliated amongst his guests. However great his political and military achievements, if he cannot control and secure the love and respect of his wife, whom he had elevated to her present position, he would be totally discredited amongst his guests.

Much discussion ensues as the king asks counsel from his closest advisors, who comment that if Vashti is allowed to get away with such disobedience, then the status of all the husbands in the kingdom would in turn be undermined. He must act decisively now. And he does this by banishing her permanently from his presence by royal decree, effectively demoting her to the status of a common serving woman.

All anger cools sooner or later, most especially that enflamed by alcohol, and in the sober light of day, he is troubled. His wise men rush to the rescue, "Find another, even more beautiful girl and make her your favourite." Now the action begins with a search for beautiful young women. And here, Mordecai comes onto the scene. He has a very beautiful young cousin, Esther, whom he had adopted on the death of her parents. He promotes her as a suitable candidate. She is accepted into the harem and prepared with great care amongst the other candidates. Once again, her beauty and her demeanour win her favour with the man in charge, who begins her beauty treatment and her diet, which lasted for a year. When she finally is taken into the king's presence, she wins his affection, and he favours her above all the others and finally makes her his queen. But on her cousin's advice, not a word that she is a Jewess.

Mordecai is now being promoted within palace circles, and he happens to tell Esther about his having saved the king's life by disclosing a plot against him, and she in turn tells the king, who orders the fact to be entered in the royal records.

Sometime later, Xerxes promoted a man named Haman to the position of prime minister, and all the court officials are ordered to honour him, to kneel and bow to him. Mordecai refuses on principle because he is a Jew, and when Haman hears this, he decides to destroy Mordecai, and while he is at it, to destroy all the Jews as well, promising that the king will profit from the seizure of all their property.

The King listens to Haman's plan and approves it with a public decree, that in law cannot be revoked, and orders it to be published throughout the empire, naming the day on which all the Jews are to be killed and their property to be seized. Mordecai now enlists the help of Esther, telling her that she alone can save her race, her nation, from extinction. All the Jews are called to prayer. Meanwhile, Haman is so outraged by Mordecai's refusal to bow to him that, on his friends' advice, he orders a giant gallows to be built, on which he proposes to hang him.

Esther now, at the risk of her life, goes to the king. Even as his wife, she can only approach him if he favours her. He does, asking her what it is that she wants. She then invites him to a special feast to which she also invites Haman, who unknown to her is building his gallows for Mordecai.

Unable to sleep that night, the king orders the official court records to be brought and reads about Mordecai's discovery of the plot against his life. "Has this man been honoured?" the king asks. "No," is the reply. So when Haman comes in, the king asks Haman what should be done to honour a man who has rendered a great service to him. Haman thinks it is he whom the king will honour, so he outlines the magnificent public procession which he imagines would elevate him in the eyes of the citizens, only to be told that the recipient is to be Mordecai. In utter horror and embarrassment, Haman hurries to Esther's banquet. After the wine has circulated, the king asks Esther to tell him what she really wants, and she explains that she and all her race are due to be exterminated and that by the king's decree, on a given day, all the Jews are to be slaughtered.

"Who did this?" the king asks. "Our enemy is this evil man Haman!" Esther replies, and the king gets up in a fury and leaves the room. Seeing what was about to happen, Haman falls at Esther's feet to beg for his life, and at that moment the king returns, sees Haman apparently about to rape his queen. The officials cover his head, and one of them tells the king that Haman had actually built a giant gallows outside his house on which to hang Mordecai who had saved the king's life. Exit Haman on the same gallows. His property is given to Esther, and Mordecai is promoted to the position of prime minister in Haman's place.

Now, how to save the Jews? Esther, therefore, requests the king to spare her people from their imminent fate which, because of the royal decree, cannot be altered. In response, he allows Esther to write whatever she wishes. Mordecai then dictates a letter to be sent out post-haste, giving the Jews the right to defend themselves, if attacked, and to destroy anyone who attempts to harm them. When the day came, the Jews all armed themselves, and aided by the local governors who were all afraid to offend Mordecai because of his position, the slaughter was averted. Yes, the Jews did kill their known enemies, but it was a limited action. In all, throughout the empire, some 75,000 known enemies of the Jews died, but there was no looting of property.

These events were recorded by Mordecai, who issued a proclamation to all the Jews, that each year, the day known as Purim should be celebrated forever as a testimony to the great deliverance by which God had saved the Jews from being exterminated.

Job

The book of Job is a remarkable dramatic poem, discussing the fate of one man, Job, who becomes the victim of events outside his control, and it focusses on what was a burning issue, why did it happen thus. To help us to understand this book, we need to remember that it was most likely written during the period when the area known as West Euphrates was under Greek control. At that time, the Greeks were themselves writing a number of dramatic poems, authors like Euripides, Sophocles and Aeschylus were themselves exploring those same issues. Why does the good man suffer? The general view was that most people suffered as a result of their own actions; therefore, their subsequent misfortunes would be a direct result of their own conduct.

However, the Greeks had come to accept that there were exceptions, cases where despite doing their best, some persons were overtaken by 'fate'. The philosophers like Aristotle, writing in his book *The Poetics* about the Greek dramatic portrayal of human suffering in these Greek plays, saw the cause of man's downfall as hubris, pride against the gods, but saw also in those dramatic representations some value, even if it was only the catharsis or purging of the emotions in the audience, resulting from seeing the dramatic enactment of these sufferings.

The Romans ascribed this fate to the actions of a goddess named Fortuna. They saw humankind as bound on a wheel, Ixion's wheel, which rotated causing the person on the wheel to go up and down, and the necessity, therefore, was – as Machiavelli recommended to the Medici ruling family in Italy whilst in decline – to seize the moment, carpe diem, that is, get off when the decline came and get back on when things were ascending.

The first problem with this book is the setting, which is a dialogue between God and Satan, in which God 'boasts' of the goodness of his servant Job. To which Satan responds by claiming that Job is only good because God is so generous to him, effectively saying, reduce him to poverty and Job will no longer worship God. The challenge then is, can Satan, through misfortune, cause Job to cease to be the good little boy he appears to be? Satan claims that his goodness is only the result of his great fortune and wealth.

OK, but can this be a true story? Was there a man called Job? Do God and Satan discuss the welfare of humans on earth? And does God allow Satan to attack people purely to prove a point?

Here we get back to the point which I made in the introduction to this book. For a story to make a very important Truth clear, it does not have to be literally true. Jesus, for example, taught using parables which were illustrative stories explaining, in an easily understood manner, an important truth. Here we have, not a typical Greek drama but, a religious drama which discusses certain essential truths for humanity – about human suffering, about man's relationship to God, with its consequences and its triumphant possibilities.

So when Job is reduced, first by the loss of his family and possessions and then by personal suffering, to the point where his wife tells him to curse God and die, his first reaction is the simple one. When God sends us something good, we welcome it; how then can we complain when He sends us trouble? In other words, we can only passively accept what life brings; we cannot alter what is God's will for us. Then we are introduced to his 'friends' who come to see him, and they sit, at first, reduced to silence by the magnitude of their friend's suffering. Finally, Job breaks the silence to curse the day he was born. He cannot accept what has happened.

Then the first of his friends, Eliphaz, speaks out. Basically, he says, "You, Job, know full well that you need to be philosophical about all this. You yourself have encouraged people in such circumstances to be resolute and have confidence in God. Think Job, has any righteous person ever met with disaster, and as for you, can anybody be truly righteous in the sight of God when even his angels were not perfect? Evil does not spring from the ground; no, people bring trouble on themselves. So humble yourself because God gives hope to the poor and needy, and happy is the person whom God corrects like a dutiful father with his children. So admit your faults, and God will bless you with many children and prosperity, and you will live to a ripe old age."

Job's response is to say that God has treated him so badly that he were better dead. Further, in these circumstances, whether he has forsaken God or not, what he needs in this time of distress is loyal friends, "But you are deceiving me, as a mirage in the desert deceives the thirsty traveller... All right, tell me my faults and I will listen, but you are just talking nonsense. Stop condemning me. I am in the right, but you think I am lying, that I cannot tell right from wrong."

Bildad, friend number two, cuts off Job's very longwinded reply and introduces another aspect. His advice centres on two things. "First, if you are righteous as you say, then your children must have sinned; they are the cause. Plead with God, and he will come to your rescue… God will never abandon the faithful."

Job replies to that with, "How can a human being win a case against God?" In a very longwinded account, he proclaims the greatness of God, as a reason why God will not listen to him a mere human. "I am innocent but I am beyond caring. Clearly, God does believe that I am guilty, as you say, so why should I bother to challenge God, who is no human being to argue with?" He then goes on to rail against God, asking him to tell him what is wrong and not to complain against something which He, God, has made. He says that God has been watching him carefully, waiting for him to do something wrong, just so that he could refuse to forgive him and punish him. In any case, Job says, "I am going to die soon so what does it matter?"

The third friend, Zophar, then speaks, "Will no one stop this man's arguments? Words do not make things right. I just wish that God would answer you and tell you that wisdom and the knowledge of God are too great for you to understand. If God, in His wisdom, brings you to trial, then He knows all things. Stupid people will start being wise when wild donkeys are born tame. Stop sinning, Job; put away evil and face the world, then all your troubles will disappear.

"Yes, you are the voice of the people," says Job, "but I am as wise as you are. God used to answer my prayers, but you who have had no trouble are just making fun of me. Even the animals could teach you; they know that God directs their lives. Everyone's life is in his power. Old people have wisdom, but God has wisdom and power. Old people have insight, but God has understanding and the power to act on it… I have heard everything you say, before. I know as much as you, but my dispute is with God not you, and I want to argue my case with God because you have words but little real knowledge. What you are saying does not advance God's cause at all."

Job then challenges God, "Are you coming to accuse me, God? If so, I am ready to be silent… Speak first God, and I will answer, or let me speak and you answer." He then asks God to tell him what he has done wrong, and after more self-justification, he says, "I will wait for better times... then you will call and I will answer."

Eliphaz then returns for a second round, in which he reiterates his former premise. "Can any human being be really pure? Can anyone be right with God? "Why, God does not trust even His angels; even they are not pure in his sight." To which Job, in reply, goes on to berate him for repeating what he had already said, that those who do evil things will reap their reward. "I have heard words like that before," continuing, that people take the evidence of his physical affliction as proof of his guilt. "I am not guilty," he says, and then come words which imply that he is learning a new kind of wisdom, the essence of Christian teaching. "There is someone in heaven to stand up and take my side... I want someone to plead with God for me, as one pleads for a friend."

Bildad then intervenes to tell Job to stop talking and to listen to them. But all he does is to add fuel to the fire, "That is the fate of wicked people, the fate of those who care nothing for God," implying once again that the fault lies with Job.

Now at last, Job is coming to a greater understanding, rejecting what his friends have argued, "You are my friends! Take pity on me." Then he returns to his previous idea with, in the words of the King James Bible and repeated so musically by Handel, "I know that my redeemer liveth and that even though after death my flesh is consumes by worms, yet in my flesh shall I see God, whom I shall see for myself and not someone else." This is the fundamental Christian New Testament statement of faith.

However, Zophar has not finished and he reasserts his position. "You have insulted me. You know that since humans were first placed on the earth, no wicked people have been happy for any length of time. In the end, they are destroyed. This is the fate of the wicked."

To this, Job's response is to remind him that his, Job's, quarrel is with God not with mere mortals. "The wicked don't want anything to do with God because they do not believe in him. You say that what I am experiencing is nothing more than God correcting me like a parent with his child. Don't you know from your travels that it is the wicked who prosper, and at their death, they are honoured. Your answers are nonsense."

Eliphaz now returns to the attack, saying that whatever Job may think, God knows everything and He is punishing him for what he has done; therefore, the solution is to humble himself, repent, accept His rules, and in return, God will bless him.

Job equally restates his own position, which is that he is searching for God in order to direct his questions to Him because, even in his misery, he knows that God is just, that he is acting in accordance with his plan and all that he asks is that God sets a time for all things to be judged and the balances drawn. To which Zophar asserts that, in truth, even though the wicked may prosper for a time, in the end, they are destroyed. Bildad now also asserts God's justice, saying that He is all powerful; humans are like insects, of little value to God. Bildad adds to his friend's words, that even the dead are subject to the justice of God who is greater than we can know.

Job now agrees with this, in that, although he may have suffered injustice, because God is so great, he accepts that all things are part of God's plan, yet he will always maintain that he is innocent and right. Zophar's final word at this point re-echoes the theme, that God does ultimately punish the wicked.

Now the whole tenor of the book alters, and we have a lengthy discourse on the value of wisdom and where it is to be found, summed in the words, "To be wise, you must have reverence for the Lord, to understand, you must turn from evil."

Here we have a very lengthy discourse from Job, which is ultimately an attempt at self-justification, with the added element of 'if only', but still accusing God of, in his case, acting unjustly. At this point, his three friends give up trying to challenge him because he still insists that he is right, but a bystander Elihu, who has overheard the arguments, becomes very angry with Job and also with his friends, for failing to know how to silence Job, which made it look as though God was at fault.

In his speech, Elihu introduces a new element into the debate, namely that age is not the source of true wisdom because true wisdom comes from the spirit of Almighty God, and he is highly critical of Job's friends. They had failed to disprove Job's arguments because they lacked the true wisdom; therefore, God must answer him, and he Elihu proceeds to tell Job what the real truth is. He begins by equating himself with Job, made from the same clay, but he continues to claim that Job is wrong. God is greater than any human is capable of comprehending, and he does speak, but no one pays attention. God corrects people to stop them sinning. He may then send an angel to rescue them, so that they will then pray to him, and then when God answers, they will honour him.

Now we must decide the case. Job claims that he is innocent, that God refuses to give him justice; but look at him, he never shows any respect for God, and God rewards people for what they do, and we would blame him if he ignored that fact. If God did nothing, who could prevent evil?

"Job," he says, "have you repented and promised to alter your way of life? Since you object to what God is doing, how can you expect Him to do what you want? It is not right, Job, for you to say that you are innocent in God's sight or to ask God, 'How does my sin affect you? Or what have I gained by not sinning?'

"Now I am going to answer you and your friends. Look how great God is. Do your actions affect God in any way? He needs nothing from you. In the same way when people are in trouble, they are too proud to ask for help, when you say that God is ignoring you, you are demonstrating your ignorance. Listen to me, God protects the righteous. He blesses those who serve him. He teaches people wisdom through suffering. In the past, God had blessed you; now your punishment is what you deserve."

Elihu then goes on to describe God's greatness in what we can observe of the world around us. Little wonder then that we poor mortals cannot approach him; we are so much in awe, and no wonder he ignores those who claim to be wise.

Now, in the narrative, we are told that at last God speaks to Job, "Who are you to question my wisdom with your ignorant words?" And then follows a remarkable account of God's wisdom and knowledge, as he challenges Job with how little he, Job, actually knows about him. To which Job humbly replies, "I spoke foolishly, Lord. What can I answer? I will not try to say anything else. I have already said more than I should." And God continues, "Are you trying to prove that I am unjust – to put me in the wrong and yourself in the right?"

Here, God does not directly answer Job's question as to "Why," but in a further remarkable (for its time) display of knowledge, God shows just how much wiser He is than any man. In response, all Job can do is to humble himself and confess that he was discussing subjects which were beyond his ability to understand – which is what we frequently do even today! Further, he states that he, Job, was replying on received wisdom, whereas now he was in the presence of the source of all wisdom.

Having finished his lecture to Job, God then rebuked the three friends, telling them to make a sacrificial offering, after which Job would pray for them. And when Job did just that, God restored to him all that he had lost and more.

A happy ending? Yes. God is a loving God who longs to forgive and forget, and to this end, He has sent His son, Jesus, to bear our guilt and our punishment in his death on the cross, that justice might be seen to have been done.

Psalms

There is not a lot which I can add to this book because, largely, it is self-explanatory. The Psalms comprise one hundred and fifty poetic songs which, since they were written, have provided a thoughtful basis for worship and for private prayer. They largely fall into two separate categories, those written by David, particularly when he was in the wilderness escaping from Saul, and which are often very intimate and personal expressions of his emotions and his relationship with his father, God; and those written by others, particularly the tribe of musical Levites named Korah. All of them are recommended for reading and reflection.

We know that David was a skilled musician, who came into prominence after being anointed by Samuel to replace King Saul who had been rejected by God because of his disobedience. He first became involved with the court of King Saul because of his ability as a skilled musician. After David was anointed as the new king, God's spirit left Saul and settled on David, and it was this combination which enabled his music to calm the troubled Saul. Later, after his remarkable victory over the giant Goliath, who was holding the Israelite army to a challenge of personal combat, which Saul's older and highly experienced soldiers had refused to accept because the fate of the whole nation hung on the result, it became clear to all that David was a unique person chosen by God. He celebrated his victory over Goliath with a song of praise to God.

As we know, Saul's jealousy caused him to try and kill David who was forced to flee into the desert. During this time, we have an intimate record of David's emotions. He very skilfully records his unhappiness, his resentment that he was being sought like flea or a rabid dog, all for no real reason. And these psalms reveal his utter dependence on God for deliverance. The opening psalms, God's chosen king, A Morning Prayer for help, An Evening prayer for help, A Prayer for help in time of trouble, a Prayer for Justice and so on, all give us a very intimate understanding of David's spiritual and emotional battles during the time of his rejection by Saul – experiences which would be of immeasurable help in his later life as king, as he expresses his confidence in God Ps 11 and 16. Then in Ps 18, we have a repetition of David's Song of Victory over his enemies, and even his last words, though not recorded as a psalm, are phrased as a song. Many of the following psalms have been of great assistance to others in time of trouble, for example, Ps 46 and 91. However, most of the psalms are simply written to express David's love for God, his majesty, his justice and his glory. But many were also used in worship by the nation because they expressed feelings which summed up the nation's ongoing relationship with their God.

But there are also darker moments such as David's cry of anguish Ps 22, his desire for forgiveness Ps 32, and most notably, Ps 51, after his adultery with Bathsheba and the murder of Uriah, Ps 70 which is a desperate cry for help. One could go on to list each psalm, but the beauty of the collection is that many of them remain a treasure store of worship and praise, expressions of a very personal nature, written by a man who knew his God but who notwithstanding, and until the time of his acceptance as king, suffered a great deal of persecution – as we also find with those written at the time of his son Absalom's rebellion. Others, like Ps 139, express deep penitence and a desire for a closer walk with God.

The rest of the psalms are largely composed by the Levitical tribe of Korah, the appointed musicians, and were written for the Israelites to sing at time of worship. Some, like Ps 119, the longest, were probably written to encourage the study of the law, whilst some were written during the period when the nation was in exile.

Proverbs

This interesting book is a collection of wise sayings often attributed to King Solomon because he was recorded to be a very wise man, wiser than anyone else of his age. However, many of these sayings would possibly have been current before or during his reign, some were probably said or written by the king, but the book is really a collection of wise sayings gathered over a period of time and written down, simply because they made sense and would constitute a guide to conduct and a good way of life. They reflect both advice on personal conduct and wisdom for groups or nations, but they are as applicable to us today as they were when they were written or spoken.

An interesting point is that they show that human wisdom, as opposed to divine wisdom, was there, known and available even to a relatively primitive people, whom we disregard at our peril. Recent discoveries in archaeology and exploration of known monuments reveal a scientific awareness which to ignore is to fail to understand the achievements of past ages. Our own Stonehenge is an example of 'primitive' astrology, and the Pyramids are an example of mathematical precision. Therefore, it will pay the reader to pause, to reflect and to read the sayings with a degree of understanding.

Whilst not specifically a religious book, there are many references to man's relationship with God. For example, 1:7, "To have knowledge, you must first have reverence for the Lord." Which is repeated in 9:10, "To be wise, you must first have reverence for the Lord. If you know the Holy One, you have understanding." In 2:6, "It is the Lord who gives wisdom; from him come knowledge and understanding." In 3:5, "Trust in the Lord with all your heart. Never rely on what you think you know. Remember the Lord in everything you do, and he will show you the right way." "Reverence for the Lord is an education in itself." "We may make our plans, but God has the last word." "Ask the Lord to bless your plans and you will be successful in carrying them out." "The Lord has determined our path; how then can anyone understand the direction his life is taking?" "Do what is right and fair; that pleases the Lord more than bringing him sacrifices."

Ecclesiastes

As the introduction to Ecclesiastes in the Good News Bible says, these are the collected thoughts of one known as The Philosopher that, by his claiming to have been king over Israel in Jerusalem, are sometimes attributed to Solomon. It is true that the sayings tend to be deeply negative, but as the introduction states, they are included in the canon for a purpose, thought worthy of being there and demonstrate, first, that Christian faith is able to accommodate such thoughts, second, that there are many positive aspects offered, and third, we have to face the fact that the Christian life is no 'bed of roses'. In other words, we have to accept that even the best of us is still very human.

The Song of Songs

Here again, we have a very poetic book written as a dialogue between two lovers and comprising, as a song, their thoughts and desires. It is included within the canon possibly because the Jews regarded it as symbolic of the relationship which exists between God and his people in scripture because God does take that stance, calling his people his children and his beloved nation. And that relationship was emphasised by Jesus when he calls his followers the children of his father and which is picked up by the apostles, "if sons, then heirs."

Isaiah

This book is one of the four main prophetic books in the Bible, directed at the Nation of Israel and it, together with the book of Jeremiah, gives us a very different view of this troubled period, from that which is presented in the Chronicles, a period which will bring to an end the unity of the Nation of Israel. For, although it covers the final period of the two independent nations, it focuses most on the fate of the chosen Southern kingdom of Judah. It is very important because not only does it foretell the future of that nation, but it comes with dire warnings that unless the people change their ways, God has had enough and they will have to learn the hard way, that is, through suffering. These warnings are coupled with reminders that Israel was loved by God, just as a father will love his child.

Although they as a nation had already experienced suffering as had happened during their 470 years in Egypt, they are told to remember that, in the past, God had delivered them from their slavery. In addition, he had also given to them a bountiful land, flowing with milk and honey, and had made them, under their kings David and later Solomon, a mighty nation, wealthy and powerful, one to be reckoned with internationally. Even more important was the fact that God had made a specific covenant with these people, under which he had promised to bless and prosper them and make them an example to the other nations of His, God's, power, His love and His presence with them. All these things were now at risk.

It is, therefore, written against this historical background of being a chosen nation which had begun with God's promise to one man, their ancestor Abraham – a man whose faith in God and obedience to his commands had brought him into a very personal and precious relationship with the creator God, which was unique at the time and was intended to have continued forever. The problem now was that Abraham's descendants, the twelve tribes named after Jacob's sons, had rebelled and had disobeyed the conditions of their covenant with God, with the result that the nation had been split into two parts. And whilst the Southern kingdom of Judah and Benjamin had had a less troubled past, they too were steadily following in the path of their Northern brethren which, as Isaiah foretold, resulted in the Northern tribes being overrun by the Assyrians and their people exiled, as happened in the year 722 BC.

The book covers a period one hundred and fifty years until after the time when the prophet lived, including the introduction of the reference to the suffering servant of the final chapters, which has given rise to the theory that there was more than one author for the book. But it is not our place here to discuss authorship, simply to look at what the book says. It is not beyond the power of God to give a vision of the future, but Isaiah's chief concern was the state of the nation in his day.

The book naturally divides itself into three parts, before the exile, during the exile and then a look at the future. The first part covered by this book is clearly stated in the opening, the reigns of five kings from 781 to 687 BC. And it begins with some extremely dramatic statements, "The Lord said, 'Earth and sky, listen to what I am saying! The children I have brought up have rebelled against me. You are doomed you sinful nation, you corrupt and evil people! Your sins drag you down! You have rejected the Lord, the holy God of Israel and have turned your backs on him.'" Not much doubt about that, and the blistering words are directed particularly at Jerusalem, the home of the Temple and the centre of worship.

However, in an interlude (Chapter 2), God does offer the hope that at some future time, Jerusalem and the Temple will once again become a place of pilgrimage. And it is this repeated foretelling of a better future which characterises this denunciation and indeed the whole book. Then, after a further and more detailed denunciation of their arrogance, the vanity and lewd behaviour of their women in 4:2, we have the prospect of a future holiness. This is followed by a song of a vineyard in which all the grapes harvested were sour.

It is not until Chapter 6 that we have details of Isaiah's own personal and very dramatic call, in which he has a mighty vision of the holy God. Then in the following chapter, after the failure of an attack on Jerusalem, Ahaziah the king is told to ask for a sign that things will ultimately improve. He refuses, and in reprimand, Isaiah tells these descendants of David that the sign will be the birth of a son to a young woman, and that before that time, their enemies will have disappeared but that also Israel will have experienced trouble greater than at any time in its history.

However, the following warnings are interspersed with various predictions such as 9:1–7 the promise of a successor to King David, as a king who will rule "until the end of time." But because of their refusal to repent, Israel is facing serious trouble. Many of their errors are specified, and God even warns that he will use the nation of Assyria like a club to punish them. Then, again, after this dreadful warning comes hope, "A time is coming when the people of Israel who have survived will truly put their trust in the Lord, Israel's holy God." (Chapter 11) "The royal line of David is like a tree that has been cut down, but just as new branches sprout from a stump, so a new king will arise from among David's descendants... A day is coming, when the new king from the royal line of David will be a symbol to the nations." Please note this statement and mark it for future attention. Then follow warnings to the other nations, interspersed with promises for Israel's future. (Chapter 13–14) This is followed in the next chapters by a solemn warning to some of the other idolatrous nations, specifically, Babylon, Moab, Syria, Ethiopia, Egypt, Edom, Phoenicia. Followed by a final a warning (Chapter 24), "The Lord is going to devastate the earth and leave it desolate."

Then by contrast, in Chapter 25, we are given a remarkable 'hymn' of praise with a tremendous message of hope. "Here on Mount Zion the Lord Almighty will prepare a banquet for all the nations of the world," in which we have the words, quoted in Revelation, "The Lord will destroy death forever! He will wipe away all tears from everyone's eyes." Now follows (Chapter 26) another remarkable series of projections about the future state of Israel – peace, prosperity and new life for those who have died (verse 19), with punishment for the people on earth who continue in sin. At this time, there is a clear distinction between the Lord's people who have sinned and the rest of the world who continue to sin. As in Chapter 28, a warning to the Northern tribes of Israel is followed (Chapter 30) by the promise of consolation for Judah, "You people who live in Jerusalem will not weep any more... The Lord will make you go through hard times, but He Himself will be there to teach you."

An interesting fact is, that whilst the Southern tribes were allowed to return under Cyrus, the only record of the ten Northern tribes is in the people called Samaritans who, as we also see during our Lord's ministry on earth, were despised by those from Judah who had returned and were now called Jews.

In Chapter 32, we have more promises of a better future, "Someday, there will be a king who rules with integrity." In 33:17, "Once again you will see a king ruling in splendour over a land that stretches in all directions."

Then once again trouble (Chapter 36). In the fourteenth year of King Hezekiah, whose reforms had changed the nation, we read of the threat from the Assyrian Emperor Sennacherib. When Hezekiah heard the boasts of the Assyrians, spoken in Hebrew so that all the inhabitants could hear, he turns to Isaiah for advice and help. The prophet assures the king that his prayer has been heard, and sure enough, God intervenes and responds to the threats and their boasts of these Assyrians, "The city of Jerusalem laughs at you." Of the Assyrian's boasting of their success, he said, "Have you never heard that I planned all this long ago? And now I have carried it out." The next day, 185,000 of their soldiers lay dead! Hezekiah the king then falls ill but is promised fifteen more years of life, in evidence of which the sun moved back ten steps on the stairway built by King Ahaz. But on recovering, Hezekiah falls into the trap of boasting to the king of Babylonia, and it is these Babylonians who will ultimately overrun Judah and take their inhabitants into exile for seventy years.

Chapter 40 is quite unique. It begins with the well-known words, "'Comfort my people,' says our God. 'Comfort them and encourage them.'" Then follow a series of statements which magnify the Lord their God, in words reminiscent of the words of God to Job. God is the incomparable God who created the heavens and the earth and verse 31, "… those who trust in the Lord for help will find their strength renewed. They will rise on wings like eagles; they will run and not get weary; they will walk and not grow weak."

Now, Chapter 42, we have the promises, "Here is my servant, whom I strengthen – the one I have chosen, with whom I am pleased. I have filled him with my Spirit, and he will bring justice to every nation." This, together with the promise of a descendant of David to rule as King forever, links these verses to Jesus himself in the New Testament. All of which points to the unity between the books of the Bible, indicating a common theme and a foretelling of the future, not only for the nation of Israel but also for the world. Chapters 43 and 44 continue the theme, and then in Chapter 45, reference is made to Cyrus, who as King of Persia will order the return of the exiles to Jerusalem, the rebuilding of its wall and the Temple under Nehemiah and Ezra the scribe.

We then have details of the judgement on Babylon, with the call for all people to repent in 45:22, and in 46:10, "From the beginning, I predicted the outcome; long ago I foretold what would happen." Which is a clear indication that all the events outlined in the book were proposed, planned and executed by the Lord himself, that they were not the result of human machinations. This message is further supported by 48:3, "Long ago I predicted what would take place; then suddenly, I made it happen." Time and place alike are at His command.

The following chapters, right up to Chapter 55 are messages of hope and encouragement and, in particular, we have mention of the future place of Jerusalem, and of the future role of the servant king for Israel, 49:6, "The lord said to me, 'I have a greater task for you, my servant; not only will you restore to greatness the people of Israel who have survived, but I will also make you a light to the nations so that all the world may be saved" – words quoted over the child Jesus by Simeon in the Temple when he was presented there for his rite of circumcision, Luke 2:29–32. And so, the next six chapters all continue the theme of the restoration of Israel, with hints of the nation's future role in respect of the Gentile nations also, including Chapter 56, the promise that in the future all nations will be included as God's people. Hence the command of Jesus, "Go into all the world, preach the gospel and make disciples of all nations," at the end of Mark's gospel.

The remaining chapters of Isaiah continue the theme of restoration and, as a means to this end, sin and idolatry are condemned, the law is to be upheld and we have words such as (59:21), "I have given you my power and my teachings to be yours forever." Which is a reminder, as Jesus himself said, that although he would in his life on earth become the fulfilment of the law, the precepts of the law were eternal. At the heart of which stand the two commandments which embody all the others, "Thou shalt love the Lord thy God with all thy heart and thy neighbour as thyself." In 61:1–2 we then have the words which Jesus read in the synagogue in Nazareth, Luke 4:18–19 at the commencement of his ministry, and which firmly place him as the 'one who was promised', "The spirit of the Lord is upon me…" in contrast to the words of the congregation "Is not this the carpenter's son?"

And then the book of Isaiah ends with further warnings, our Lord's final victory over the nations (Chapter 63), a prayer for God's help (Chapter 64), punishment for the rebellious (Chapter 65). "The Lord said, 'I was ready to answer my people's prayers, but they did not pray. I was ready for them to find me, but they did not even try." We then have some visionary words in 65:17

121

which are echoed in Revelation. "The Lord says, 'I am making a new earth and new heavens. The events of the past will be completely forgotten'" And in 66:22, a very interesting prediction for the nation of Israel, "Just as the new earth and the new heaven will endure by my power, so your descendants and your name will endure!" And thus the book ends.

In summary, the ten Northern tribes, right from their rebellion under Jeroboam, were less responsive to God, were more committed to evil, as with King Ahab and his wife Jezebel, whilst in the South, the two tribes, Judah and Benjamin, were more consistently loyal to the worship of God and the rule of the Mosaic Law as imposed under King David. Many of their kings were reformers, removing the altars and idols of the idolatrous nations, but even they, in total, were disobedient, and later, like their Northern neighbours, they were finally captured and exiled in Babylon. However, it was they, Jews from the tribe of Judah, who were allowed to return under the decree from the Persian emperor, Cyrus, whereas the Northern tribes lost their identity.

Jeremiah

This, the second book of the critical period in Israel's history, deals with the trauma of the nation of Judah in the years between the 13th year of Josiah's reign, around 627 BC, until the capture of Jerusalem and the fall of the nation in 587 BC roughly from 626 to 586 BC, beginning some seventy years after Isaiah. Like Isaiah, which covers a much longer period, it is not a record of miraculous events as with Elisha and Elijah; it is a record of the declamations of a prophet whose words were regarded as the word of God. "The Lord said to me, 'I chose you before I gave you life; and before you were born, I selected you to be a prophet to the nations. I am giving you the words to speak.'" Jeremiah obviously takes his role very seriously, often at great personal cost, but through it all his love for his nation is exceeded only by his love for God.

That the prophet was a man of great poetic imagination is clear in the fact that many of the revelations were in the form of visions of a graphic nature. An almond branch and a pot boiling over are examples of the way in which God is making the message dramatic through everyday details. But the message is clear; the nation is in great danger and his message will make him unpopular, "But I, God, will make you a fortified city, an iron pillar, a bronze wall" – reassurance! Jeremiah is so personally involved in his messages that he is even personally directed to act out various scenes.

The chronology of the book is somewhat confused, implying that more than one person was responsible for the text. Beginning with Jeremiah's prophetic warnings, it moves on to some personal details of the prophet's life, and then, in the concluding chapters, we have a retelling of previous events. However, what is so striking is that, like its predecessor Isaiah, it is full of the most glorious predictions of a period when Jerusalem will be greater than ever before. And these promises of an unparalleled future are interspersed amongst the dire warnings of the present, in a similar manner to that in Isaiah, most especially during the period when the nation was in captivity, as though it was intended to create faith and confidence in the almighty power of God towards a chosen people, with their specific place in the Divine plan for the world.

The first public message reminds the nation that they are a cherished possession from the time of their ancestors. What then caused them to turn away? And the first layer of blame is directed at the priests, "My own priests did not known M" (2:8); the second against the rulers and finally the prophets, "The prophets spoke in the name of Baal and worshipped useless idols." (2:8) " No other nation has changed its gods." (2:11) Travel where you will, but nowhere else will you find a people who changed their gods. Then comes the result, they have lost their status by their own actions and become slaves to evil passions, the idolatry of the other nations.

To reinforce this message, the prophet quotes the situation of a man who divorces his wife but is legally unable to take her back. The adultery of the nation is their idolatry; they have forgotten their first love, the Lord, and whored after false gods. (Chapter 3). Their only hope is repentance. To reinforce this, Judah the nation is threatened by invasion, indicating that their former success was from their husband, God, and the divorce has left them at the mercy of their enemies. Dramatic but politically and spiritually true.

4:19 then shows how personally involved Jeremiah is with his message "The pain! I cannot bear the pain... I cannot keep quiet." "My people are stupid... They are experts at doing what is evil, but failures at doing what is good." Jeremiah goes on to add that Judah's sin is so great that the whole earth will be affected (4:27). Jerusalem the city is at the heart of their sin because that is the site of the worship of God, the Temple. The situation now is so bad that the people deny that God is involved, and they disregard the prophetic message saying of God, "He won't really do anything," and of the prophets, "The prophets are nothing but windbags." Now God, through Jeremiah, does not mince His words (5:20–22), "Tell the descendants of Jacob, tell the people of Judah, 'Pay attention you foolish and stupid people, who have eyes but cannot see and have ears but cannot hear. I am the Lord; why don't you hear me? Why don't you tremble before me?"

These messages are dramatic, violent even, because the situation is becoming desperate. God has abandoned His people, and they have rejected His way. Now the enemy from the North is approaching, but still God's message is that they are being tested. There is still time to alter their behaviour. However, their rank disobedience is such that God even tells Jeremiah not to pray for them. If you do, I won't listen (7:16).

And so we come to the heart of the matter. God says that in their early history there were no commands about sacrifices (7:22); all He wanted was their obedience, for them to live as He wanted. But the evil in their natures overcame them, and the more God did for them, the worse they became. He even tells Jeremiah that the people will not listen to him. Then follow graphic details of the people's sins and Jeremiah's deep sorrow which even leads to his questioning God's purpose which, at the end of the day, is to test the people's faith and trust by putting them into situations where the choice is theirs. At this stage, the narrative balances the issues out, with Chapter 10 which is a song of the majesty and glory of the God of power and love, which in turn contrasts Him with the miserable false gods who are nothing more than human creations of wood and stone.

Now the spiritual conflict intensifies as Jerusalem is warned of coming exile, and the people are reminded of the terms of the Covenant under which God had blessed them and which now they are breaking. It reaches the point where the prophet's life is threatened, and he questions God's justice (Chapter 12), in response to which we have even more dramatic imagery – the linen shorts which become rotten, then the wine jars as symbols of their intoxication. The pressure is on now, and God warns against pride, and then with the dramatic image of the empty jars in time of drought, he shows their true condition. Now, there are signs of a response from the nation, but the situation is so bad that, "Even if Moses and Samuel were standing here pleading with Me, I would not show these people any mercy" (15:1). And now Jeremiah himself complains that he is being victimised because of the people's sin, to which God's reply is that if he, Jeremiah, will personally retrieve his own trust in God then He, God, will bless him in spite of everything – a picture through Jeremiah of the nation's situation.

Following this, Jeremiah is given a vision of hope, the possible return from exile, and Jeremiah's confidence in God is restored (16:19). At this point, the whole issue of the possibility of renewal is raised, with the image of the potter, in which via the potters actions, God is portrayed as being able to remake, to renew broken or damaged vessels and to produce an end which is better than the previous state (18:1–4), which would make the suffering, the crushing and reshaping, justifiable. This is followed by the salutary message of the broken jar which cannot be restored.

Jeremiah's troubles are multiplied when the priest Pashhur, son of the chief officer of the temple, has him beaten and chained up overnight. At this, Jeremiah complains bitterly to God that he is suffering through doing what God told him (20:7), and he sings a song, strangely reminiscent of Job, in which he complains but still praises God.

We then have a whole series of warnings to other people and nations. Jerusalem will be captured; the royal house will pay the price of their failure in the kings Josiah and Joahaz, Jehoiakim and Jehoiachin. They together with the godless priests and prophets will share the fate of the other nations. These prophecies continued until finally Jeremiah is captured because, at the Lord's bidding, he proclaimed doom in the Temple courtyard and had been brought to trial. Fortunately for him, some speak in his favour, reminding the judges that in previous reigns, prophetic utterances had proved to be right, and he is released. So back to work, this time to wear an ox yoke to speak to the various ambassadors who were visiting King Zedekiah. The message: God is the one who controls all things, and he is going to use Nebuchadnezzar of Babylon to fulfil His purpose for the nations.

At this point, we are dealing with the prophet's own personal life, as opposed to his public appearances as the voice of God, and here there is a challenge to Jeremiah's authority from a prophet named Hananiah who declares an entirely different message, and taking the ox yoke from Jeremiah, he breaks it saying this is how God will destroy Nebuchadnezzar's power within two years! Jeremiah rebukes him, warning him that he will die because he is misleading the people, and die he does. The narrative then jumps ahead to the time when the nation is in exile, which suggests that some of this narrative may have been compiled from his secretary, Baruch's, notes.

Now what follows is a letter which the prophet wrote to the Jews who were in exile, promising that after seventy years, the nation will be restored and, shades of the potter, the restored nation will be the better for its suffering. There is, in other words, a future ahead of them, provided they repent and obey. The chapters 29 to the end of 31 outline the hopeful outcome of their troubles and remind them of God's great love for them.

31:1, "The Lord says, "The time is coming when I will be the God of all the tribes of Israel." "Sing with joy for Israel, the greatest of the nations" (verse 7). "I scattered my people, but I will gather them" (verse 10). "Israel, you are my dearest son, the child I love best" (verse 20). And vitally important, verse 32,

"The Lord says, 'The time is coming when I will make a new covenant with the people of Israel and with the people of Judah. The new covenant that I will make with the people of Israel will be this: I will put my law within them and write it on their hearts. I will be their God and they will be my people.'" Verse 36, "He promises that as long as the natural order lasts, so long Israel will be a nation." On the strength of this prophecy, Jeremiah is told to buy a field as an illustration, or act of faith, that one day the people will return from exile and the land will, therefore, be valuable again, even though at that time, he was a prisoner of King Zedekiah for prophesying defeat under Babylon.

Now we have, first, Jeremiah's prayer and the promise of Hope, even though he is still imprisoned (33:1–2), "While I was still in prison in the courtyard, the Lord's message came to me again. The Lord who made the earth, who formed it and set it in place, spoke to me. 'Call to Me and I will answer you; I will tell you wonderful things and marvellous things that you know nothing about.'" "I will make this land as prosperous as it was before" (verse 11).

The next chapters show events from a different perspective. As Nebuchadnezzar's army is assaulting the city, Jeremiah reminds Zedekiah that his behaviour, and that of his ancestors, was responsible for the trouble they were in. God's patience had run out because of the insincerity of their repentance. So serious was the situation, and so determined was God that the people should know and remember, that Baruch, Jeremiah's scribe, was ordered to write down all of the prophet's warnings and to read the words out in the temple. (Chapter 36) Result, the king burns the scroll, repudiating all that had been said. So Jeremiah, or his scribe, wrote another scroll.

The next events show what happened as Nebuchadnezzar's army takes control. First, the king, Jehoiakim, is replaced by his son Jehoiachin, and then three months later, Nebuchadnezzar replaces him by his choice, Zedekiah. Events move swiftly as we are not certain of the timing. Apparently, at this time, Jeremiah is still free, and the king asks him to pray for the nation. Result, the Egyptian army, recruited to help, crosses the border and the Babylonian army withdraws, but as the prophet had warned, the Egyptians turn back, the Babylonians then capture the city and burn it. In this interval, the prophet goes out of the city to take possession of the land he has just bought and is accused of treachery. Zedekiah asks for his "word from the Lord," which is simply that the king will be captured and the city looted and burnt. The king objects to this and, first, the prophet is imprisoned. The officials say that he is undermining the loyalty of the army, so he is put into a dry well to silence him, not killed as some wanted. In secret, Zedekiah asks Jeremiah's advice as to what will happen. Jeremiah refuses, saying, "If I tell you, you will kill me," but on the promise that his life would be spared, he explains in some detail what the fate of the city and the king will be. And after a period of a nearly two-year siege, that is exactly what happened.

Fortunately, on Nebuchadnezzar's word, Jeremiah is released and put into the care of Gedaliah who is to be the new governor of Jerusalem. This was an illustration of the way these emperors controlled such large areas, simply by using some of the elite officials of the nation, allowing them to bear the brunt of any complaints. The Romans adopted the same system, hence in our Lord's day, Jerusalem was governed on a day-to-day basis, under Roman authority, by the religious leaders. Even the tax officials were largely Jews who accepted Roman authority and were hated for it; and the great historian of the period, Josephus, was a Jew who became a Roman citizen and, therefore, could live and move freely and record events.

Following the fall of the city, we have a very turbulent time, which gave the people a reputation for rebellion. Gedaliah is murdered and Ishmael the leader of the rebellion has to flee to Egypt to avoid punishment from the Babylonians and, during this very story, in this rebellious period, the people who were left appealed to Jeremiah to intercede with God on their behalf. The gist of his message was that the people should stay in their own land and not flee to Egypt. In return, God promised that he would restore the nation as he had previously foretold. However, they disobeyed. God then told Jeremiah to warn them that he would destroy Egypt as well, because in going to Egypt, they had returned to the idolatry of the gods of Egypt.

In Chapter 45, we return to Jeremiah's scribe, Baruch, whose records of Jeremiah's words appear to be our source in these closing chapters. These tell of the defeat of Egypt's forces under their king Neco at Carchemish, which is close to the river Euphrates, by Nebuchadnezzar's forces and the subsequent invasion of Egypt to put an end to their pride. And incidentally, it was also the beginning of the end of Egypt's position as a mighty empire, which will finally come about through the Romans, with Cleopatra's ill-advised liaison with Mark Anthony, and their naval defeat at the battle of Actium.

The final chapters of this remarkable book deal with God's punishment on a great number of other nations who had caused problems to the Israelites and angered God by their dreadful and sacrilegious idolatry, which is a repetition of previous condemnations of these nations, such as Egypt, Philistia, Moab, Ammon, Syria (Damascus), and finally on Babylon itself (Chapter 50) – intermingled with various repeated promises that God would deliver His people from these nations and restore their prosperity. And it ends (Chapter 52) with a repetition of the fall of Jerusalem in 586/7 BC.

Lamentations

The value of this book, written as it was after the devastating destruction of Jerusalem the city together with the temple, lies in its dramatic expression of the strength of the emotion which the loss of the Temple created. It is not really possible for us, in the twenty-first century, to understand just what that meant to the Jews. The city was important; it was their ancestral home, yes, but the Temple was the place where their God dwelt, where the sacrifices for the forgiveness of sins were made and where, daily, the priests offered the incense of prayer. The light of God's presence was there. To lose the Temple was to be cut off from God.

We know from the witness of other writers in this period, such as Daniel, Ezra and Nehemiah, that emotions ran high. Here in this poetic outpouring, we have a sense of the desolation, the agony, the shame, the depth of emotion, expressed so powerfully that, even today, the poems are read to prevent that feeling of loss from ever being forgotten. Because, remember, the Temple destroyed by the Romans in AD 70 has never been rebuilt. The agony and the pain are still there in these five dramatic and poetic expressions of human feeling.

The poems need to be read to be appreciated. All I can do is tempt you with some of the more challenging words which speak to any open heart today.

The poems commence with the dramatic personification of the city. Verse 1, "How lonely lies Jerusalem." And one is immediately drawn to the image of a woman weeping, bereft, unable to find comfort or assurance. "All night long she cries, tears run down her cheeks. Of all her former friends, not one is left to comfort her." Verse 6, "The splendour of Jerusalem is a thing of the past." Verse 20, "Look, O Lord, at my agony, at the anguish of my soul!" But also, "My heart is broken in sorrow for my sins."

2:1, "The Lord in his anger has covered Zion with darkness." This is the recognition that behind the suffering and pain, the fault lies with the people who lived there. And verse 5, "Like an enemy, the Lord has destroyed Israel." And the writer goes on to focus the blame, to level it at the door of the offenders. Verse 14, "Your prophets had nothing to tell you but lies; their preaching deceived you by never exposing your sin. They made you think you did not need to repent."

But then in Chapter 3, "I am one who knows what it is to be punished by God." Verse 13, "He shot his arrows deep into my body. People laugh at me all day long." Yet hope is there, despite the humiliation and heartbreak. Verse 22–24, "The Lord's unfailing love and mercy shall continue, fresh as the morning, as sure as the sunrise. The Lord is all I have, and so I put my hope in him." Verse 32, "The Lord is merciful and will not reject us forever. He may bring us sorrow, but his love for us is sure and strong." Verse 49, "My tears will pour out in a ceaseless stream until the Lord looks down from heaven and sees us."

4:6, "My people have been punished more than the inhabitants of Sodom." Verse 13, "But it happened because her prophets sinned and her priests were guilty of causing the death of innocent people." But look out you other nations, take heed of what has happened to us. Verse 21–22, "Laugh on, people of Edom and Uz; be glad while you can. Your disaster is coming too; you will stagger naked in shame. Zion has paid for her sin; the Lord will not keep us in exile any longer. But Edom, the Lord will punish you; he will expose your guilty deeds."

Then finally, in Chapter 5, we have the prayer to the Lord for mercy. "Remember, O Lord, what has happened to us. Look at us and see our disgrace." Verse 4, "We must pay for the water we drink; we must buy the wood we need for fuel." Verse 15, "Happiness is gone out of our lives; grief has taken the place of our dances." Verse 17, "We are sick at our very hearts and can hardly see through our tears." Verse 20–22, "Why have you abandoned us so long? Will you ever remember us again? Bring us back to you, Lord! Bring us back! Restore our ancient glory. Or have you rejected us forever? Is there no limit to your anger?"

Did the Lord hear? Did he respond in loving kindness and forgive and restore the nation? Why yes, he did, as you can read in the coming books.

Ezekiel

Chronologically, this book, like its fellow Daniel, fits in before Ezra and Nehemiah, in that it covers the period of Israel in exile; but its character, its content and its message is much wider than that relatively small period of the Nation's history. As we begin to study what the book is saying, we must not be diverted by the very dramatic visions which the prophet saw. There is no way we can interpret those realistically, in modern terms; rather we must see them as relevant to the prophet, indicating as they did the awesome splendour, the power and the majesty of the Lord himself. This was the dazzling light which shows the presence of the Lord (1:28.). Ezekiel saw a violent storm coming from the North – in just the same way Moses, on Mount Sinai, was overpowered by the enormity of what appears to us to be like a violent volcanic eruption – and through this, the Spirit of the Lord took control of him. Whilst the period covered is that of the exile, the prophet also takes us back to the warnings issued prior to the invasion by the Persians, probably as part of the reason for the Lord's anger.

So then, Ezekiel is living in exile in Babylon during the period around the time of the fall of Jerusalem in 586 BC, and his message is largely to the nation of Judah, but also to the exiles and to any Jews who were still in the land of Israel, and the first part of the message is delivered like a scroll to be eaten. He is told not to be afraid to speak; further, he is reminded that because the people speak his language, there is no difficulty in communication. The problem lay with the refusal of the people to listen, yes, but the burden of the message was laid on the prophet, who was told that, if he failed to deliver the message, the guilt would be on him, whereas once the message was delivered, the issue of guilt lay with the hearers. Ezekiel is rendered silent.

First (Chapter 4), he is told to dramatize his message, to act out the siege of Jerusalem. However, the first 390 days were for the Northern tribes and the shorter period of 40 days for the Southern tribes. His diet was restricted and his hair shaven as part of the message, but at the heart was the fact that by their disobedience, by their idolatry, by their following the customs of the other nations they, God's own people, have publicly defiled, besmirched, God's holy name. Therefore, their sin is worse than that of the other nations who did not know God. The punishment which will result will be that Israel will be humiliated publicly, their sin so great that what will happen to Jerusalem will be above all belief. In terms of human suffering, they will starve till they eat their own children. So great will be the punishment that the other nations will not merely sneer, they will be terrified. The anger of God is expressed so forcibly that it will even be reflected in the land itself, which will witness their punishment as God destroys their hilltop altars, and the unburied bodies will litter the hillsides until the remnant are forced to accept God's authority, and even they will be scattered among the nations in exile (6:8).

In fact, we know from biblical history, that the Jews who returned were from the Southern tribes, until by the time Jesus came, the only remnants of the North were the hated Samaritans who were not part of the Temple-worshipping community at Jerusalem. (See the story of the woman of Sychar).

So great is God's anger (Chapter 7), "This what I, the Sovereign Lord, am saying to the whole land of Israel: 'This is the end for the whole land. Israel, the end has come.'" Verse 10–11, "The day of disaster is coming for Israel. Violence is flourishing. Pride is at its height. Violence produces more wickedness. Nothing of theirs will remain, nothing of their wealth, their splendour or their glory." Verse 24, "I will bring the most evil nations here and let them have your homes." No wonder God had to make a terrific impact on the prophet at the start. Here ends the first vision given to the prophet.

The second vision comes six years into the exile, when the prophet had the leaders with him in his house. (Chapter 8) The power of the Sovereign Lord came upon him so much, that in a vision of brilliant, majestic splendour, he was caught up in the air and taken to the city of Jerusalem where he was shown an idol "which was an outrage to God." Then, amidst the dazzling light of God's presence, just as at the river Chebar, he is shown in dramatic form the disgusting things that the nation were doing, which were driving away God's holy presence. Images of awful strange gods were there, and women too. Here names were named of the priests who were complicit in this demon worship, doing it in secret and saying, "It does not matter, God cannot see it." Not content with spreading their pernicious idolatry in the countryside, they have to come and do it here, where they pollute the sacredness of God.

In the vision, Ezekiel sees God punishing these men, killing them within the precincts of the temple itself. So great was the force of God's anger, that Ezekiel falls on his face to plead with God. The reply (9:10), "I will not have pity on them; I will do to them what they have done to others." At that, the man in linen clothes who had been ordered to carry out this dreadful punishment returns to say to the Lord, "I have carried out your order." Then, still in the vision, the prophet sees that the dazzling creatures give live coals to the man in linen and he scatters it over the city. At this point, the strange creatures rise in the air, and the glorious light of God's presence goes above them, and they leave the temple. Ezekiel comments that these creatures were just like the ones he had seen in the first vision of judgement, each having a face like the first creatures and what appeared to be human hands.

The next part of this vision takes the prophet to the East gate of the Temple, where he sees twenty-five named men, who are actually replicating the evil advice given by the false prophets in Jeremiah's time, namely that his, Jeremiah's prophecy, is wrong, the siege of Jerusalem will soon be over. 11:3, "The city is like a cooking pot and we are like the meat in it, but at least it protects us from the fire." Just as today, these false leaders thought that their false religion would protect them from God's wrath, and God throws their words back at them, verse 7, "This city is indeed a cooking pot," but the meat is the corpses of their victims, and God warns that He will throw them out of the city. "While you were following the laws of the other nations, you were breaking my laws." And as Ezekiel was uttering this prophecy, one of the men fell dead. God then warns him that he and the exiles are being vilified, that those few remaining are feeling secure because they are left, suggesting that God is helping them.

God now reassures the prophet that, although He has exiled the people, He is still with them and will bring them back. Ah, at last the promise of hope for a future (11:17–20), in which God promises that the returning exiles will have been purified of their evil. And then a repetition of the words in Isaiah and Jeremiah, verse 19, "I will take away their stubborn hearts of stone and will give them an obedient heart. Then they will keep my laws and faithfully obey all my commands. They will be my people and I will be their God."

Now the vision goes, and the following morning, God speaks directly to Ezekiel with, in Chapter 12, some remarkable statements, which we need to consider, predicting the events recorded in the previous books. God said that the people were saying that, "Time goes by and predictions come to nothing" (verse

22). Tell them, no more false or misleading prophecies, "There will be no more delay. "I will do what I have warned you I would do." Verse 25 "The Israelites think that your visions and prophecies are about the distant future. So tell them there will be no more delay."(verse 27-28)

Then follows a long diatribe against false prophets, male and female, much of it echoing previous warnings given through Isaiah and Jeremiah, about the false prophets and God's contempt for them. The same in Chapter 14, as God warns Ezekiel against the false prophets who came to him to seek God's will. Again, reinforcing what had been said about the false prophets who were misleading the people and promoting idolatry, a warning that He, God, will remove both false prophets and those who consult them, in order to purify the nation. Saying, further, that if Noah, Daniel and Job were living in the land, they would be unable to save even their own children, just their own lives. In the image of a dead vine, only useful as firewood, God will burn up those Jews who are unfaithful.

At this point, after the visions of Jerusalem, we now have in Chapter 16, the condemnation of Jerusalem, which is described as a prostitute, which again reinforces the earlier condemnation of the city by previous prophets, and the damning words that Sodom and Samaria had not sinned as greatly as Jerusalem. Salutary words, but emphasising that Jerusalem's sin was all the more pernicious because of its prominence as the place where God dwelt. But Chapter 16 ends with a repetition of the words of the previous prophetic books, that ultimately God will restore the city and make a covenant with Israel (Judah). "But I will honour the covenant I made with you when you were young, and I will make a covenant with you that will last forever" (verse 60).

Now comes a most remarkable parable about an eagle (Chapter 17) which broke off the top of a cedar tree in Lebanon and placed it in a city of commerce. Then he took a young vine plant from Israel and placed it in a fertile field, where it grew, flourished and reached up towards the eagle. Now there was another giant eagle, and so the roots of the vine reached out to it in hope that it would receive more water than it was already getting. But surely, the first eagle will simply uproot it and let it die. Ask these rebellious Jews what this means, and then tell them that when the king of Babylon came, he took the king and his officials back with him, made a treaty with one of the king's family, and made him swear loyalty to him, but he kept the important men hostage. What did this king do? Why, he sent messengers to Egypt to hire a great army. Can he succeed?

Can he break a treaty just like that? No! And I, the living God, will punish him for breaking that treaty, which he swore in my name. He and his forces will be scattered and killed in battle. In contrast, God offers hope to the nation. Continuing the parable, he says that he will take a tender sprout from the tree and plant it on Israel's highest mountain, where it will flourish and become magnificent. "I the Lord have spoken. I will do what I say." So once again, God is promising a glorious future for Israel.

Chapter 18 continues the theme of personal, individual responsibility Verse 30, "I will judge each of you by what you have done." This is followed, Chapter 19, by a series of parables in song, each illustrating the false pride of the nation. Then, Chapter 20, we have the leaders of the nation coming to Ezekiel to ask about God's will, only for him to be told to rebuke them by reminding them of their past defiance of God's will despite all the miracles which he had performed for them. Looking back to the period of Moses, during which their conduct was appalling, to the point where God had suggested to Moses that he would simply destroy them and start again, their conduct at that time led to forty years wandering in the wilderness during which all the rebellious generation died. Even when they reached the promised land, they did not keep the holy laws but followed false gods. "You have made up your minds that you want to be like the other nations, like the people who live in other countries and worship trees and rocks. But that will never be" (verse 30).

The importance of this cannot be overstated. Israel as a nation was unique in God's purpose, but they were frustrating that purpose by their blatant rejection of his covenant. What was happening now was in fact a result of their sin. However, yet again, we see expressed, the love, the mercy, the forgiveness of God but also the necessity of their submission. For He continues, saying that (20:37), "I will take firm control of you and make you obey my covenant. I will take away from among you those who are rebellious and sinful. I will take them out of the lands where they are living now, but I will not let them return to the land of Israel." These are powerful words and open to much interpretation. Does this refer to a part of the Southern nation, Judah and Benjamin? Or does it refer to the Northern kingdom only, whose deeds were much more rebellious, and whose whereabouts now is the subject of much speculation? Perhaps the future will reveal all. Verse 42, "When I bring you back to Israel, the land I promised I would give to your ancestors, then you will know that I am the Lord. You will be disgusted with yourselves because of all the evil things you did."

Now follows a series of denunciations against Jerusalem, containing also quite specific details of how the Babylonians will come against them. In spite of the various treaties which they have made, God will punish the city, but only at the hands of the one whom the Lord has chosen to do this, even though they don't believe it. It is important to note here, that Persia is God's servant in this. Then follows a warning to the Ammonites, before we have a reiteration of the crimes committed by Jerusalem, and the fact (illustrated by the account of the potter in Jeremiah) that the nation will only be of use after the refiner's fire has broken and remade them.

Further chapters then describe the sins of Israel as an adulterous relationship with other nations, because Israel coveted the splendour of the other nations – here, specifically, the nation of Egypt, which was admittedly, as we now know, a very splendid and elaborate, highly cultivated and advanced society. But one from which they had been delivered because they cried to God for help. These are mixed with parables of purging, of cleansing, and for example, the reason why the temple was taken from them which was the fact that they had misused it.

Then follows a prophetic list of nations against whom God's anger will be seen. Ammon, Moab, Edom, Philistia, Tyre and Egypt, which was a reminder of what God had previously stated, but amid it all there is a reminder also of God's future plans for Israel (28:24). Interestingly, in 29:17, it is Babylon under Nebuchadnezzar who will restrict the power of Egypt, although we know that Egypt was not finally reduced until her ill-fated attempt at union with then emerging Roman empire, the Persian empire being succeeded successively by the Greeks, under Alexander, and then by the Romans. This, the potential weakness of Egypt, was made ironic in the way that Israel had turned to them for help against Assyria and Babylon. God had described them at the time, as a 'broken reed'.

When we reach Chapter 33, Ezekiel is reminded of his responsibilities as a watchman to the nation of Israel, to warn them, even though they will not heed his warning (33:33), "But when all your words come true – and they will come true – then they will know that a prophet has been among them." (Even if it is too late.) Against God's commission to the prophet is set his denunciation of the Israeli leaders. 34:2, "You take care of yourselves, but never tend the sheep," followed by the description adopted by Jesus so many years later, verse 11, "I, the sovereign Lord, tell you that I myself will look for my sheep and take care of them." "Everyone will know that I protect Israel, and that they are my people. You, my sheep, the flock that I feed, are my people, and I am your God," says the Sovereign Lord.

There now follows a further assurance that God will bless his people and that their persecution by the surrounding nations will no longer happen, together with that frequently quoted line, "It is true that people say that the land eats people, and that it robs the nation of its children, But from now on, it will no longer." And the prophecy continues that, in spite of their pollution of the land, God will bring them into a new relationship with himself, "... what I am going to do is not for the sake of you Israelites but for the sake of my holy name... I will take away your stubborn heart of stone and give you an obedient heart. I will put my spirit in you, and I will see to it that you follow my laws and keep all the commands I have given you." In other words, through suffering, they will learn obedience and, when refined and cleansed by the fire of persecution, God will then, by his Holy Spirit, give them a completely new attitude so that they will follow Him from their hearts and not by means of external ritual. See Joel 2:28, where the idea of renewal through God's Spirit within them is explored in some detail.

We have not yet finished with dramatic visions, and the next one is often quoted, in which the prophet is given a vision of a great army lying as scattered bones in a valley of dry bones. Then, at God's command, the prophet prophesies over the bones, God blows with the wind of his spirit and the dry bones come to life as a mighty army, as will the nation of Israel. Following this, a key passage, in Chapter 37, tells that God will unite Judah and Israel in one nation again, verse 22, "They will have one king to rule over them, and they will no longer be divided into two nations or split into two kingdoms."

Whether that has already happened or is yet another vision of the future, we cannot be certain. What is certain is that it will be accompanied by the restoration of the temple, and "A king like my servant David will rule over them forever". Which takes us back to Isaiah's prophecy regarding the time we are now dealing with, see Isaiah 7:17–23; 9:6–7, and, in fact, Ezekiel here is saying exactly what Isaiah had said some one hundred years earlier. One interlude here concerns the defeat of Gog, the ruler of the nations of Meshech and Tubal, which we cannot exactly place, but then we return to news of the restoration of Israel and another vision in which Ezekiel sees a 'man' measuring the temple in great detail. And we then see what is obviously a vision of a new Temple, a new priesthood, and the almighty presence of the Holy God is there, with a stream flowing East from the renewed temple, which will flow into the Dead Sea and bring fresh life to it. The book then ends with a redistribution of land amongst the tribes. Clearly here in this, we have an admonitory vision of a potential, or actual city, with a nation behaving correctly, as was originally intended.

Daniel

The book of Daniel is set during the period of exile of the Jews under Babylon and Persia, and in part, it shows the faith and resolution of Daniel and three others who were amongst the elite of the Jewish nation, whom Nebuchadnezzar intended to use in the administration of the district known as West Euphrates, which included the land of Israel.

We begin by seeing how the four men make a stand against the licentiousness of that empire by refusing to become ritually unclean through eating and drinking the royal fare, choosing instead to remain ritually clean, by a diet of vegetables and water, in order that their lives might bear witness to the God of the Jews. Surprisingly, for Ashpenaz, who had the ordering of them, we find that God gave them superior understanding in literature and philosophy and, for Daniel, the ability to interpret dreams and visions (shades of Joseph), which gave them ten times better understanding than the king's own officials.

The first major incident concerns the threat to the king's advisors, who were challenged to interpret the king's troublesome dream. To test their ability to understand, rather than merely speculate on what they were told, the king requires the men to tell him what he had dreamt. Only Daniel is able to do this, stating clearly that this understanding comes from his God, not himself. The dream foretells the rise of four empires, of which the Babylonian was the first and then most probably the second the Persian under Cyrus, the third the Greek under Alexander and, finally, the Roman empire, which under Constantine would intermingle with the Christian church, following the vision which the emperor experienced.

The result of this was that Daniel was mightily rewarded, and given prominence in the kingdom, whilst at Daniel's request, his three comrades, Shadrach, Meshach and Abednego, were promoted to high office in the provinces.

Following this, in pride at his own achievements, Nebuchadnezzar orders a giant statute of himself, 27 metres high and three wide, to be set up, saying that all the people of all the provinces should, at a given signal, bow down and worship his image. This was an immediate challenge to the strict beliefs of the Jews, and they refused to obey, which in turn gave an opportunity to their detractors, to denounce the Jews as failing in their respect to the king. Shadrach, Meshach and Abednego were told, "bow or burn," at which command, their own response was to honour their God by refusing to bow to the idol, saying, "If the God whom we serve is able to deliver us, He will, but if not, we will certainly not worship any other god or bow to the statue." Result, a very angry king and three men thrown, fully dressed, into the superheated furnace. And the result of that was, that the king saw not three men in the fire but four walking about unharmed, with the fourth looking like an angel. And the further result, the three men's God was given high honour in the kingdom.

Now the king dreams again, and only Daniel can explain it. Referring as it did in the image of a tree cut down leaving the stump in the ground, it referred to the king himself who, at the height of his powers, would suffer humiliating madness and be driven from his throne for seven years, which happened twelve months later. God, through this, was teaching the king that He, God, is supreme, and at the end of the seven years when the emperor's sanity returned, the result was that the king publicly honoured God.

Now the years have passed, and Nebuchadnezzar's son Belshazzar is king. He one day holds a drunken orgy for a thousand of his noblemen and, at the height of their folly, a human handwrites a message on the palace wall, at which the drunken king was terrified and asked for his magicians to tell him what the message meant. They could not. However, the queen mother remembered Daniel, and he was sent for. His first reaction was to severely criticise the king for his behaviour and then to read the three words on the wall which were 'number', 'weight', 'divisions'. Meaning: God has numbered your days and brought it to an end; you have been weighed in the scales and found too light; your kingdom will be divided and given to the Medes and the Persians. Daniel was highly rewarded for this, but that same night, Belshazzar died, and Darius the Mede took the throne.

Under Darius, Daniel was given a senior position. His ability was no doubt on record. However, his outstanding ability under the new ruler earned him the jealous hatred of his Persian subordinates, who plotted against him, using his loyalty to his God as the key. To undermine him, they suggested that an order be given by the king that for thirty days no one should ask anything from any god or human being, except the king, knowing that three times a day Daniel went to his room, faced Jerusalem from his window and prayed to his God! As a result, the king was deeply upset, but a law having been issued by the king, could not be countermanded.

So in punishment, Daniel was arrested, bound and thrown into the pit of lions. However, the king could not sleep. So he arose early and went to the pit, only to find Daniel still alive; his God had saved him by sending an angel to shut the lions' mouths. The king was delighted and had Daniel plucked out, and the false accusers and their families were thrown in. This time, their bones were crushed by the lions, even before they reached the bottom of the pit. Once again, Daniel's God is highly praised and an order sent throughout the kingdom that Daniel's God should be honoured and respected because his power and authority will never end. In fact, Daniel's reputation continued during the Persian dynasty, right through to the time of Cyrus.

Now we are told that Daniel has had a vision during the first year of Belshazzar's reign. This mysterious vision was of four beasts, representing four empires which will arise on earth, and then that God's people will receive royal power and keep it forever (7:17–18). However, it is the fourth empire which gives rise to questions because it is different and will lead to terrible conflict between his authority and that of God's people. Yet ultimately, it will result in the royal people of the supreme God being enabled to overcome and given authority and power which will last forever (7: 27), the power of that final king having been utterly and completely destroyed. The visionary dream was really alarming, and Daniel was so terribly frightened that he kept silent about it. Many people have attempted to put time and place to this dream, but only one thing emerges as indisputable from this vision – namely, that in the end, whatever happens, God and his people will be triumphant.

Now we are told, Daniel has another vision of a ram and a goat representing two world powers, in which the goat overcomes the ram and then goes on to challenge the Holy Land and the Heavenly powers, until the temple is desecrated and became the place of irreligious practice. Daniel overhears the angels discussing this and asks when it will happen. The answer is that a specific period is determined, given as 2,300 days, during which time no sacrifices will be offered, and then the Jewish temple in Jerusalem will be restored. (Chapter 8).

The angel Gabriel is sent to explain to Daniel that the ram represents the kingdoms of the Medes and the Persians, and the goat, the kingdom of Greece. The first of its horns, its first king, would be replaced by four horns representing four divisions of the kingdom, but not as strong. When those kingdoms come to an end, they will be replaced by a stubborn, vicious and deceitful king, who will cause terrible destruction, and, in his pride, he will defy the greatest king of all, but will ultimately be destroyed without the use of any human power. Daniel is then told to keep this vision secret, because it will not happen for a long time. Gabriel had said that the vision refers to the end of time.

Now we come back to the immediate present to Daniel who, during the reign of the Babylonian king Darius, is thinking about the seventy years of Jeremiah's prophecy during which time Jerusalem would be in ruins. His prayer then is for his people. He admits their sins, their errors of disobedience and neglect, which have brought about the downfall of God's nation. He admits that Jerusalem's fault is very great, but also that even now the people have not changed their ways. So thinking back over God's goodness in the past, he pleads with God to help, not because the people deserve it but because God is a God of love and forgiveness (9:18).

At this, the angel Gabriel is sent to him again, to explain the situation in answer to his prayer. And now we have more details: 490 years being the time before Jerusalem will be free, the people's sins forgiven and the temple worship restored. From the time the order to rebuild the temple is given until God's chosen leader comes, 49 years will pass, Jerusalem the city will be rebuilt and last for 434 years, which will be years of troubles. At the end of this time, God's chosen leader will be killed unjustly and the city and the temple destroyed by a powerful ruler. He, in turn, will have an agreement with many people for a further seven years, and when that time is over, he will end all sacrifices and offerings and place The Awful Horror on the temple mount, which will remain there until the one who put it there meets the end which God has prepared for him (9:27). Interpreting this has kept many people busy for many years.

Now, in the third year of Cyrus, Daniel, also called Belteshazzar, was given a message which was true but hard to understand. Daniel is undergoing a three-week period of mourning, during which he and some others will be fasting. Standing on the banks of the river Tigris alone, he saw in a vision a man dressed in linen with a gold belt, whose presence was awesome, flaming, bright like polished jewels, and whose voice was, "like the roar of a great crowd." The others with him heard the sound and were terrified, running away, but they saw nothing (as in Paul's vision on the road to Damascus). Daniel is overpowered by this vision and becomes unconscious, lying there until roused by an angel who tells him that God loves him, has seen his humility and his longing for understanding and has sent him a message, to which he is to pay careful attention.

Daniel is then told that the message has been delayed for 21 days because he, the angel, opposed by the angel prince of Persia, was left stranded in Persia until Michael, one of the chief angels, came to help him. Interestingly, we are told that the angel had the appearance of a human being, who took hold of Daniel to stop him shaking with fear. He told him that he had come to tell him what was written in the Book of Truth, but that now he must return to fight the guardian angel of Persia, after which the angel of Greece would come. "There is no one to help me except Michael," Israel's guardian angel who was responsible for helping and defending him."

Now comes the message. Three more Persian kings will be followed by a fourth who will challenge Greece. Then, a heroic king will rule over a huge empire as an autocrat, but at the height of his power, the empire will break up into four parts. The king of Egypt will be strong, but one of his generals will be stronger. Later, the king of Egypt will make an alliance with the king of Syria, giving him his daughter in marriage. This alliance will not last long and she and her child will be killed, but later, one of her relatives will become king, and he will attack Syria and seize his possessions and gods, taking them back with him to Egypt. Some years later, Syria will attack Egypt without success. Sons of the king of Syria will gather a great army and attempt to reconquer Egypt, only for one of them and his huge army to be defeated by an angry Egyptian monarch who will boast of his victory. However, later, the king of Syria will gather an even larger army supported by Egyptian rebels, and even some of the more violent members of the Israelite nation who have seen a vision will rebel but be defeated. Syria will finally defeat Egypt and occupy Israel. Not content with this, he will attempt to challenge the nations by the sea, only to be defeated by a foreign leader who will humiliate him, driving him back to take refuge in his own fortresses where he will end by being destroyed.

The angel then continued to say that the next king of Syria would be an evil man with no right to be king. He would seize power by trickery, sweep away all opposition including God's High Priest, and by making treaties with other nations, he, by trickery, despite his only having a small kingdom, will seize a more powerful and wealthy province and then prepare to attack Egypt, whose king will be ruined by the deceit of his own advisors. The Syrian king will return home with all his loot, determined to destroy the religion of God's people. Later he will invade Egypt yet again, but this time, he will be frightened off because the Romans in ships will oppose him, and he will turn back in anger and try to destroy the worship of the Israelis, aided by rebels from within that nation. His soldiers will desecrate the temple and set up the Awful Horror, leading to civil war between the rebels and the true worshippers. Through the ensuing troubles, God's people will receive some support and will be purified, religiously, by the ensuing conflict. This will continue until the time of the end which God has determined.

The King of Syria will boast of his success, claiming to be greater than the Lord God of the Jews, ignoring even the other false gods because he will claim to be greater than them all. He will continue until his own end comes, which is already determined by God. Finally, the king of Egypt will launch a massive attack, and in response, the king of Syria will attack and invade many countries, including the Promised Land. He will conquer Egypt, Libya and Ethiopia but then frightening news will come from the North and East, which will so enrage him that he will set up camp between the Temple and the sea, but he will die.

Chapter 12, now the angel wearing linen clothes declares that there will be a time of great trouble, the worst since the nation (Israel) came into existence, but all those whose names are in God's Book will be saved. Some of the dead will live again to judgement, whilst those who have lived and served the living God will, "shine like the stars forever." Daniel is now told to seal the book until the end of the world (verse 4), with the very potent warning we do well to heed, "Meanwhile many people will waste their efforts trying to understand what is happening." How very true.

Asked when these things would happen, the angel replied, "It will be three and a half years. When the persecution of God's people ends, all these things will have happened." Daniel is now told to go because these words are to be kept secret. Verse11–13, "From the time that the daily sacrifices are stopped, that is, from the time of the Awful Horror, 1,290 days will pass. Happy are those who remain faithful until 1,335 days are over. And you, Daniel, be faithful to the end. Then you will die, but you will rise to receive your reward at the end of time."

Symbolic, yes, and no doubt many of his contemporaries would have understood the references. We must avoid any attempt to construct theories to explain what is not made clear. Jesus himself confessed that he did not know when the end would be.

Hosea

Although the writer was living in the tribal area of the Northern kingdom, this message was addressed to both of the two kingdoms, prior to the invasion of Israel by Sennacherib of Assyria, warning them that, because of their continued sin and disobedience, God was determined to discipline them severely. But once again, the message is also full of the love of God for the wayward nations.

As was customary with these messages, many of the prophecies were illustrated dramatically to speak to a people who were reluctant to listen to simple words. Remember that they would have been largely illiterate, at a time when communication was limited and restricted mostly to spoken accounts, so that dramatic illustration via symbolism was one way of attracting their attention.

In this case, Hosea was told to get married to a woman who would then be unfaithful to him, but whose children's names would also reinforce the prophet's message. The first child was named Jezreel, after the city where Jehu had killed the remainder of the wicked King Ahab's family. The second child was named 'Unloved' because God said that he would no longer love Israel, although he still loved Judah! Quite a distinction. The third child was then named 'Not my People' because God had rejected them, although that is followed by the comment that one day they would again become 'the children of the living God'. As his wife becomes unfaithful, the prophet begs with his children to plead with their mother to stop her adultery – a very clear message, indicating that the ordinary people of the nation should have acted to stop what their leaders were doing. However, Hosea declares that despite her conduct, he will ultimately win back her love, just as God will pardon the sins of the people and restore then to a right relationship with himself.

Hosea is then urged to buy a prostitute but not have any relations with her for a long time, illustrating the point that there would come a time when, at some future date, the Nation would be restored under a king who would be a descendant of the first king David.

The dire warnings now continue, with a statement that the people's sin will result in damage to their environment, and a direct rebuke to the priests who have become unfaithful to their God, in their worship of wooden idols, and he ridicules their behaviour with the words, "A stick tells them what they want to know." He further adds that their behaviour has got such a firm hold on them that they are unable to acknowledge God.

In a separate message, he compares the conduct of Judah favourably, compared to the Northern nation, but then he goes on to condemn that nation also, for their behaviour towards their neighbour, Israel, in attempting to seize part of their territory.

Hosea then comments that when Israel does try to reform, they do so in such a way that it shows their insincerity, to the point where God comments, through the prophet, 6:5, "I want your constant love, not your animal sacrifices. I would rather have my people know me than burn offerings to me."

In Chapter 8, the prophet is even more specific. Their sin is not just idolatry but, when in trouble, instead of turning to God and keeping his covenant, they chose their own leaders. They insisted on having kings like the other nations and then turned to idols of wood and stone to provide guidance. And the more they constructed their places of idolatrous worship, the more they increased their ability to sin. Their idolatry was compounded because they abandoned their God to rely on other nations, like Egypt, to help them. Even the name of the god they chose, Baal, could be rendered as 'husband'. Hence the metaphorical use of 'marriage' and 'adultery.'

Again, there are further warnings and predictions, warning that they will not only lose God's presence, but they will also be evicted from their national homeland, for which they had fought so hard. And here, again, the message is in poetic form, "When I first found Israel, it was like finding grapes growing in the desert… like seeing the first ripe figs of the season. But when they entered the promised land, they began to worship Baal." In fact, as God tells them, their sinning began at Gilgal, where they camped and set up memorials after they had crossed the river Jordan, by Jericho, and as they began their occupation of the Promised Land. And in Chapter 10, the judgements continue only, in Chapter 11, for God to reiterate his love for them, verse 8, "How can I give you up, Israel? How can I abandon you?"

The prophecy then comes to its conclusion with 13:9, which is God's final judgement on the nation of Israel, "I will destroy you, people of Israel! Then who can help you?" And this message is firmly driven home by the words of the prophet in a final plea. Chapter 14, "Return to the Lord your God, people of Israel… Let this be your prayer, 'Forgive all our sins and accept our prayer, and we will praise you as we promised. Assyria can never save us… We will never again say to our idols that they are our God." And of course, the prophecy ends with the remarkable repetition of God's position, "I will bring my people back to me. I will love them with all my heart." To which is added the addenda, that this should be a lesson to all who witness these events.

Joel

This very short book is interesting in that, although we do not know when it was written, the likely time is during the Persian period of their exile. It uses very dramatic imagery, again, to illustrate or symbolise the dire condition of the nation. Directed mostly at the Southern kingdom, because it speaks of Jerusalem, it describes the nation as being like a country devastated by an enormous invasion of locusts, one of the pestilential scourges of the area, leaving everyone destitute and mourning, even the Temple sacrifices would be deprived of gifts.

However, what is so important is that the prediction is set in a potential future time, which is described as 'The Day of the Lord', which will be a day of justice and retribution, when the Lord's army, 2:10, will be so frightening that even the earth and the heavens will tremble at the terrible judgement. The prophet then calls upon the nation to repent, but to repent sincerely from the heart not simply in outward expressions, as in tearing their clothes. "Call the people together; weep and pray in the hope that God will 'change His mind'. Then follows a picture of a restored nation becoming prosperous again, delivered from their enemy in the North, which was Assyria.

At this point, the prophet, like all the others, speaks of a day which is coming when Israel will once again accept that it is their God who has delivered them. Here too we have a variation on one of the continued themes found in other prophets, that at some time in the future, the nation would be obedient and worship in sincerity because their hearts have been changed. Here we are told how and why, and when. 2:28, "Afterwards, I will pour out my Spirit on everyone. Your sons and daughters will proclaim my message;" which is commonly accepted as the outpouring of God's Holy Spirit on the disciples on the Day of the feast of Pentecost (Acts 2:1), which transformed the frightened disciples into the men and women who would so boldly, and at great personal cost, spread the gospel across the then known world, evidenced by miraculous power.

However, the time when this will happen is described by certain events, verse 30, "I will give warnings of that day in the sky and on the earth; there will be bloodshed, fire and clouds of smoke. The sun will be darkened and the moon will turn red as blood before the great and terrible day of the Lord comes." This appears to be linked with our Lord's prediction of a time of suffering and destruction, as in Matthew 24 and repeated in Mark 13 and Luke 21. Whether this was a reference to the time, in AD 70, when the Roman emperor Vespasian ordered that Jerusalem be destroyed because of Jewish rebellion against Roman authority, and his son Titus burnt the city and totally destroyed the Temple, or whether it refers to sometime in the future, is an open question.

What we are told is that it will be a time when Israel is restored, and the nations judged by their actions towards Israel. Certainly, the message is reinforced by a warning to the nations to prepare for war (3:9), but just before this, Joel makes mention of the Jews being taken from their land and sold to the Greeks (verse 6).

Then the prophecy ends, as do most of the other prophetic books, with the promise of a glorious future for Israel. Verse 22, "But Judah and Jerusalem will be inhabited forever, and I the Lord will live on Mount Zion."

Amos

Here in this book, we have the emphasis of the prophecy directed at the Northern kingdom of Israel, even though the prophet Amos lived in Judah. Most of the prophetic books were related to Judah. Whether this was because, of the two nations, only Judah would eventually be restored from exile to rebuild the Temple and the city of Jerusalem, or whether it was because the Southern kingdom was seen as more important because the Temple was there, the place of sacrifice and the place where God 'dwelt', we cannot be certain. It may even be simply that most of the priests and scribes were from the South.

The burden of this prophecy of Amos appears to have been written before the North was engulfed by Assyria as part of their military expansion, and it does also speak of judgement against Israel's neighbours, notably Syria, Philistia, Tyre, Edom and Moab, before Israel is mentioned. This would be supported by our knowledge of the military campaign waged by the Assyrians as they extended their borders of influence down through Western Israel en route to block, to cut off, the Egyptian access to the region of West Euphrates.

Once again, the prophet appeals to the history of the nation, to the way in which God had led, provided for and brought them into a fertile country, as reasons for Israel to be grateful, not arrogant and proud. 3:2,"Of all the nations on earth, you are the only one I have known and cared for. That is what makes your sins so terrible, and that is why I must punish you for them." They were unique, chosen as special, as God's representatives on earth, an example to the other nations of God's power, yes, but also of his mercy and love – which echoes Moses' appeal to God on behalf of Israel, when they were so badly behaved and made to wander for forty years in the wilderness, simply because they were disobedient, ungrateful and prone to fall back into primitive religious beliefs. God wanted them to have a better relationship with Him.

After heavy and specific criticism of Samaria, their capital, Amos goes on to speak of their failure to learn from past experience, from their own history. In resounding words, the prophet goads them, 4:3–5, "The Sovereign Lord says, 'People of Israel, go to the holy place in Bethel and sin, if you must! Go to Gilgal and sin with all your might! Go ahead and bring animals… Go ahead and offer your bread in thanksgiving to God, and boast about the extra offerings you bring! This is the kind of thing you love to do.'" Verse 12, "So then, people of Israel, I am going to punish you. And because I am going to do this, get ready to face my judgement." 5:6, "Go to the Lord, and you will live. If you do not, he will sweep down like fire…" And amidst all this talk of doom and gloom the prophet praises the majesty of God the great creator.

This powerful denunciation was to people who were guilty of injustice, greed, and living in idle luxury, whilst their poor people suffered. 5:12, "You persecute good people, take bribes and prevent the poor from getting justice in the courts. And so, keeping quiet in such evil times is the clever thing to do." Verse 18, "How terrible it will be for you who long for 'the day of the Lord'! What good will that day do you? For you, it will be a day of darkness and not of light." And so the message builds to a climax, verse 21–24, "The Lord says, 'I hate your religious festivals; I cannot stand them! When you bring me burnt offerings and grain offerings, I will not accept them; I will not accept the animals you have fattened to bring me as offerings. Stop your noisy songs; I do not want to listen to your harps. Instead let justice flow like a stream, and righteousness like a river that never goes dry." And now the intensity of the message increases, verse 25–27, "People of Israel, I did not demand sacrifices and offerings during those forty years that I led you through the desert. But now, because you have worshipped images of Sakkuth, your king god, and of Kaiwan, your star god, you will have to carry those images when I take you into exile in a land beyond Damascus." In fact, during the 470 years of captivity in Egypt and the forty years in the desert, we have no record of God making any demands on them, although clearly worship was observed because the priesthood remained and, later, such occasions as Passover were instituted, and their excuse for leaving Egypt was so that they could worship God and sacrifice to him.

Now come further warnings of impending disaster and God's rejection of their pride and their luxurious living. Israel was, of the two kingdoms, the most prosperous and numerous.

Amos, like Joel, also had a series of visions, of locusts followed by fire, as destructive forces would ravage the nation. And a builder's plumb line to show that they were not straight and true. Now, Amaziah, the priest of the shrine at

Bethel, betrays Amos to the king Jeroboam, accusing him of treachery, "His speeches will destroy the country… This is what he says, 'Jeroboam will die in battle, and the people of Israel will be taken away from their land into exile.'"

Amaziah then told Amos to go back to Judah and do his preaching there, saying, "Let them pay you for it. Don't prophecy here at Bethel anymore. This is the king's place of worship, the national temple." Amos replied, "I am not the kind of prophet who prophecies for pay. I am a herdsman, and I take care of fig trees. But the Lord took me from my work as shepherd and ordered me to come and prophecy to His people Israel. So now you listen to what the Lord says to you, 'Your wife will become a prostitute on the streets, and your children will be killed in war. Your land will be divided up, and you yourself will die in a heathen country. And the people of Israel will certainly be taken away, into exile."

Then the prophesy ends with a further condemnation of Israel and severe warnings of the consequences of their sins, which would include the overthrow of the temple, 9:9, "I will give command and shake the people of Israel like corn in a sieve," but verse 11, "The Lord says, 'A day is coming when I will restore the kingdom of David, which is like a house fallen into ruins. I will repair its walls and restore it. I will rebuild it and make it as it was long ago.'" Verse 14–15, "'I will bring my people back to their land. They will rebuild their ruined cities and live there. I will plant my people on the land I gave to them, and they will not be pulled up again.' The Lord your God has spoken."

Obadiah

This very short book appears to have been written sometime after the Babylonians had overrun the Southern kingdom of Judah, and it is directed specifically at the nation of Edom, whose territory lay to the South of Israel below the Dead Sea and, therefore, directly on the route which the Israelites had taken on their way from Egypt to the promised land. There is little question that, as Numbers 20–21 had recorded, the Edomites, like the Moabites, had refused to allow the Israelites to pass through their land, on their journey to their future in the Promised Land.

We are told that the inhabitants of Edom were descended from Jacob's brother Esau (Genesis 36), so whether their refusal to allow them passage was a result of the feud between the brothers, which appeared to have been resolved when Jacob returned from his years of exile with his uncle Laban, as described in Genesis 33, or whether, as has been suggested, it was because Edom lay across a major trading route, the Way of the Red Sea. If the latter, then for a relatively strong and prosperous nation, as Edom was, to have to face continual invasions from other nations looking for fertile land, the prospect of allowing a vast horde of nomadic people to cross, with the inevitable depredations for fodder and sustenance, would have been likely to have been resisted.

What we do know is that, for the Israelites, the journey from Kadesh Barnea to their entry into Canaan took some thirty-eight years. Travelling, as they did, with so much livestock and human lives to feed, their journey must have involved prolonged stops en route whilst they searched for fodder or even planted and grew new crops. The refusal to allow the Israelites to travel through the land of the nations on their way would add much to the problems of that long, long, journey.

Whatever the cause, the Edomites had incurred the wrath of God, and this prophetic book very dramatically describes what will happen to them and why. In this case, the stated reason was because, when the Southern kingdom of Judah was facing the challenge of the Babylonian invasion, they took advantage of the situation to rejoice, to gloat (verse 12), and to stop anyone trying to escape from the invaders, while at the same time looting the towns whilst the inhabitants were too weak to resist.

When the time comes for God to judge the nations (verse 15), Edom is singled out for special mention. The prophet warns that Judah will, at some time in the future, take revenge and that Edom, like all the other surrounding nations, will be destroyed. Whilst for Judah the promise is, verse 21, "The Lord himself will be King," which prophecy emphasised the fact that at some time in the future, the glory for Judah will be re-established under a new king.

We now know that, historically, these nations have vanished, leaving no trace, their land being occupied by the modern nations which supplanted them, whereas Israel has now been restored to her land again, as happened in the creation of modern Israel in 1948.

Jonah

This is another short book with a specific purpose, for it tells of a prophet who was initially sent to warn the inhabitants of Nineveh, the capital city of the Assyrian empire and bitter enemy of Israel, that God – that is, not their gods but Jehovah, the supreme Lord of all creation and 'father' of the nation of Israel – was bringing judgement on them for their sin.

Here the story becomes very interesting. First because Jonah was convinced that if he preached to the citizens, they would repent and God would change his mind and not destroy them – and that was something quite remarkable because neither Israel North nor Israel South had heeded God's prophetic warnings. Here is an ungodly nation, and yet the prophet is so convinced that in absolute mercy, God will let them off because they will listen and obey him. This is because, ultimately, God is a God of mercy and love and does not want to destroy anyone, even those who bitterly oppose him, provided only that they repent, that is, alter their way of life. What an object lesson for Israel. Meanwhile, however, Jonah is the naughty boy. He refuses to obey, seeks out a ship going in the opposite direction, and has to pay his own fare, before he then heads for Spain. But God is not mocked. Because God is almighty and omnipotent, because He is the creator of all things, not only can Jesus His son still the storm on Lake Galilee, but God the father can create a storm to reprimand a disobedient servant, Jonah.

Honest enough to own up, when the ship in which he is travelling is caught in a sudden and precipitous storm, Jonah accepts responsibility (he had been asleep so even here he is not afraid) and is thrown overboard. The sailors were reluctant to do this, but Jonah insists. The storm is calmed, the sailors convinced of God's greatness and Jonah is swallowed by a great big fish.

Jonah's prayer from inside the fish is eloquent, as one would expect, from a man in such a desperate situation. However, essentially, he acknowledges God's greatness and his mercy. His comment (2:8) is also interesting. "Those who worship worthless idols have abandoned their loyalty to you. But I will sing praises to you; I will offer a sacrifice and do what I have promised. Salvation comes from the Lord."

Now back on dry land, God again issues the order to Jonah, "Go to Nineveh," which was a great city so large that it took him three days to cross it. There he proclaimed the message, "In forty days Nineveh will be destroyed." When the king heard that, he got off his throne, put on sack cloth and issued an order, 3:8, "Everyone must pray earnestly to God and must give up his wicked behaviour and his evil actions. Perhaps God will change his mind." "God saw what they did; He saw that they had given up their wicked behaviour, so he changed his mind and did not punish them."

Now, Jonah is very unhappy about this, because it was just the reason why he did not want to go in the first place. 4:3, "Now, Lord, let me die. I am better off dead than alive." He is having a good old-fashioned sulk. So another lesson – the whale had not been enough. A plant to shield Jonah from the heat of the sun grows up and then dies off. Then God sent a hot East wind. Jonah has had enough, "I am better off dead than alive." He is angry enough to die, but God rebukes him, "You feel sorry for the plant which you did not make grow. How much more should I be sorry for that great city of Nineveh with its more than 120,000 innocent children."

God is a God of mercy and love, and the citizens of Nineveh had repented sincerely, that is, they had altered their sinful ways. Remember that when asked for a sign that he was the Messiah that was to come, Jesus said that the only sign that would be given was that of the prophet Jonah, presumably the concept of returning to life after three days.

Micah

Writing as he does some ten or fifteen years before the fall of the Northern kingdom, Micah's words are very dramatic, as he foresees the approaching downfall of the Northern kingdom being a direct result of their behaviour, and he singles out their rebellious and sacrilegious conduct, their lavish lifestyle, contrasting as it did with their oppression of the poor, and he makes use of highly symbolic language to emphasise his message. 1:5 "All this will happen because the people have sinned." Verse 3, "The Lord is coming from His holy place; He will come down and walk on the tops of the mountains. Then the mountains will melt under Him like wax in a fire." He also sees that Jerusalem, the Southern kingdom, is heading the same way, verse 13, "You imitated the sins of Israel and so caused Jerusalem to sin."

Micah then goes on to elaborate his condemnation of their actions in Chapter 2, "How terrible it will be for those who awake and plan evil! When morning comes, as soon as they have the chance, they do the evil they planned."

What exacerbates the situation is that the people reject his 'preaching' at them, 2:6,11, "These people want the kind of prophet who goes about full of lies and deceit and says, 'I prophecy that wine and liquor will flow for you.'" 3:5, "My people are deceived by prophets who promise peace to those who pay them, but threaten war for those who don't." And then, "But as for me, the Lord fills me with his spirit and power and gives me a sense of justice and the courage to tell the people of Israel what their sins are." Verse 10, "You are building God's city, Jerusalem, on a foundation of murder and injustice."

Not content with predicting that punishment will soon be meted out, Micah then goes on to follow his predecessor, Isaiah, in predicting a day of great blessing, which will come at some time in the future (Chapter 4). The prophet had already explained exactly why the nation of Israel will suffer. "But these persons do not know what is in the Lord's mind. They do not realise that they have been gathered together to be punished in the same way that corn is brought in to be threshed" (4:12). But in verse 7, the prophet has already stated that, "They are crippled and far from home, but I will make a new beginning with those who are left, and they will become a great nation." In other words, there is a greater purpose in God's intentions. When Israel will return from exile, not only will their nation be restored, but a new, righteous and just king will be born to the house of David, in Bethlehem. "The Lord will abandon his people to their enemies until the woman who is to give birth has her son." (5:3–4). To some, this was fulfilled in King Hezekiah, but for the promise to be truly fulfilled, the coming king would have to achieve far more than the temporary benefits under Hezekiah – which is why the Church today sees in this a foretelling of the birth of Jesus, in Bethlehem.

Now in the next Chapter 6, the prophet again states the Lord's case against Israel, that they had ignored the circumstances which had given them prominence, God's deliverance from slavery in Egypt, and the prophet repeats the Lord's accusation, verse 3, "My people, what have I done to you?" The prophet then states clearly what the Lord is looking for in response to a posed question, "What shall I bring to The Lord?" (verse 6), answering with, "The Lord has told us what is good. What he requires of us is this: to do what is just, to show constant love, and to live in humble fellowship with our God" (verse 8). No questions, a simple statement, which corresponds with similar statements through previous prophets, such as in Amos 5:21, "I hate your religious festivals." Verse 23, "Stop your noisy songs... Instead let justice flow like a stream and righteousness like a river that never goes dry."

Before the book ends, there is a damning condemnation of Israel's immoral and corrupt behaviour, but again Micah finally concludes with a conditional promise, 7:9, "We have sinned against the Lord, so now we must endure his anger for a while. But in the end, he will defend us and right the wrongs that have been done to us." And then a final plea for the Lord's help in verse 15, "Work miracles for us, Lord, as you did in the days when you brought us out of Egypt." And verse 18, "There is no other God like you, O Lord, you forgive the sins of your people who have survived. You do not stay angry forever, but you take pleasure in showing your constant love."

Nahum

This very brief book is a fascinating complement to the previous book of Jonah, in which the prophet was sent to warn Nineveh of impending doom and destruction but at first refuses to go because he claims they will repent and God will forgive them – which is exactly what does happen when, finally, the prophet obeys and goes.

Now we see that in spite of a temporary respite, in the period around the end of the seventh century BC, the nation of Assyria, of which Nineveh was the capital and which had caused so much trouble to Israel, is finally overwhelmed by the Babylonians under Nebuchadnezzar. With the result, first, that it was the Babylonians who over ran the Southern kingdom of Israel, destroying Jerusalem in the process, but were in turn, as we see here, themselves overrun by the Persians.

The prophet here states quite clearly that it is the Lord God who is responsible for the destruction of the Assyrians because, although they had been instruments used to punish Israel, their conduct was a reproach to the holiness of the Lord. They were both proud and arrogant and acted most cruelly. 1:12, "This is what the Lord says to his people Israel: 'Even though the Assyrians are strong and numerous, they will be destroyed and disappear. My people, I made you suffer, but I will not do it again. I will now end Assyria's power over you and beak the chains that bind you.'" As of course happened under the Persians. This event here introduces another theme which can be traced through the prophetic books. These other nations who so bitterly opposed and troubled Israel would disappear; and they have historically, whereas the Nation of Israel is still extant – not just in the numbers of Jews scattered throughout the world but, since 1948, they have existed as a nation.

The prophet then repeats this assertion (2:2), "The Lord is about to restore the glory of Israel, as it was before her enemies plundered her," which is then followed by very dramatic imagery describing the fate of Nineveh, comparing her to Egypt (3:8) who, although stronger and more easily defended, had also been destroyed and her power over the nations ended. "Emperor of Assyria, your governors are dead, and your noblemen are asleep forever. Your people are scattered on the mountains and there is no one to bring them home again."

Habakkuk

This urgent plea from this prophet is a challenge to the Lord. He asks why it is that he should be confronted with such injustice, violence and evil doing – even the good people are being overpowered by the evil people to the point where justice is never done, and the law is powerless. The perpetrators? The Babylonians. Who else at this period in history? Writing around the same time as the previous prophets, that is, around the time that the Babylonians were attacking Egypt and devastating the Northern kingdom of Israel, as had happened under Sennacherib who had even threatened Jerusalem, Habakkuk's concern is simply that the Lord appears to be doing nothing to deal with the situation.

However, 1:5, the Lord's reply, "Keep watching the nations round you, and you will be astonished at what you see. I am going to do something that you will not believe when you hear about it. I am bringing the Babylonians to power!" To this, the prophet replies, "Lord from the beginning you are God. Holy and eternal Lord... You have chosen the Babylonians and made them strong so that they can punish us. But how can you stand these evil and treacherous men?" His complaint is that the Babylonians are worse than they, Israel, have been, so why pervert justice by using the worse to punish the lesser? A good point!

When the Lord replied, it was to tell Habakkuk to write the answer on clay tablets, that is, to preserve it, because "the answer may be slow in coming but it will come soon." And the answer? That evildoers would perish but the righteous would live, 2:4, "Because they are faithful to God." In other words, they all would be judged on their relationship to God!

The Lord then elaborates, yes, there will be doom for the ungodly, but the day is coming, verse 14, "When the earth will be as full of the knowledge of the Lord's glory as the seas are full of water." Followed by the repeated condemnation of the folly of looking to idols of wood and stone for help.

The book then ends, Chapter 3, with another remarkable outpouring of praise and worship honouring the Lord. "I am filled with awe. Now do in our times what you used to do. Be merciful, even when you are angry." Followed by a recital of the mighty power of the living Lord God and ending, verse 18, "Even though the fig trees have no fruit and no grapes grow on the vines, even though the olive crop fails and the fields produce no corn, even though the sheep all die and the cattle stalls are empty, I will still be joyful and glad, because the Lord God is my saviour. The Sovereign Lord gives me strength."

Which brings Habakkuk to the place that Job had reached, even though everything goes wrong I will still trust in the Lord. "Even though he slay me, yet will I trust in him."

What a remarkable alteration in the man, from his bitter complaint against the Lord at the start of his vision, to an acceptance of God's will and purpose for humanity.

Zephaniah

According to the opening, this prophecy relates to the period at the end of the Southern kingdom of Israel, prior to the occupation by Nebuchadnezzar, around 640 to 610 BC. That is at a similar time to Jeremiah, and it really says what the other prophets were also declaring, namely that Jerusalem and Judah would suffer terrible punishment because their worship was totally insincere and also corrupted by practices of worship of the god Baal.

The denunciation again is dramatic, 1:2, "I am going to destroy everything on earth." Verse 7, "The day is near when the Lord will sit in judgement; so be silent." He is also critical of those who say that the Lord is indifferent, verse 12, "… who say to themselves, 'The Lord never does anything, one way or the other.'" Whereas verse 17, "The Lord says, 'I will bring such disasters on mankind that everyone will grope about like someone blind.'" The inference is that the fate of Jerusalem will affect the whole world, typical of Zephaniah's vehemence.

Chapter 2 introduces the possibility of reconciliation, verse 3, "Turn to the Lord, all you humble people of the land who obey his commands," but goes on to issue warnings of doom to the nations surrounding Israel, including the nation which is the strongest threat to Israel, Assyria. Verse 13, "The Lord will use his power to destroy Assyria. What a desolate place it will become." No hope of repentance or forgiveness there, unlike the hope which is always offered to Israel.

No hope here, though, of restoration for Jerusalem. Chapter 3, "Jerusalem is doomed, that corrupt, rebellious city that oppresses its own people." Verse 6, "I have wiped out whole nations… I thought that then my people would have reverence for me and accept my discipline, that they would never forget the lesson I taught them." And verse 8, "'Just wait,' the Lord says. 'Wait for the day when I rise to accuse the nations.'" Verse 9, "Then I will change the people of the nations, and they will pray to me alone." And of Israel, "I will leave there a humble and lowly people who will come to me for help." So there is hope that a remnant will survive.

But then Zephaniah's mood changes equally dramatically, verse 14, "Sing and shout for joy, people of Israel. Rejoice with all your heart, Jerusalem. The Lord has ended your punishment; he has removed all your enemies. The Lord, the King of Israel, is with you; there is no reason to be afraid." And then follows verse 20, "The time is coming! I will bring your scattered people home; I will make you famous throughout the world and make you prosperous again."

To make such a prediction at a time when the nation was being warned so severely, both by the prophets who spoke in the name of the Lord and by the existing political situation, required either an extraordinary faith or the voice of God. And remember, history tells us that it happened, just as Zephaniah had predicted.

Haggai

This book is a record of a number of messages specifically directed at the people who had returned from exile under the Persian king, Cyrus, and who were, during the reign of his successor Darius, simply dragging their feet, not getting on with the work which they had been returned to Jerusalem to do. Particularly, having built themselves houses on their return, some of which were palatial, they had ignored, or forgotten, the Temple, which implied that it was less important to them than their own wellbeing. Further, the prophet attributes their poor harvest to their failure to honour the Lord. Verse 9, "When you brought the harvest home, I blew it away. Why did I do that? Because my Temple lies in ruins while every one of you is busy working on his own house. That is why there is no rain, and nothing can grow."

Alarmed by Haggai's rebuke, three weeks later they got to work. However, still there were problems, and one of those was the fact that those who had known the previous temple, the one built by Solomon and which had been magnificent, could see that this one was nothing like as splendid. And they were discouraged by that fact. 2:3, "How does it look to you now? It must seem like nothing at all. But now don't be discouraged, any of you. Do the work, for I am with you. When you came out of Egypt, I promised that I would be always with you. I am still with you, so do not be afraid."

And then follows a remarkable promise for the future not, this time, of a future king to restore their fortunes but a promise for the Temple. Verse 7, "I will overthrow all the nations, and their treasures will be brought here, and the Temple will be filled with wealth. All the silver and the gold of the world is mine. The new Temple will be more splendid than the old one, and there I will give my people prosperity and peace."

Then follows a religious issue, of what is defiled and the effect a defiled person would have on food if he touched it. The lesson, that by themselves being defiled, that is not 'clean', they also defiled anything they touched. Hence their problems over harvest and their failure to rebuild the temple, in spite of the warning signs of drought and poor harvest. Verse 18, "Today is the twenty fourth day of the ninth month, the day that the foundation of the Temple has been completed. See what is going to happen from now on. Although there is no corn left, and the grapevines, fig trees, pomegranates and olive trees have not produced, yet from now on, I will bless you."

The message was, if the people want God to bless them and their efforts, they must stir themselves and get on with his work. Result, verse 20, "On that same day, the twenty-fourth of the month, the Lord gave Haggai a second message." And this message was to Zerubbabel the governor, saying that he, the Lord, was about to shake heaven and earth and overthrow kingdoms and end their power, but that he would elevate Zerubbabel his servant to rule in the name of the Lord his God.

Zechariah

Here we have a collection of prophecies from the time of the exile, dealing with the restoration of the Jews, the rebuilding of the Temple and then the reforms under Ezra and Nehemiah – namely, the renewal of their religious relationship to the Lord. Then we have a series of prophetic utterances, concerning a time in the future when God's Messiah would be revealed. This is interesting because after the next prophet Malachi, there are no more prophecies, no word from God recorded for some four hundred and fifty years until the Messiah, the Son of God himself, appears, born as a baby in Bethlehem, as the prophet Micah had foretold. In other words, as we shall later see, following the dreadful disobedience and idolatry prior to the great punishment of the seventy years in exile, there is of necessity a time of renewal, of cleansing morally and spiritually before John the Baptist will call the people to repent in preparation for the advent of Jesus.

Where the prophecies of Zechariah become so very interesting is that they use almost identical imagery to that used at a similar period by Ezekiel, imagery which is both dramatic and dynamically startling, possibly terrifying, in the implication that over and above our lives here on earth there is another sphere of influence. The poet and theologian John Milton, following his blindness, writes in similar terms in his monumental work *Paradise Lost*, and of course, we find very similar imagery used by John the Apostle some five hundred years later, in his book The Revelation, interpretation of which has the pundits at a loss.

So the message to Zechariah begins, "The Lord Almighty told Zechariah to say to the people, 'I the Lord was very angry with your ancestors, but now I say to you, "Return to Me, and I will return to you." Do not be like your ancestors… Your ancestors and those prophets are no longer alive. They disregarded my commands and suffered the consequences.'" Then they repented. And now follow a series of very dramatic visions, similar to those received by Ezekiel and, to a lesser extent, Daniel.

The first visions of the four horses followed by that of the four ox horns and the four workers with hammers, appear to reveal that the prophet is to understand that it is the Lord himself who is controlling events, and that He has heavenly beings in charge of and supervising what is happening.

In Chapter 2, the vision of a measuring line suggests an architect preparing for redevelopment or simply checking to see if things are correct. The statement that angels are at work here reinforces the concept of a controlling power but also creates a sense of anticipation for better things to come. Further explanation is in 2:6, "But now, you exiles, escape from Babylon and return to Jerusalem," which connects the vision directly to current events, but then goes on to predict, verse 11, "At that time, many nations will come to the Lord and become his people," which suggests a time in the future.

The next chapter 3, then refers directly to the High Priest Joshua being accused by Satan and being rebuked by an angel, who passes on the Lord's message, "If you obey my laws and perform the duties I have assigned to you, then you will continue to be in charge of my temple," which is double edged. Either reform or be dismissed. In other words, whilst God is promising restoration for his people, to be successful, it must be accompanied by drastic reforms to the people's relationship with God. The High Priest has dirty clothes which must be replaced by clean ones. Then and only then will God take his place amongst his people again.

This is followed by further imagery from a renewed temple, in which the utensils are seen as illustrative of a supernatural God. Following this comes a message. Zerubbabel who was in charge of the rebuilding of the temple, which we have been told appeared to be not as good as the one built by Solomon, is told directly, "You will succeed, not by military might or by your own strength but by my Spirit. Obstacles as great as mountains will disappear before you. You will rebuild the temple, and as you put the last stone in place, the people will shout, 'Beautiful, beautiful.'" And this was direct encouragement for Zerubbabel because he was being criticised. 4:10, "They are currently disappointed because so little progress is being made. But they will see Zerubbabel continuing to build the Temple and be glad."

This is then followed by a series of visions: the scroll of condemnation, the idolatrous woman in a basket sent to Babylon, and then the vision of four chariots, which symbolised the anger of the Lord. Now Joshua the High Priest is made symbolic of a new High Priest, who will be called The Branch, who as a king will 'rebuild the Temple' or re-establish true worship.

Condemnation of the insincere worship which occurred during the exile is repeated, 7:4–6, "Tell the people of the land and the priests that when they mourned and fasted... and when they ate and drank, it was for their own satisfaction." And further reference is made to their disobedience which was the underlying cause of the exile.

Like all the other prophets of the period, Zechariah is told, Chapter 8, that impossible though it might appear, the Lord will return to Jerusalem and be worshipped there. Verse 6, "This may seem impossible to those of the nation who are now left, but it is not impossible to me." Words reflected by our Lord himself in response to Nicodemus, "With men it is impossible, but with God, all things are possible." The chapter then enlarges on the promise of future blessing and prosperity for Jerusalem, whilst Chapter 9 begins with a repetition of judgement on the nations who had caused so much trouble to Israel, followed by a very fulsome, poetic picture of a future King and what his reign will achieve.

This very positive foretelling of the future in Chapter 10, reverts to ordinary language, albeit still using symbolic expressions, verse 6, "I will rescue the people of Israel... and bring them all back home. They will be as though I had never rejected them."

By Chapter 12, we have a prophecy which is clearly of a future time, as also referred to by other prophets, when a successor to the king David will lead his people, verse 8, "The descendants of David will lead them like the angel of the Lord, like God himself." And then in what appears to be a reference to the 'suffering servant' of Isaiah, verse 10, "I will fill the descendants of David and the other people of Jerusalem with the spirit of mercy and the spirit of prayer. They will look at the one whom they stabbed to death, and they will mourn for him like those who mourn for an only child."

Chapter 13 commences with a view of the future. "'When that time comes,' says the Lord Almighty, 'A fountain will be opened to purify the descendants of David.'" Chapter 14 then speaks of a time, clearly in the future, when Jerusalem will become prominent. Physical changes, such as the Mount of Olives being split in two to create a freshwater valley, will make the city open to all comers. Verse 6, "When that time comes, there will be no more cold or frost." Verse 8, "When that day comes, fresh water will flow from Jerusalem, half to the Dead Sea and half to the Mediterranean." Verse 9, "Then the Lord will be king over all the earth; everyone will worship him as God and know him by the same name."

In some senses, this book is a precursor to the words of John in his Revelation at the end of the New Testament. However, as with Revelation and the prophetic books, it is impossible for us to put a date to the events, although many have tried.

Malachi

This prophetic book appears to have been written after the return from exile, and following the rebuilding of the Temple, because it is written as a reminder of the past blessings which they had enjoyed and the fact that they were God's chosen people. They were the descendants of Jacob not Esau. When the people ask, "How have you shown your love for us?" the Lord replies, "Esau and Jacob were brothers, but I have loved Jacob and his descendants and have hated Esau and his descendants." It is Paul, writing later in his letter to Romans 9:13 who comments, this is not injustice but God's choice.

But the nation had fallen into disobedience and idolatry, through their failure to uphold the law and obey it. Therefore, to avoid a repetition of the disaster from which they were now recovering, it is imperative that they renew their vows, obey the covenant with its laws, and this work must begin with the priests. Chapter 2, "The Lord Almighty says to the priests, 'This command is for you: you must honour me by what you do.'" Verse 7, "It is the duty of priests to teach the true knowledge of God. People should go to them to learn my will, because they are the messengers of the Lord Almighty." The people are also told what they must do, as Ezra had earlier indicated. For example, men married to foreign wives must divorce them (verse 11).

Then the prophet is told to move on, and in Chapter 3, he speaks of a future time. "The Lord Almighty answers, 'I will send my messenger to prepare the way for me. Then the Lord you are looking for will suddenly come to his Temple. The messenger you long to see will come and proclaim my covenant.'" And verse 5, "The Lord Almighty says, 'I will appear among you to judge.'"

The people are then reminded, in respect of the rebuilt temple, verse 10, to "Bring the full amount of your tithes to the Temple so that there will be plenty of food there. Put me to the test, and you will see that I will open the windows of heaven and pour out on you in abundance all kinds of good things."

Verse 16, "Then the people who feared the Lord spoke to one another, and the Lord listened and heard what they said. In his presence, there was written down in a book a record of those who feared the Lord and respected him. 'They will be my people,' says the Lord Almighty."

The book ends with the challenging words, 4:5, "But before that great and terrible day of the Lord comes, I will send you the prophet Elijah. He will bring fathers and children together again; otherwise I would have to come and destroy your country." Jesus would later imply that the coming of John the Baptist fulfilled this role.

The Gap Years

In order to understand the period in which our Lord, the Son of God came to earth, we must of necessity look at what has happened between the close of the book of Malachi and the birth of Jesus Christ, because this period of over 400 years was for the Jews a time of great change, of challenge and tumult.

The exile from Israel was complete by 586 BC, the Northern kingdoms under the Assyrians and the Southern kingdoms by the Babylonians, and the Temple had been destroyed. Cyrus the Persian emperor then conquered the Babylonians (circa 538), and the return of the Southern tribes, which began under Cyrus, was continued during the reign of his successor Darius. The rebuilding of the Temple was completed around 515 BC, and by this time, the Jews were somewhat chastened. The return was marked by much greater religious fervour under Ezra and Nehemiah. However, not all the Persians were so well-disposed towards the Jews, as the story of Esther under Xerxes illustrated. This Persian dispensation lasted for some 200 years and enabled the Jewish nation to re-establish itself, before the rapid expansion of the Greeks under Alexander the Great introduced new learning which also created new problems.

One other important factor emerges and that is the rise of the Samaritans as they became known. These were remnants of the Northern tribes returning from Assyria but intermingled with the peoples with whom the Assyrians had replaced the ten tribes. In our Lord's day, the Samaritans were despised and outlawed by the devout Jews. These remnants had brought with them some of the forbidden idolatry of the other nations, even though they retained a semblance of the Jewish faith. For this reason, under Nehemiah, their offers of help in rebuilding the Temple were refused. As a result, they created their own place of worship on Mount Gerizim, equating this with the place of worship mentioned in the books of Moses. However, some good was to emerge from this because the Samaritans based their assertions on the first five books, the Pentateuch, but only on those books, which in turn inspired the Southern Jews to pay much more attention to their own faith – which inspired our Lord's words to the woman at the well of Sychar (John 4:22), "You worship what you do not know; we know what we worship, for salvation is of the Jews."

This period also led, ironically, to the decline in importance of the Temple, its role in part being taken by the institution of local synagogues with their emphasis on the regular reading of the scriptures. The Jews were later to become known as 'the people of the book'.

When, in 336 BC, Alexander the Great came to power and brought the Greek states under Macedonian authority, he determined to drive the Persians out of Asia Minor. As a result, Greek culture became dominant in the cities like Alexandria and up the Western seaboard of Asia Minor. Alexander also thrust South, through the West coast of Palestine, to reach Egypt. It is said that he actually travelled to Jerusalem, but whether true or not, the Holy Land came under the influence of the Greeks.

In his conquest, one effect was to strengthen the Jews in their observance of their ancient faith. However, apart from other influences, it created a demand for the Hebrew scriptures to be translated into the Greek language. It also gave rise to some conflict between the emerging philosophical ideas embraced, for example, by Alexandrian Jews and those of Palestine, but it also opened the Jewish faith to other nations. However, what we are ultimately exploring is the way in which God was preparing His world for the ultimate revelation of himself in the person of Jesus Christ, something which would now be able to be understood by people other than those educated exclusively in the Jewish scriptures. If Rome built the roads, someone said, the Greeks provided the language for the spread of the Gospel.

Unfortunately, after the death of Alexander, the empire was split between his generals, and the land of Southern Syria and the lands down to the border of Egypt changed hands five times. Fortunes were about to change again as the Syrians gained more influence over Judea, and the Syrians were more influenced by Greek culture. However, it was the outrageous behaviour of the Syrian Antiochus Epiphanes who, frustrated by his failure to eliminate the Jewish religion, laid waste much of Judea and Jerusalem, circa 168 BC. This led to a rebellion by a Jewish priest Mattathias, leading to what became known as the war of the Maccabees which was a rebellion against the might of Syria under Judas Maccabeus, one of the sons of Mattathias, which gave a measure of independence to the land for the first time in some 400 years.

However, it was not until the time of John Hyrcanus that the Jewish people were able to throw off the Syrian yoke altogether, and under his guidance, the Jews achieved a prosperity not known since the days of Solomon. It was during this period that the two elements of the Jewish faith came to prominence, the Sadducees and the Pharisees, of whom the latter were the more restrictive whereas the Sadducees denied immortality and resurrection of the dead.

However, the Romans who, by 270 BC, dominated the Italian peninsula, struck out into Macedonia, defeating them in Thessaly in 197 BC. Then under the emperor Pompey, the Romans extended their territory quite rapidly, and in 63 BC, having ostensibly come to the aid of the Jews in Jerusalem who were under siege, Pompey captured the city. So the Promised Land was once again occupied territory. However, the Jews were allowed a degree of autonomy, because the Roman idea of subjugation was to enlist the aid of sympathetic or renegade citizens to carry out their dirty work. Hence, at the time of Jesus, the Roman taxes, separate from the Temple tax, were collected by collaborators. Effectively, the religious affairs were still controlled by the two rival factions, Sadducee and Pharisee, and Herod, who was nominally a Jew, was supported by the Pharisees. But he largely remained in power by ingratiating himself with the Romans, by developing the civic powers of the province, by placating the Jews by restoring the ruined Temple and by largely refusing to be drawn into any religious matters.

The main point of interest arising from this four-hundred-year interval between the close of the Old Testament and the coming of Christ is that during that period the nation had undergone a period of uncertainty, of rebellion and change. In fact, the Romans had taken authority over the area largely because of insurgency and political unrest, which is why Pilate the Governor had troops stationed within the walls of the city, and to some extent, it explains the reaction of the authorities to our Lord's teaching. "Better that one man suffer than the whole nation perish," was a relevant comment by the Jewish religious leaders who were walking a political tightrope to maintain their authority in the city. In fact, during our Lord's lifetime, mention is made of more than one contemporary uprising. Later Paul's preaching would be seen as a threat to the national and religious integrity of the nation.

What we need to remember, as we approach the New Testament, is that whereas in many ways the Old Testament is man centred in the sense that it focusses on man's response to God, the New Testament is God centred because it focuses on the life and work of His son Jesus and on what he, Jesus, has done for us and what he will do for us in the future. For the Old Testament, the hope was that Israel would be restored. In the New Testament, we have the promise of a new world with Jesus as Lord.

One last point before we move to the text. After the exile, only the Southern tribes had been restored, and whilst the old tribal loyalties were still there, under Roman rule, the nation was divided into three provinces: Judea in the South which included Jerusalem, Samaria in the centre, where worship was focused on Mt Gerizim, and Galilee in the North, which was the area around the lake where much of our Lord's ministry occurred. Over the Jordan, in what had been the land given to the tribes of Reuben, Gad and half Manasseh, were now the Ten Towns of the Decapolis, which included Gadara and Gerasa.

Matthew

When we move from the writings of the Old Testament prophets, we find a noticeable change. No longer the fiery and dramatic first-person rhetoric of Isaiah. Here we have an account written by a Jewish tax collector working for the Romans, whom Jesus met, "As he walked along" 9:9. We are told that Matthew invited Jesus to a meal at which tax collectors "and other outcasts" were present. In fact, the other disciples, who were present at the meal, heard some very heavy criticism of Jesus from, "some Pharisees who saw this." It is Mark who gives us a little more insight into who this Matthew was when, in 2:13–17, he comments that the meeting took place on the shores of lake Galilee and that his family name was Levi son of Alphaeus. Luke also enlarges on this, 5:27, and he too remarks on the adverse reaction of the Pharisees, all of which implies that the writer is avoiding references to himself, as far as is consistent with the narrative. This is not a personal account of his time with Jesus; it is a carefully considered record which lays emphasis on the person, the teachings and the role of Jesus as the Messiah chosen by God. In consequence, Matthew, as an individual, fades into the background to focus on the person of Jesus.

The reason why the first Gospel begins with the list of the ancestors of Jesus is simply stated. Matthew was writing some years after the life of Jesus had ended and when a new generation had arisen, who had not been present and were, therefore, not familiar with the details, at a time when the validity of our Lord's claim to be the Messiah was in question by the Jews. He was establishing, as fact, that Jesus, whom the disciples claimed was the Jewish Messiah, was actually a descendant of the famous King David and ultimately a descendant also of Abraham, the father of the Jewish line, although in this case through his mother. This was very important because, for the Jewish critics of the Christian message, there was one key requirement for anyone to be able to claim to be the promised Messiah of Old Testament prophecy – he must be a descendant of the royal tribe of David.

Therefore, Matthew begins by setting the record straight. Chapter 1:1, "This is a list of the ancestors of Jesus Christ, a descendant of David, who was a descendant of Abraham…" not just a common criminal crucified under Roman law. He then goes on to mention the circumstances surrounding Jesus' birth, and he is careful to mention that this Jesus was born in Bethlehem, as foretold by Micah 5, even though he was brought up and lived in Nazareth. Matthew also links other similar prophetic detail, such as the 'virgin' birth mentioned by Isaiah 7:14, although in the original, the word translated virgin did not mean an unmarried girl or one not sexually active; it simply meant a young woman of marriageable age, which age would have been anything from puberty at 14 to, say, 16. Marriage to an older man was commonplace for young girls because the husband would need to be in a position to support a wife and any ensuing children. Joseph, as a master tradesman carpenter, would be an excellent choice by her family. Hence the betrothal but not yet a marriage.

King Herod's response to the visit of the Wise Men, astrologers from the East who had come looking for a king, was to slaughter all boys born at that period. If their message was true, the child would have been a threat to his, Herod's, own status. He was related by marriage to the Maccabees who had provided kings and priests during the turbulent period between Malachi and now. But he was not a descendant of David; therefore, a descendant of David would have a far stronger claim to the throne. To escape the danger, Joseph was warned by God, in a dream, to take the child to Egypt, from where the family would return on Herod's death.

The next stage in Matthew's account was the appearance in the desert near Jerusalem of John, Jesus' cousin. Having had very elderly parents, it is not impossible that John had been brought up by the very strict Jewish sect, the Essenes, whose hidden store of manuscripts, discovered by a shepherd, were ancient scripture passages. Here too, Luke provides far more detail than Matthew, telling us exactly when John's ministry began and that it began when, "At that time the word of God came to John, son of Zechariah." He was "someone shouting in the desert get the road ready for the Lord." But it is Matthew who links this to Isaiah to add scriptural validity as evidence for his account. This emphasis on John's role is important because it sets the scene for what follows, by indicating that Jesus is acclaimed by God, after the Holy Spirit come upon him, in the words, "This is my own dear Son, with whom I am pleased." So Matthew has established, first, that Jesus was born supernaturally in Bethlehem, to a family of the tribe of Judah, that he was seen by Herod as a potential Jewish king, and that his ministry was recognised by God himself. What more evidence could be needed for Jew or Gentile?

It is clear from the text that the ministry of Jesus can be divided into sections. The time from his baptism to the first Passover, roughly six months, covering also the temptation, and up to the wedding at Cana in Galilee which, it might be said, marked the beginning of his public ministry; the following period up to the second Passover, then the twelve further months to the third Passover and again up to the fourth Passover; and finally, the three days to just before his resurrection – a total of roughly three and a half years.

Matthew now moves on rapidly, from our Lord's Baptism, to the Temptation, then to John's arrest, at which point, Jesus returns to Galilee, but not to his hometown of Nazareth. He makes Capernaum his base, not Nazareth, choosing as his first disciples, four fishermen, and beginning his teaching ministry.

It is noteworthy that in this period, most of our Lord's teaching concerned the law, but he interpreted the law very differently from the Pharisees, having clearly stated that (5:17) he had not come to do away with the Law of Moses or the teachings of the prophets, but to make their meaning clear, that is, the purpose which underlay the law. Hence, verse 27, adultery is far more than committing the act. To contemplate the act is to sin. He also condemned the hypocritical attitude behind the public giving of charity, and he healed the sick as evidence of his authority, the Roman Officer's servant at Capernaum (8:5) being an example. And his ability to forgive sins is shown in 9:1–2, when he demonstrated that he could heal physical deformity, a feat much more difficult than mere words.

It is at this point that Matthew tells us that he was called by Jesus as a disciple and, by Chapter 10, we are told that the number of followers, called Apostles, has risen to twelve, and they are now commissioned to go out and preach, teach and heal the sick, but only to Jews – not to Gentiles at this stage. Here too the disciples are warned that they will face persecution, suffering and that the time is short. A first indication is here of the future work of the Church, with the promise of the enabling of the Holy Spirit, and they are told that ultimately, their ministry will take them to the Gentiles, but not yet.

Chapter 11 then tells of John the Baptist sending some of his disciples to question Jesus. Obviously, our Lord's ministry was very different from that of

John, and he wanted reassurance, which Jesus gives from the evidence of his miracles. Jesus also praises John, stating he was the Elijah, whose coming had been predicted in scripture.

It is at this point that Jesus begins to challenge the authority and teaching of the Pharisees, to whom he will later say, quoting Isaiah 29:13, "You have made the word of God of no effect by your traditions." He does this by healing a man in the synagogue on the Sabbath, after having previously justified his disciples picking and eating corn on the Sabbath, by quoting King David's actions when his men were hungry and quoting to his critics Hosea 6:6. "The scripture says, 'It is kindness that I want, not animal sacrifices.' If you really knew what this means, you would not condemn people who are not guilty" (12:7). The response of the Pharisees to this is to accuse Jesus of using satanic power and then by asking him to validate his actions for them by performing a miracle. His reply, the only miracle they will be given is that of Jonah. He will be three days and nights in the earth before rising to life. He also comments that Nineveh repented at Jonah's preaching! A great dig at their pompous, self-important, self-righteousness. The authority behind Jesus' teaching was the Old Testament scripture which the Pharisees found hard to refute.

This period is now followed by a series of teachings, via parables, as Jesus explains some of the mysteries of the kingdom, with also some difficult ideas expressed, as implicit in his feeding of the five thousand and later by a further four thousand. All of which was leading up to the major issue, in his question to Peter, "Who do people say the Son of man is?" Which elicited the answer, "You are the Messiah, the Son of the living God," which Jesus told him had been inspired by the Holy Spirit; it did not come from human wisdom.

After this, Peter, together with James and John, share the experience of seeing a 'transfigured' Jesus talking with Moses and Elijah on the top of a local mountain. In other words, the revelation of God through Jesus is reaching its climax, as we are being given glimpses of the true nature of the Son of God, who had for a little while become the Son of Man. The vision concludes with Jesus telling the three men, 17:9, "Don't tell anyone about this vision you have seen until the Son of Man has been raised from death."

Now follows further teaching, and Jesus speaks again about his forthcoming death, before his triumphant ride into Jerusalem on a donkey, as prophesied by Zechariah 9:9. The teaching of the next three days focusses now on the coming Kingdom. It also reminds us of our Lord's defence of the doctrine of the resurrection of the dead, 22:23, which silenced the Sadducees who did not believe it, to the great pleasure of the Pharisees, who then proceeded to attempt to trap Jesus themselves with questions of their own, such as, "Which is the greatest commandment in the law?" And our Lord's question to them, "How can the Messiah be David's descendant?" which question reinforces Matthew's words at the beginning.

All of which brings us to the great questions of Chapter 24 as, sitting on the Mount of Olives, looking at the splendour of the great temple rebuilt by Herod, Jesus explains to them three things that will happen in the future. The destruction of the Temple, which took place in AD 70 when Titus the son of the Roman Emperor Vespasian, incensed at the rebellious actions of the Jews, was ordered to destroy Jerusalem and, in doing so, accidentally – according to the Jewish historian Josephus – burnt the Temple to the ground. In the years following this disastrous three-year siege of the city, the Romans would systematically remove all the Jewish people from the city and scatter them in other provinces of their empire. The setting up of the sacrilegious Awful Horror on the site of the Temple would follow that, and then finally, the time of the coming of the Son of Man as Son of God in power and glory would arrive. Jesus used the further illustration of the blooming of the fig tree, a symbol of the Jewish nation, which would be a sign that the final days were about to begin. However, when that will happen, verse 36, "neither the angels in heaven nor the Son; the Father alone knows."

Now more teaching in the Temple takes place. The plot by Judas to betray Jesus is agreed with the priests. The final Passover meal, which we call The Lord's Supper, takes place in which Jesus, taking the ceremonial bread and wine, announces the he is the true Passover victim whose broken body and shed blood will bring redemption for humanity. 26:26–30, and which is quoted later by Paul in 1 Cor 11:23–25.

Then follow in rapid succession, our Lord's seminal prayer in the Garden of Gethsemane, in which, in prayer, he surrenders himself to the will of God in the words, verse 30, "My Father, if it is possible take this cup of suffering from me! Yet not what I want, but what you want." The arrest led by Judas the betrayer follows, and the trial at which Peter denies his Lord. Our Lord is then questioned before Pilate, and then come the sentence, the crucifixion and our Lord's death on the cross. Joseph, from Arimathea, begs Pilate for, and then buries in his own tomb, the body of Jesus, the guard is set at the tomb; and then, early on the Sunday morning, the wonder of the resurrection.

Mark

As we have previously indicated, the person to whom this Gospel is attributed is probably John Mark, whose mother, Mary Mark had played host to Peter. It was there, in her house, that Peter found refuge after being set free from prison by an angel. Possibly the house of the upper room last supper. Mark was possibly also the young man in the Garden of Gethsemane at the time of our Lord's arrest who fled leaving his robe in the hands of the soldiers. Cousin to Barnabas from Cyprus, he had accompanied Paul and Barnabas on their first missionary journey but left to go home at Perga in Pamphylia. Paul then refused to take him on the second journey, which led to the dispute between Paul and Barnabas, Paul taking Silas, whilst Barnabas took Mark with him (Acts 16).

Mark's Gospel is the shortest of the Gospels and, possibly, much of the earlier material may have come from Peter, who calls him 'my son'. It begins without any preamble, at the point where John the Baptist, preaching the baptism of repentance, announces that, verse 7, "The man who will come after me is much greater than I am… I baptise you with water, but he will baptise you with the Holy Spirit." Cousin to Jesus, born six months earlier, John obviously had no up-to-date news of his cousin, but was expecting the Messiah to come. His mission was to prepare the way. Later, he will have some doubts, expressed as questions, but initially, the evidence he needs, that the Messiah has come, will be the voice from heaven which he heard, "You are my own dear Son. I am pleased with you," followed by the vision of heaven opening and the Holy Spirit, like a dove, descending. This was immediately followed by the forty-day temptation, which was to be a major preparation for our Lord's ministry which was to follow, and in which Jesus, aged thirty, would have had to come to terms with the spiritual battle which would follow him throughout his remaining three years.

Most of the material in this Gospel has a parallel in Matthew and Luke, but the focus here is on particular aspects of our Lord's ministry – his miracles of healing, the authority of his preaching and his ability to rebuke evil spirits and to deliver the victims from their power. These aspects would have appealed to the very practical and outspoken, almost impetuous, nature of Peter. The writer describes the call of the four Apostles, Simon (Peter), Andrew, and then James and John, who were to form the core of his disciples, and immediately he tells of the deliverance of a man possessed by an evil spirit. Then we are taken to the house of Peter and Andrew, where Jesus healed Peter's wife's mother who was sick of a fever. By sunset, all the village had heard the news and gathered outside the house, with their sick and demon-possessed relatives and friends. This immediacy of action is typical of a man like Peter, as is his reaction next morning when Jesus having risen very early and gone out alone for prayer, Peter mounts a search for him.

The scene now is Galilee, and Capernaum the focus. Matthew is called. The issue of the disciples not fasting like John the Baptist's disciples raises yet another distinction between the ministry and teaching of Jesus, as compared with the rather strict nature of John's message. Then follows a very brief mention of the disciples eating corn in the field on the Sabbath and then the healing on the Sabbath, in the Synagogue, of the man with the withered hand, in which Jesus challenges the Pharisees' attitude to the law about keeping the Sabbath, "You have made the word of God useless by your traditions." Then almost immediately, we are confronted with the choice of the twelve apostles. Home again, and there Jesus is challenged by some teachers of the Law who had come up to Galilee from Jerusalem to question him about his ability to control evil spirits.

It is this rapid relation of events, ignoring any unnecessary detail, which characterises this Gospel. There is none of the ordered progression found with the other writers. Here is a burning need to cover as much of the important detail as possible, without wasting time on any irrelevances, as we are now led through a number of parables, with only a brief explanation of why Jesus used them. Then we are into the calming of the storm on the Lake, indicative of our Lord's power and authority as the creator of nature, before we are back with a serious case of actual demon possession again, and the consequent loss of a vast herd of illegal pigs, two thousand in all. We are then introduced to an interesting interlude, where Jesus, on his way to visit Jairus and heal his twelve-year-old daughter who is sick, is delayed by a woman who had suffered with a serious medical condition, also for twelve years. The woman is healed because she believed, and the young girl, who had died by this time, was restored to life. This was the first example of three cases, where Jesus proved that there was the possibility of life after death, of resurrection, again through faith in the power of God.

At Nazareth, his hometown, Jesus is again rejected because the people who knew him did not understand that he was God's son, not the carpenter's son, whom they had known for so many years.

One very important issue is given some prominence here, in our Lord's confrontation with the Pharisees who had travelled up from Jerusalem to confront him. The issue they picked on this time was that our Lord's disciples were guilty of eating their food without complying with their very strict rules about how they should wash their hands. These rules were not part of the Law; they were derived from practices developed and observed by their ancestors. Jesus challenged their imposition of these totally irrelevant laws, calling them hypocrites, 7:6, by quoting from the prophet Isaiah (Is 29:13), "These people, says God, honour me with their words, but their heart is really far away from me. It is no use for them to worship me, because they teach human rules as though they were God's laws. You put aside God's commands and obey human teachings."

Further miracles and teachings follow, and then we have repeated the incident in which Peter is challenged about who Jesus is and responds, "You are the Messiah." Yet to our amazement, as Jesus begins to teach the disciples more about his forthcoming death, emphasising the fact that he will rise three days later, Peter takes Jesus aside and begins to reproach him for suggesting that he would die! Jesus is so concerned about this, seeing in it satanic power attempting to undermine what is, for Jesus, the whole purpose of his coming to earth to be our Saviour. Death, to him, was the highest moment of his life, the fulfilment of God's plan of redemption for the world. Further, these men, and especially Peter, had shown incredible loyalty and a degree of understanding, yet when faced with the real issue, Peter clearly has failed to understand. He can understand in Jesus the miraculous power of God, the remarkable understanding of human nature, the compassion, but not the death.

It is this failure to recognise the fundamental need for our Lord's death, which undermines much of today's 'modern' theology in which Jesus is seen as an example of the highest ideals of humanity but that does not deal with sin. It is Paul who, later on in his letters, will emphasise this in his words, Jesus was "delivered by the determinate counsel and foreknowledge of God," and Romans 4:25, "Because of our sins, he was handed over to die, and he was raised to life to put us right with God." This leads inevitably to the fact that the disciples were still concerned with our Lord's references to his forthcoming death which interfered with their own plans for their own future and the future of their nation, which is illustrated when Jesus challenges them about their conversation on their way home to Capernaum (9:34). And all of this following their remarkable experience of being with Jesus on the Mountain when not only was he transfigured, transformed into a supernatural being in front of their eyes, but they could have heard the conversation which Jesus had with Moses and Elijah, which no doubt was exactly about his forthcoming death, as Luke has it in 9:28–36, except that they were asleep at the time, as they were also, during our Lord's agonising prayer in the Garden of Gethsemane.

There now follows more teaching, with children as an example, before Jesus faces yet another major issue, that of the rich young ruler who wants to know what to do to 'receive eternal life'. Jesus liked this young man; there was something so compellingly honest about him yet so naïve. His wealth, probably inherited, stood in the way of his salvation, and when told this, he departed, sad because he was very rich. The disciples were shocked by the lesson which Jesus extracted from this, "How hard it will be for rich people to enter the Kingdom of God," not because they are rich but because their values are wrong; harder, in fact, than for a camel to go through the 'eye of a needle' – which is traditionally seen to demonstrate the fact that, after the main gate to the city was closed, a laden camel could enter via the 'postern,' but only by being unloaded and going through unladen, presumably to be reloaded once through.

However, despite the interlude, we are still with the subject of the disciples' ideas for the future not coinciding with God's purpose in sending his only Son to earth. This time, the subject of the future, for James and John, is introduced by them – not as in the other account in Matthew by their mother. No doubt there was much discussion on this in the quiet moments when Jesus was not there to listen. The places at our Lord's right hand and left hand, when he comes into his kingdom. What? Chancellor of the exchequer and home secretary? They claim to be prepared for whatever cost may be involved, but that cost would be far greater than they realised, and the positions of authority were not in our Lord's gift. Only the Father had that kind of authority. Jesus himself was subject to the ultimate will of God (10:39–40). And the others were angry at what they saw as an attempt to 'curry favour' with Jesus.

This is followed by an illustrative discourse, using the fig tree as an emblem of the Jewish nation, cursed and then dead. A miracle, but what enormous miracles are possible to someone with even a little faith. Then a further question about our Lord's authority, but this time from the chief priests, the teachers of the Law and the elders, which was quite in character. Jesus answers by questioning their attitude to John the Baptist, which they cannot answer without condemning themselves.

Further questions, about the validity of the Roman taxation of Jews, for which Jesus has the perfect answer, verse 17, "Pay the Emperor what belongs to the Emperor, and pay God what belongs to God," for which they had no answer. This in turn is followed by the Sadducees who try to catch him out over the issue of the resurrection of the dead, to which Jesus answers, verse 27, "He is the God of the living not of the dead."

Then, as we approach the final Passover, the disciples, named here as Peter, James, John and Andrew, sitting on the Mount of Olives and looking at the very splendid temple, ask Jesus to elucidate his comment, "You see these great buildings? Not a single stone here will be left in its place; every one of them will be thrown down" (Chapter 13). Obviously, with such a remarkable prediction hanging in the air, they want to know when, and Jesus answers, as he does in Matthew 24 and Luke 21, by outlining what will be fulfilled in the destruction of Jerusalem and the Temple by the Romans in AD 70, and events which will follow, ending, verse 24, with a prediction of the end of the world, as also recorded by Matthew and Luke. This is followed by our Lord's parable of the fig tree and the symbolism of its regrowth.

Now events are reported rapidly. In Chapter 14, Jesus is anointed at Bethany, the house of Mary, Martha and Lazarus whom Jesus had raised from death. Judas agrees to betray Jesus for money and starts looking for an opportunity which must be when Jesus is not in a public place, for fear of a reaction from the crowd. The disciples celebrate the Passover feast, the Lord's Supper, at which all twelve apostles were present and in which Jesus indicates that the bread and wine, which were symbols of the lamb sacrificed to deliver the Israelites from that last of the plagues in Egypt, was in fact a symbol of his own death, which was to be the sacrifice for the sins of the world. Following the meal, they all, except for Judas, retire to the Garden of Gethsemane, where Jesus is facing the final and most decisive moment of his life as, in extreme agony, he asks to be delivered, if possible, from his forthcoming suffering and death, only then to accept his destiny as being the Father's will.

The scenes which follow are all too familiar. The arrest, the trial before the Jewish Council, probably the Sanhedrin, at which Peter, out of sheer, absolute fear for his life, three times denies any knowledge of Jesus, only to hear the cock crow reminding him of Jesus' words foretelling this moment of betrayal, and Peter then goes out, weeping bitterly. Jesus himself makes no answer to the false charges brought against him. So now, Jesus is referred to Pilate, the Roman-appointed governor of the province, because only the Romans can pass the death sentence, which the Jewish leaders see as their only hope of avoiding a direct confrontation with the Roman authorities. Pilate is amazed that Jesus refuses to answer the accusations of the chief priests and, convinced that Jesus was being persecuted out of jealousy, attempts to release him. But the priests and the crowd reject Jesus in favour of a local, and presumably popular, leader of a recent riotous mob, Barabbas, and Jesus is handed over to the Roman soldiers who mock and jeer at him before leading him out to be crucified.

The only slight relief for the badly bruised and beaten man was that Simon from Cyrene was made to carry the cross. Then, nailed to the Cross to die, Jesus is further mocked by the chief priests and the passing crowd, 15:31, "He saved others, but he cannot save himself!" Oh, yes, he could, but he chose not to call on angelic powers to deliver him, and he died as a deliberate sacrifice in the place of a sinful humanity, supported in his suffering only by the women who had followed him and, of the Apostles, only John.

The burial, towards evening, was just before the beginning of another day, which for the Jews was from 6 p.m. in the evening. Then the women watched as Joseph from Arimathea, having begged the body from Pilate (verse 42–43), buried Jesus in his own prepared tomb, because the following day was a holy day in the Festival prior to the Sabbath. They were intending to return after the two further days had passed to perform the necessary burial customs. Then, returning early at sunrise on the third day (Chapter 16), the three women, Mary Magdalene, Mary the mother of James and Salome, coming to anoint the body, found only an empty chamber. The stone sealing the entrance, gone! Inside, where they expected to find the beaten and bruised body, a young man dressed in white who informed them that the Jesus they were looking for was not there, verse 6, "I know you are looking for Jesus of Nazareth, who was crucified. He is not here; he has been raised! Look, here is the place where they put him. Now go and give this message to the disciples, including Peter, 'He is going to Galilee ahead of you; there you will see him, just as he told you.'"

This account by Mark ends with the brief comment that Jesus also appeared to Mary Magdalene, then to the two on the road to Emmaus, and finally to the eleven, before being taken up into heaven. The other Gospel writers at this point give us far more detail, suggesting either that there are parts of this manuscript missing or that the author was not present. Either way, we have three other much more detailed accounts.

Luke

Here, in the third of the Gospels, we return to a much more detailed and slower moving record, suggesting careful preparation rather than a hurried gathering of the most important facts. Luke, who wrote the history of the early Church, The Acts of the Apostles, refers to this as an earlier account which he wrote of "all the things that Jesus did and taught from the time he began his work until the day he was taken up to heaven", Acts 1:1, which is clearly the Gospel ascribed to him here.

There are a number of personal details about this Luke recorded in the New Testament. That he accompanied Paul and Silas on some of their missionary journeys is evident from the change from the third person to the first person in Acts 16 where 'they' (verse 6) becomes 'we' (verse 11). Paul also refers to him as "Luke, our dear doctor," in his Letter to the Colossians 4:14. "Only Luke is with me," he says in his Second Letter to Timothy 3:11. And he is referred to as a 'fellow worker' in his Letter to Philemon 1:24.

What this implies is that, although not numbered amongst the twelve and not mentioned by name during our Lord's ministry, Luke was clearly closely involved with the early church growth. His opening greeting to "Dear Theophilus" at the beginning of the Acts of the Apostles states that he had already recorded his knowledge of the early life of Jesus, gained first-hand from those who were there, his Gospel, before he began his second volume detailing the events following the resurrection and ascension of Jesus. That he was so meticulous in his record of the facts also implies careful research.

The opening to his Gospel, addressed to "Dear Theophilus," states categorically, "Many people have done their best to write a report of the things that have taken place among us. They wrote what we have been told by those who saw these things from the beginning, and who proclaimed the message. (The disciples?) And so, your Excellency, because I have studied all these matters from their beginning, I thought it would be good to write an orderly account for you. I do this so that you will know the full truth about everything which you have been taught."

Which suggests that the Theophilus to whom he is writing was possibly a pupil, but probably also a person of some standing in the community. Therefore, Luke's writings can be taken to be authentic. His own personal reputation would rest on that. He was also possibly, probably younger than Paul because by this time, certainly by the time he writes the Acts, Paul would have been dead. Finally, as a doctor, he was an educated man. All right, medical knowledge was very limited in those days, but his training would have been in philosophy and history as well as physiology, and he would have learned how to discover factual detail. He probably studied Aristotle, as would have Paul, giving those two men a rapport in addition to their shared Christian experience. What a good preparation to become an accredited, factual historian, and one who was conversant with human character.

So Luke, following his address to Theophilus, begins at the beginning by appealing to external evidence, "During the time when Herod was king of Judea, there was a priest named Zachariah." Clearly, his readers would be familiar with recent history, so that was enough. He then goes on to elaborate a very detailed account of the parents, the circumstances of and the reason for, the miraculous birth of a baby, John, to these aged parents. That it was something beyond normal human experience was demonstrated by the appearance of an angel, and Zechariah's understandable and very human response, verse 18, "How shall I know if this is so? I am an old man, and my wife is old also." No wonder; Zechariah is not simply being told that he and his wife will have a baby when in purely medical terms it was not possible but is being given the angel's extraordinary details of what this child will achieve during his life, verse 15, "He will be a great man in the Lord's sight. He must not drink any wine or strong drink. From his very birth, he will be filled with the Holy Spirit, and he will bring back many of the people of Israel to the Lord their God." A tremendous amount of knowledge and faith would be required for an old man of his age to believe all that. It quite puts his work into perspective. And indeed, the angel has to take him to task, verse 19, "I am Gabriel," the angel answered. "I stand in the presence of God who sent me to speak to you and tell you this good news. But you have not believed my message, which will come true at the right time. Because you have not believed, you will be unable to speak; you will remain silent until the day my promise to you comes true." And that literally came true, all of it!

But wonders do not cease because, six months later, the same angel, Gabriel, is sent also to a young woman, living in Nazareth, contracted in marriage to a carpenter, who was distantly related to King David. Once again the visit causes consternation, not simply because Mary was not married but because what the angel told her about the child she would bear was beyond human belief, verse 32, "He will be great and will be called the son of the most high God. The Lord God will make him a king, as his ancestor David was, and he will be the king of the descendants of Jacob forever; his kingdom will never end."

Mary's response was not so much one of unbelief as, 'How?' Verse 34, "I am a virgin. How then can this be?" Undoubtedly, she would have been brought up on the Hebrew Old Testament and would be well aware of the prophetic promises, but her response is less of unbelief than 'How?' She was well aware of basic medical facts and this did not fit. Fortunately, Gabriel is ready with the answer, verse 35, "The Holy Spirit will come upon you, and God's power will rest upon you. For this reason, the holy child will be called the Son of God." And for evidence, she is told to remember her relative Elizabeth for whom, at a very old age, a similar situation was already in process. And Mary's response is that of someone who is totally submissive to the will of God, whatever the cost, verse 38, "I am the Lord's servant," said Mary, "may it happen to me as you have said."

What would any sensible girl do now? Why, go and visit her relative, of course. And when they met first, Elizabeth's baby reacted, and then, filled with the Holy Spirit, Elizabeth prophesied in a loud voice, "You are the most blessed of all women, and blessed is the child you will bear." Verse 45, "How happy you are to believe that the Lord's message to you will come true," which confirms that Mary HAD believed. And in further confirmation, Mary, now in song, says, verse 54, "He has kept the promise He made to our ancestors." And that IS faith because she is looking ahead prophetically as well as accepting her role in the fulfilment of the past.

Now, Elizabeth has her baby in due time. Zechariah gets his voice back when he insists on the boy being named John, and goes on to declare the message, that this event is the fulfilment of ancient prophesy, verse 76, "You will go ahead of the Lord to prepare his road for him" (Malachi 3:1). We are also told that, verse 80, "The child grew and developed in body and spirit," and, "He lived in the desert until the day when he appeared publicly to the people of Israel." In the meantime, Mary has her baby.

Great detail is provided here again, as we have come to expect from our source Luke. Here are all the familiar details of the Nativity scene but given external authenticity by being specifically dated, although there is some query historically over the actual date of this census. This is the only Gospel to record the account of the angel visitors and the ensuing visit to the cradle of the shepherds. Then follows the account of the circumcision of our Lord and his naming, Jesus. This is given in some detail because of the witness of a very devout man in the Temple, Simeon, who prophesies that the child will be, verse 32, "A light to reveal Your will to the Gentiles and bring glory to Your people Israel." But also, verse 34, "This child is chosen by God for the destruction and the salvation of many in Israel. He will be a sign from God which many people will speak against. And sorrow, like a sharp sword, will break your heart." One remarkable point here being the reference to the Gentiles. Anna, also a prophetess, arrives and confirms the future of the child Jesus.

The family then return home to live at Nazareth. Later we have an account of the family's visit to the Temple for the Passover Festival when Jesus was aged twelve. This is the only account of his boyhood, but it is clearly recorded because of the importance of what happened during the visit. However, Luke does not tell of the visit of the Wise Men nor of the family's temporary exile in Egypt to escape the wrath of Herod.

The account now moves on rapidly, Chapter 3, as John the Baptist is now seen fulfilling the prophecies given at his birth and preparing the people for the beginning of our Lord's ministry which, verse 21, begins with the public baptism of Jesus in the river Jordan. Baptism having been John's trademark sign, unique because it had not been part of traditional Jewish symbolism. Our Lord's baptism by John was characterised by two things. First, the descent of the Holy Spirit visible as a dove to John, and then the voice of God, acknowledging Jesus as His Son (verse 21–22) both while Jesus was in prayer.

Luke then interposes another genealogical record of Jesus' ancestry, before telling us that following his baptism, Jesus was led into the desert, Chapter 4, where, for forty days, he was tempted by the Devil. No doubt intended to either dissuade him from his ministry or to persuade him to use his obvious powers for his own personal benefit, actually quoting scripture in support of these suggestions and implying that he the Devil actually possessed the power (verse 6). Jesus simply answers by quoting scripture (verse 12).

Jesus then begins his ministry, returning to his hometown of Nazareth where he is at first acclaimed, "Isn't he the son of Joseph (verse 22), but then rejected so violently that they tried to kill him because he was critical of them, verse 24, "Prophets are never welcome in their hometown." And verse 28 follows, which lead to him moving his base of operation to Capernaum (verse 31), from where most of his Galilean ministry would be conducted. The first of these was the deliverance of a man with an evil spirit, on the Sabbath in Capernaum. The difference here being that here he was accepted and welcomed, the people being amazed at the authority with which he spoke. He also healed Peter's mother-in-law here, and such was the regard in which he was held, that the people wanted him to stay. But he insisted that he must spread his teachings throughout the country, although it was here, by the Lake Galilee, that he called to him the first four of his disciples.

Now follow a series of healings, also recorded by Matthew and/or Mark, many of which raise important issues. Such as the correct use of the Sabbath, following our Lord's healing of the man with the paralysed hand, which so enraged the Pharisees who witnessed it (6:11), that they began to see Jesus as a serious threat to their interpretation of the ancient scriptures, and consequently undermining their authority. After spending the whole night in prayer (verse 12), Jesus then chose the twelve men who were to become the chief witnesses of his ministry.

The following healings and teaching, as recorded by Luke, give us a slightly different perspective on what we have already seen. For example, in the healing of the Roman Centurion's servant, Matthew says that the Centurion himself approached Jesus; here, it is the Centurion's servants who come, telling us that the Roman soldier was a worthy man who had actually built a synagogue for them. However, the essential point, our Lord's comment that this man had more faith than the Jews, is repeated (7:9). We also learn a little about the practicalities of our Lord's itinerant life in 8:1, as we are told that a number of women, some whom the Lord had healed but others who were clearly wealthy and influential, were supporting Jesus and his disciples – important facts in such a masculine-dominated world. Yet by contrast, when Jesus' mother and brothers came to see him (8:19), they were regarded as no more important than anyone else, even though we know from the marriage in Cana that Mary was well aware of his relationship to God, and one of his brothers, James, will later become prominent in the Jerusalem Church.

Much of the next section, by repeating many of the key facts, such as Peter's confession that Jesus was the Messiah, serve to confirm the veracity of the content. Some, however, are unique here, such as 9:31 where, in an interlude referring to his final journey to Jerusalem, we hear of the refusal of a Samaritan village to receive him, apparently simply because he was on his way to Jerusalem. Whereas in his parable (10:25) illustrating the command to "Love your neighbour as you love yourself," the example is set by a Samaritan. We are also given a picture of the way in which Jesus was 'mobbed' wherever he went, 12:1, "Thousands of people crowded together, so that they were stepping on each other." Here the people were warned to beware of the hypocrisy of the Pharisees and were given a solemn warning against blasphemy against the Holy Spirit (verse 9) and warned that to serve Jesus would cause division (verse 49) even within families.

But the main the context of this gospel relates the parables and miracles which accompanied our Lord's teaching. Lessons about personal conduct and warnings that the way we live will be reflected in God's judgement of us, are mingled with parables illustrating what Jesus expects on his return to receive his kingdom, for example, 17:20. Many of these parables are unique to Luke and well worth reading, as is the story of Zacchaeus in Chapter 19.

Then, at last, we come to our Lord's triumphant entry into Jerusalem, riding on a colt, the foal of a donkey, which, because of its symbolic value, is repeated by all four Evangelists, marking as it does the nature of his message as a prince of peace not the triumphant homecoming of a great military hero – that is reserved for his second coming, as foretold later. We know that this was now the seven-day festival of Passover, and during it, Jesus spent at least three days teaching daily in and around the Temple, dealing with a number of pertinent issues such as the liability to pay tax to the Romans Chapter 20:22, his answer to which amazed the Pharisees as well as the listening crowd.

However, much of these days was occupied with words and illustrations about forthcoming events, as in 21:20, when he speaks of what will be the awful events of the AD 70 destruction of Jerusalem and the temple, and as previously in Matthew, he tells of the signs of the Coming of the Son of Man (verse 25). We then have details of the plot against Jesus (22:3), The Lord's Supper (verse 14), and our Lord's prediction that Peter would deny him (verse 31). But here, Luke explains that this is just part of the many tests which they, as disciples, would undergo, and adds our Lord's words to Peter, "But I have prayed for you Simon that your faith will not fail. And when you turn back to me, you must strengthen your brethren."

Then comes the visit to the Garden of Gethsemane at the foot of the Mount of Olives and our Lord's agony of prayer, followed by his arrest by the soldiers led by Judas. Then Peter's denial, as had been foretold, whilst he was listening to the events in the house of the High Priest. Now Jesus is questioned before the Council, brought before Pilate, sent to Herod, and then, in the final act of cowardice by Pilate, Jesus is delivered into the hands of the Chief Priests, as Pilate gives in to their demand and sentences Jesus to death. And this, despite Pilate's ringing words 23:13, "Now I have examined him here in your presence, and I have not found him guilty of any of the crimes you accuse him of. Nor did Herod find him guilty, for he sent him back to us. There is nothing this man has done to deserve death!" The crowd refuse Pilate's offer of mercy for Jesus and choose instead a criminal named Barabbas. And so Jesus is led out and crucified, being mocked by all who were there, except one of the two men being crucified with him (verse 40) whose, "Remember me Jesus, when you come as King," will secure him a place in eternity.

After the death, burial and resurrection, we have more detail, such as the journey to Emmaus, at which Jesus answers so many queries by the two disciples but is not recognised by them until he sat at supper with them and broke bread. They, then rushed back all the way to Jerusalem with the news (24:25–33), only to be greeted with the news that Peter had also seen him – which is something not explained earlier when the women brought the first news that the body was not in the tomb.

The chapter 24 then ends with some detail of the events which followed as Jesus appeared to his disciples, including his reminder to them that what had happened had been foretold in the Jewish Scriptures (verse 45), followed by his final words of instruction to them and the very strict enjoinder that they must wait in the city Jerusalem until they receive the promised gift of the Holy Spirit. Then, the walk up the Mount of Olives as far as Bethany, where he was taken up into heaven in front of their astonished eyes.

John

Immediately, as soon as one reads the opening words of this Gospel, one can see that it is very different from the other three. John, whom we believe to be the author, has an entirely and unexpected way of introducing us to Jesus. No lineage, no story of a birth, we are taken right back to the beginning of time itself, with a vision of the cosmos, which is startling for its time and suggests a real relationship with the subject of this gospel. Where did this intimate understanding come from, we might ask? And the only answer can be that the writer is inspired by the Holy Spirit. After all, the coming of the Holy Spirit on the day of Pentecost had brought new understanding and enlightenment about the nature of Jesus and God. Even Peter's declaration, "Thou art the Messiah," was, Jesus told him, given him by God the father; it did not come from human understanding.

What is unique about this Gospel is that in the retelling of events, the miracles and teachings, the writer expresses a much deeper understanding of what lies behind each incident and opens to the reader the underlying purpose behind it. For example, in Chapter 4, the detailed analysis of the encounter with the Samaritan woman at the well of Sychar reveals so much about the person of Jesus and his mission. In Chapter 5, we have much greater detail about the source of our Lord's authority and what it is that bears witness to the source of that authority. Again, in Chapter 6, which tells of the feeding of the five thousand, the writer goes on at considerable length to explain the reason behind this miracle and the significance of the symbolism, taking us back to the time of Moses and the provision of manna in the wilderness for the children of Israel, but through that, he explains how he, Jesus, becomes the source of life to us, relating it to the water of the well at Sychar which was yet another powerful symbolic image of life. If you only ever read one book from the Bible, read the Gospel of John.

"In the beginning, the Word already existed, the Word was with God and the Word was God," is startling enough but that is followed by verse 3, "Through him, God made all things; not one thing in all creation was made without him." And verse 10, "The Word was in the world, and though God made the world through him, yet the world did not recognise him." So what does the word "Word" mean? Well, John soon answers that in verse 14, "The Word became a human being and lived among us." So John is talking now about someone who, to them, was a human being but who was also God!

Inevitably, to the thoughtful reader, what John is saying is that he has realised that Jesus was not, as everyone thought, the carpenter's son from Nazareth at all. He is an eternal being, not created or born but part of what they knew of as God. Even more than that he, Jesus, had, as God, actually created the cosmos itself, but yet when he entered it, the world he had created did not recognise its own maker! Stupendous statements! Yes, but John, now an old man, is telling us what he has come to realise after a lifetime of experience is the actual truth. Telling us NOW, because it took him so long to come to terms with it himself, and he wants us to benefit from what he has discovered.

Following these somewhat startling assertions, John refers us to the testimony of John the Baptist who said, verse 15, "This is the one I was talking about when I said, 'He comes after me, but he is greater than I am because he existed before I was born.'" As Jesus was his cousin and John was only some six months older than Jesus, the remark is also startling, reinforced as it is by the Baptist's background knowledge of Old Testament prophecy. To all this, he adds verse 17, "God gave the Law through Moses, but grace and truth came through Jesus Christ." Verse 18, "No one has ever seen God. The only Son, who is the same as God and is at the Father's side, he has made Him known."

We then have a memo about the message which John the Baptist preached in which he plainly states, quoting the Prophet Isaiah (40:3), "I am the voice of someone shouting in the desert: make a straight path for the Lord to travel." He also said that "Among you stands the one you do not know". And the following day when Jesus came to John to be baptised, he confirmed that he had been told that the one on whom the Holy Spirit came down like a dove and stayed, was indeed the Son of God.

We now have a different account of how Jesus called his first disciples. The following day, Andrew, here one of John the Baptist's disciples, follows Jesus after hearing John say again, "There is the Lamb of God." And in turn, he goes and fetches his brother Simon. Then the next day in Galilee, Jesus found Philip and Philip found Nathaniel. It may make easier the other account which is that

Jesus saw Andrew, Peter, James and John by the Lake in Galilee and called them. Thus, it may well be that they had already met or heard about Jesus from John the Baptist, in which case their immediate response of leaving nets, boats and families might make more sense. However, how it happened is less important than the fact that they did leave all to follow Jesus, in a commitment which, unknown to them at the time, would revolutionise their lives and lead them to a path of ministry and suffering which, in turn, would transform the world.

John now points to the wedding feast in Cana, a small town by the lake, at which Jesus and his disciples, together with his mother, were invited guests, as the beginning of our Lord's ministry. For it is here that he performs the miracle of turning water into wine. John states that this miracle was the point at which our Lord's mother and his disciples first realised that he was different, and how different.

The action now moves to Jerusalem for the Feast of the Passover where Jesus, amongst other things, orders all the merchants and traders in the Temple to leave, 2:16, "Stop making my Father's house a marketplace." Here it was that the Jewish authorities first challenged our Lord's authority to act like this, saying verse 18, "What miracle can you perform to show us that you have the right to do this?" to which Jesus responded in a remarkably contentious statement, which they tended to believe he meant literally, "Tear down this Temple, and in three days, I will build it again!" But we know that Jesus was here referring to his subsequent death and resurrection but, at the time, was completely misunderstood.

Presumably whilst still in Jerusalem, Jesus has the interesting conversation with a leading Pharisee named Nicodemus, in which he tells him that, "flesh is flesh," 3:6, "A person is born physically of human parents, but is born spiritually of the Spirit of God." Which explains his earlier comment, verse 3, "No one can see the kingdom of God without being born again." And then Jesus goes on to elaborate that, as with the children of Israel bitten by snakes in the desert because of their sin, the cure was to look at a bronze snake which Moses put on a pole; so in the same way, the cure for sin will be the Son of God lifted up to die on a Cross. Salvation then comes from believing both who the Son of God is and why it was necessary for him to die.

The action now moves South to the Jordan in Judea where John the Baptist is preaching and baptising, and when Jesus arrives, John's disciples are puzzled. John resolves the situation very directly, in acknowledging that his own ministry is ending and that from now on Jesus will take preference, because John can do no more than point to the one who is in fact the person to which his own ministry had been a rallying cry. His had been the "voice crying in the wilderness, prepare."

Chapter 4 then deals with a very challenging conversation between Jesus and a Samaritan woman whom Jesus had asked for a drink of water. Our Lord's revelation of himself to that woman, as one who knew all about her private life, resulted in the village coming out to listen for themselves to the one who was claimed to be the source of the 'water of life', the source being the Holy Spirit who would bring 'life-giving water' so that that those who drank would never thirst again. Jesus had also answered her query about whether it was better to worship God on the mountain in Samaria (as the Samaritans did) or in Jerusalem (which was where the Jews worshipped) with the profoundly prophetic statement in verse 23, "The time is coming, and is already here, when by the power of God's Spirit, people will worship the Father as He really is." Verse 24, "God is spirit, and only by the power of his Spirit can people worship Him as He really is." Which is the remarkable prophetic statement, shortly to be fulfilled, that true worshippers in future will worship God not via external means, such as the demands of the Law with its ritual and sacrifices, but by personal contact with the living God, through the mediation of the new High Priest, who is Jesus Christ himself. As Paul will say later, "There is but one mediator between God and man, the man Christ Jesus" (1 Tim 2:5).

The miracles and parables, now following, are all indicative of the role to be played by Jesus in determining the future both of the 'world' and of humankind; demonstrating his authority over illness, disease, and even the elements themselves. Followed by the miracle of the feeding of the five thousand in which, symbolically, Jesus himself is the bread of life, just as to the Samaritan woman he was the 'water of life'. As later, in the final 'Last Supper' Passover meal, Jesus will be seen as the reality behind the 'symbolic' sacrifice of a lamb, the shedding of whose blood ensured deliverance from the plague of death in Egypt.

Now the action moves back to Jerusalem for the Festival of Shelters. Warned that the Jewish authorities are out to get him, Jesus says, first, that he will not go, but then, quietly and unnoticed, he appears in the Temple, to the amazement of the people who know that their leaders are out to get him. And indeed, the temple guards are sent to arrest Jesus but are puzzled by his words, 7:33, "Jesus said, 'I shall be with you a little while longer, and then I shall go away to Him who sent me.'" And in fact, Jesus teaches and preaches quite openly, telling the Pharisees, "I am the light of the world. Whoever follows me will have the light of life and never walk in darkness," with the implication that those who followed the teaching of the Pharisees would be walking into darkness.

He also dealt with a woman taken in the act of adultery, the punishment for which was stoning to death. His method of dealing with the need for justice was simply to say, "Let him that is without sin cast the first stone." And as he wrote in the dust, the eldest slunk out first, presumably with more on their conscience and, possibly, recognising their own deeds written in some of the words in the dust. This was yet another example of our Lord's very acute exposure of their hypocrisy.

Another most revealing discussion takes place when the Pharisees attempt to investigate the healing of the man who was born blind (Chapter 9). The deduction of the Pharisees was that because the healing took place on the Sabbath, contrary to THEIR law, the perpetrator could not be from God. The Pharisees then question both the man, whose healing was visible to all, and his parents, trying to implicate them in some irreligious practice, but to no avail. The parents even commenting, verse 21, "But we do not know how it is that he is now able to see nor do we know who cured him of his blindness. Ask him; he is old enough, and he can answer for himself."

Following further teaching, we are then told of Jesus in the Temple at the Festival celebrating its dedication. Asked to answer honestly whether he was the Messiah, Jesus answers simply, 10:25, "I have already told you, but you would not believe me." "I know my sheep and they follow me." At which the people, in a final act of rejection, took up stones to throw at him. But he walked away, returning to the place of baptism at the Jordan, where those who did believe came to listen.

Now comes the greatest miracle of all. His friend Lazarus, brother of Mary and Martha, was ill and now has died. Jesus is criticised for delaying his visit for three days, by the surrounding crowds but also by Mary and Martha. 11:21, "Martha said to Jesus, 'If you had been here, Lord, my brother would not have died.'" They too were puzzled by Jesus' further delay of three days after Lazarus had died. Oh yes, they knew that their brother would rise 'at the last day'. However, it is then that in the presence of the two sisters and their relatives and the crowd, that Jesus tells them to open the tomb, and in a loud voice commands Lazarus to come out. Lazarus does come out, but he is still bound hand and foot with the grave clothes which then had to be removed. This was to be the most dramatic of the three cases of the dead being raised to life by Jesus. Of the others, Jairus' daughter, had only just died. The son of the widow of Nain, who had just died and was not yet buried. Later in that house at Bethany, Jesus will be anointed with costly ointment by Mary, in preparation for his own burial. But from now on, the pressure is on for the authorities to find a way to get rid of this 'man' who is undermining their authority and, in their view, threatening to disturb the fragile peace which existed between them and their Roman overlords.

It is precisely at this juncture that Jesus is seen to spend much time with his disciples, explaining to them his role as a 'servant' (Chapter 13) by washing his disciples' feet, and warning of his betrayal by Judas, and of Peter's denial, which Peter hotly denies (verse 38). In the next three chapters, we have a very personal and confidential account of our Lord's last words to his disciples as he prepares to face his forthcoming trial and ensuing death. These are most precious disclosures, showing as they do, our Lord's deep concern for his disciples in the traumatic period during and after his trial and his crucifixion.

Chapter 14 describes their forthcoming relationship with him after his resurrection. Philip's request to be shown 'the Father' is met with, verse 9, "Whoever has seen me has seen the Father. Why then do you say, 'Show us the Father'? Do you not believe, Philip, that I am in the Father and the Father in me?" Verse 13, "And I will do whatever ask for in my name, so that the Father's glory will be shown through the Son. If you ask me for anything in my name, I will do it." And then Jesus makes the profound promise, verse 16, "I will ask the Father and He will give you another helper who will stay with you forever. He is the Spirit who reveals the truth about God." Verse 29, "The Holy Spirit, whom the Father will send in my name, will teach you everything and make you remember all that I have told you."

Then follow more intimate details of this forthcoming relationship, and in Chapter 16, the work of the Holy Spirit, who will enable the disciples to overcome the world, is outlined. And that is followed in Chapter 17 by the deeply moving account of our Lord's prayer for his disciples. Chapter 18 gives us first-hand details of our Lord's arrest in the Garden of Gethsemane, which is followed by Jesus appearing before Annas, the previous High Priest, father-in-law of the current Caiaphas. Peter, having followed the 'other disciple who was well-known to the High Priest' into the courtyard. More questions, then Peter's repeated denial that he knew Jesus, and then the confrontation with Pilate, the

Roman governor, who, seeing no fault in Jesus, does his best to avoid sentencing Jesus to death and washing his hands of the matter hands Jesus over to the Jewish Authorities with consent for crucifixion.

A couple of points worth noting here. First, that standing by the Cross was 'the disciple whom Jesus loved' standing with Jesus' mother and some other women. It is presumed that this 'other disciple' is in fact John. Out of humility, he does not name himself, but the close relationship with Jesus is shown by the fact that Jesus commends the care of his mother to him. The other is the fact that when, in order to take the bodies down before the Sabbath, they break the legs of the other two men crucified with Jesus, when they come to Jesus, he is already dead. So none of his bones were broken, as had been foretold by the prophets.

Then, on the Sunday morning, an empty tomb. Here we are told that Mary Magdalene was the first there, followed by Peter and 'the other disciple'. John looks in but does not enter. Peter (who else?) "went straight into the tomb," (20:6) and found only the linen wrappings lying there. Later, in the garden, Jesus appears to Mary who did not recognise him, thinking him to be the gardener – sorrow, pain, grief, had altered his appearance; his face was "so disfigured that he hardly looked human" (Isaiah 52:14) – until he spoke. Then Mary knew. Later that evening, Jesus appeared to all the disciples except Thomas, whose own doubts were resolved later. Jesus also appeared to the disciples in Galilee at which time Jesus heals Peter's broken heart by giving him an opportunity to confirm his love and give him a mission.

The book then ends with further personal confidences from 'the one whom Jesus loved' giving credence to the authorship of this Gospel, 21:24, "He is the disciple who spoke of these things, the one who also wrote them down; and we know that what he said is true."

The Acts of the Apostles

In his opening words, the author identifies himself as the writer of Luke's Gospel, which is his very detailed record of the birth and life of Jesus. We can also identify him as the 'beloved physician' and later companion of Paul the Apostle. This book takes over the written record of Jesus from the moment in time where the four Gospels end and, it begins with some very important detail of the days following the crucifixion, and prior to our Lord's ascension back to his Father, which we do not in find the Gospels. Here, for example, we are told that for forty days after his death, Jesus had appeared to his disciples, instructing them, encouraging them and cautioning them not to begin their work or leave Jerusalem until after they had received the promised gift of the Holy Spirit. In fact, it is Paul (1 Corinthians 14:6) who comments that Jesus was seen by more than five hundred of his followers after his resurrection, and last of all by Paul himself in a vision on the road to Damascus.

We then are given specific details of the ascension of Jesus, after the disciples had yet again asked him whether this was the time for the restoration of the nation, verse 6, "Lord, will you at this time give the kingdom back to Israel?" To which our Lord's response was, that the time was known only to the father in heaven, not for them to know, verse 8, "But when the Holy Spirit comes upon you, you will be filled with power, and you will be witnesses to me in Jerusalem, in all Judea and Samaria and to the ends of the earth." And as he said this, Jesus was taken up into heaven in front of them, and they watched until he disappeared in the clouds. As they looked up, two angels appeared, telling them that, "This same Jesus would return in the same manner."

Leaving the Mount of Olives, the disciples returned to Jerusalem, and there, in the upper room (Chapter 2), the Holy Spirit came down in visible flames. And in the most remarkable transformation, these timid, fearful, doubtful men were transformed into the bold, brave, fearless unto death witnesses who, "turned the world upside down," with their message and began what we now know as the Church.

Noteworthy now is the first message of Peter (2:14) in his address to the crowd in explanation of this unique event. This was a very detailed and comprehensive resume of the biblical events leading up to this spectacular demonstration. These were uneducated working men, who were addressing the crowd but speaking directly in some sixteen foreign languages, all telling about this Jesus whom they, the Jewish people, had so recently crucified, which also stated in a very clearly expressed statement, where the guilt lay (verse 36). "When the people heard this, they were deeply troubled and said to Peter and the other apostles, 'What shall we do, brothers?'" (verse 37).

Now follows an account of the daily life of the new 'church', which was in many respects a continuation of their Jewish religious practices, but which were transformed by the remarkable healing of the man who lay, lame from birth, at the beautiful gate of the Temple. Once again, Peter's spoken message in the Temple is a remarkable statement of the facts, based on their existing Jewish scriptures, confirming that it was Jesus, whom they the Jews, had crucified in ignorance of who he really was, who had healed this lame man, and that this Jesus was the Jewish Messiah, long promised, who was now alive in Heaven from where he would soon return to earth. These statements so incensed the priests, and the Sadducees who did not believe in resurrection, that they sent Temple guards who arrested Peter and John and put them in jail. Brought before the Council next day, they confirmed what to them were the facts, that it was this same Jesus who had healed the man. The Council were unable to ignore the fact because the man who had been healed was there in the Temple. So they were cautioned by the Council not to speak in the name of Jesus, and then set free.

Released, they re-joined the others, who shared in praising God, and prayed for further boldness to speak out. With the result that the number of the believers, previously thought to be around 120, rapidly increased to over five thousand, with further believers added daily to their number. So now they had become a substantial, fully committed group; they were no longer a just small band of fishermen and other relatively unknown men and women, surrounded by a curious crowd of sightseers. (Chapter 5)

Believing that Jesus would very shortly return to establish his Kingdom on earth via the Jewish nation, the believers were totally committed to this new way of life. To the extent that many sold all their possessions, pooled the money and ensured that a co-operative community of believers were able to work and worship. However, this, sadly, gave two 'converts' an idea. They would win plaudits from their generosity, but secure their own financial position, by selling their land but only giving part of the sale price to the community. Peter, warned by the Holy Spirit, challenged Ananias. Why make such a deceitful compromise? Either give the money or state that you are only giving part, even keep the money, but however, whatever you do, be honest. Sapphira his wife was a party to the deception, and both died. Result, fear amongst the community as they realised that here they were dealing with God not humans. As a result, outside the community, even more converts joined, and many miracles and wonders occurred. Clearly this was no ordinary social grouping; this was the beginning of the new 'kingdom'. New rules applied and judgement was no longer in the hands of corruptible men.

There were disputes, inevitably, such as the complaint that the Greek-speaking widows, who were probably expatriate Jews from outside Jerusalem, were being neglected in the daily distribution of money. The twelve disciples were too busy to be occupied with administration, so seven helpers, men full of the Holy Spirit, were appointed as administrators, leaving the twelve free to dedicate themselves to their ministry of preaching, teaching and healing. However, one of those chosen, a man named Stephen (6:8) described as, "A man richly blessed by God and full of power, performed great miracles and wonders among the people." For this, he was opposed by certain Jews, members of the synagogue of the Freedmen, who criticised him and, unable to refute what he was saying, falsely accused him of speaking against the Jewish faith. Hauled before the Council, Stephen was asked to speak, and his message (Chapter 7), based on the Old Testament scriptures, is quite remarkable for its depth of understanding and was obviously inspired by the Holy Spirit.

In his message, Stephen goes back to the founder of their faith, Abraham, looking at the history of their race, reminding his hearers that their ancestors had rejected Moses' leadership, so that Moses had to spend the next forty years out in the desert keeping sheep, yet he was the one whom God had appointed to lead the people out of slavery. It was Moses, Stephen said, who prophesied that God would send his people another prophet, verse 37, "God will send you a prophet, just as he sent me, and he will be one of your own people." And continuing, he reminded them of the sad history of their nation through their disobedience and sin. He then went on to talk about David their great king, and his desire to build a Temple, "But God does not need a Temple made by hands," then verse 51, "How stubborn you are, how heathen your hearts, how deaf you are to God's message? You are just like your ancestors; you too have always resisted the Holy Spirit." At this point, Stephen reminds them that their ancestors killed the prophets who announced the coming of, "The righteous servant" (verse 52). "And now you have betrayed and murdered him." This stated plainly that in crucifying Jesus, they had killed God's chosen messenger. They were horrified.

In the end, the only way for them to silence Stephen was to accuse him of blasphemy and stone him, which they did, laying their coats at the feet of a very zealous Pharisee from Tarsus named Saul who was studying here in Jerusalem.

A further example of the way in which this new teaching was spreading is seen in the encounter of Philip with the Ethiopian official, who, returning in his chariot from worship in Jerusalem, was reading Isaiah 53 but not understanding who the suffering servant was until Philip, sent by the Lord, showed him that the words prophetically speak of this Jesus. All of these, as Luke demonstrates in The Acts, are the work of the Holy Spirit in confirming that Jesus was the promised Saviour, promised to the Jewish nation by their prophets but killed by them.

Arising from the death of Stephen, Saul of Tarsus, enraged by what he saw as blasphemy against their Jewish religion, is now on his way to Damascus to persecute the followers of the new 'Way', when he is stopped by a brilliant light and a voice from the sky which challenged him, "Saul, Saul, why do you persecute me?" "Who are you Lord," he asked. "I am Jesus, whom you persecute." (Chapter 9). So now, Saul is forced to accept that in persecuting the Christians he is persecuting the Son of God himself. Blinded, led into the city, Saul is told by a very nervous Christian, Ananias, who knew exactly why this Pharisee Saul was coming to Damascus, "Go, because I have chosen him to make my name known to Gentiles and kings and to the people of Israel. And I myself will show him all that he must suffer for my sake" (9:13).

Now we see a vitally dramatic shift in emphasis, in the way this 'good news' will spread. What had previously been seen as a Jewish variant on their existing traditional faith, is now becoming a message for the non-Jews (Gentiles) as well. "A light to lighten the Gentiles, and the glory of my people Israel" Luke 2:32. Simeon's prophesy was about to be fulfilled.

Following his conversion, Saul preached Jesus in Damascus and was forced to flee by angry Jews, being lowered over the city wall in a basket. Saul then travelled to Jerusalem, but the disciples there were afraid of him, his reputation being that of a betrayer of the faith. However, Barnabas, a Greek-speaking Cypriot believer, vouched for him and Saul did preach but was himself threatened with death by other Greek-speaking Jews, and so he was sent away to Tarsus.

In the meantime, the church was growing. Peter, travelling abroad to spread the news, went to Lydda, to Joppa and surrounding districts, where he preached and many remarkable healings took place. Then the Holy Spirit spoke to a devout Roman army captain named Cornelius, stationed in Caesarea, telling him, in a vision, to send for a man named Peter who was staying in the house of Simon the Tanner by the sea at Joppa. In preparation for this, God gave Peter a remarkable vision, which he did not understand, of a sheet let down from heaven containing animals, reptiles and birds. 10:13, "A voice said to him, 'Get up, Peter, kill and eat.' 'Certainly not Lord! I have never eaten anything ritually unclean or defiled.'" Verse 15, "Do not consider anything unclean that God has declared clean." This vision happened three times and then the vision ended. At that very moment, the messengers from the Roman soldier were knocking at the door and Peter was told to go with them.

Now more drama. Reaching the house of Cornelius in Caesarea, Peter hears of the vision given to Cornelius, and he now realises the significance of his own vision and preaches Jesus to the assembled household. 10:44, "While he is speaking the Holy Spirit descends on the listeners," just as it had on the one hundred and twenty follows in the Upper Room in Jerusalem. Peter, understanding now that this is of God, a work of the Holy Spirit, agrees to baptise them as believers, even though they were not Jews.

Chapter 11, Peter now returns to Jerusalem to report this staggering news, verse 12, "The Spirit told me to go with them without hesitation. These six fellow believers from Joppa accompanied me to Caesarea." So it was not just Peter's word; there were other witnesses to what had happened. The response from the Jewish Christians in Jerusalem, verse 18, "When they heard this, they stopped their criticism and praised God, saying, 'Then God has given to the Gentiles also the opportunity to repent and live.'" But there was more trouble to come.

Following the persecution which arose after the stoning of Stephen, many of the believers were scattered, travelling as far afield as Phoenicia, Cyprus and Antioch, telling the message only to Jews. But other believers, coming from Cyprus and Cyrene, went to Antioch and proclaimed the message to Gentiles also (verse 20), and the power of the Lord being with them, a 'great number of people believed and turned to the Lord.' Which caused some consternation back at HQ, so they sent Barnabas to sort things out. He encouraged the new believers there, and then set off for Tarsus to find Saul and bring him back to Antioch, where they stayed and preached with much success for twelve months. It was here that the name Christian was first applied to these converts. Then, following news of a famine in Judea, the new believers decided to send money to Jerusalem by the hands of Barnabas and Saul.

The early church had been accepted by the Roman authorities as a 'sect' being regarded as still part of the authorised Jewish religion. Now, Chapter 12, King Herod begins to persecute some of these 'converts'. Verse 2, "He had James, the brother of John, put to death by the sword. When he saw that this pleased the Jews, he went on to arrest Peter," intending to interrogate him publicly later. Overnight, an angel awoke Peter and took him out through the barred gates, where he made his way to the house of John Mark's mother, Mary Mark. Rhoda heard him knocking but was so excited that, at first, she failed to open the door. Great excitement for those in the house, but Herod, as one would expect, was extremely angry and had the guards put to death. Then, later, Herod left for Caesarea, where he was due to make a speech and would die, by God's hand, for blasphemy. Meanwhile, Barnabas and Saul had finished their mission and returned to Antioch, taking John Mark with them. There in Antioch, the Holy Spirit calls the two to begin the ministry for which God had called Saul, now called Paul, which for Paul was the first of his great 'missionary' journeys.

So the three men, Barnabas, Saul and John Mark travelled first to Seleucia and thence to Cyprus, having great success there. Then to Perga where John Mark left to go home, leaving Saul and Barnabas to travel on to Antioch in Pisidia, where in the synagogue by invitation, Paul, as he is now called, preached with mighty power, tracing the coming of Jesus back through Old Testament (Jewish) prophecy and showing that this Jesus was indeed the Son of God. So effective was their ministry that they were invited back, and the following Sabbath, most of the city came to listen, being especially encouraged by the message that Gentiles also were included in God's promise. But whilst the word of God spread rapidly, some of the Jews were incensed, both at the fact that they were being blamed for the crucifixion of the Son of God, and also the fact that by including Gentiles, the Apostles were undermining the exclusiveness of their faith. So they were persecuted and thrown out. But the believers in Antioch were full of joy and the Holy Spirit at the message.

On then to Iconium where the same thing happened again; believers multiplied but, 14:2, "The Jews who would not believe, stirred up the Gentiles and turned them against the believers." Paul and Barnabas stayed for some time with increasing success, but threatened with stoning, they left and went to Lystra and Derbe, cities in Lycaonia. Here, after a miraculous healing in Lystra, they were hailed as gods, Zeus and Hermes, and were about to be worshipped. Saved in fact by the arrival of some Jews from Pisidia and Iconium, who stirred up animosity against the two men, Paul was stoned and left for dead. However, Paul recovered and they left for Derbe. Here they had great success and were much emboldened so they returned to the scene of their former problems and again preached with power, but also warning the converts that followers of Jesus must expect suffering. Then, finally, back to the Antioch from which they had started out, to be greeted with much joy, (verse 28), especially at the news that God had opened the way for the Gentiles also to believe.

However, this remarkable inclusion of Gentiles in the Faith was to suffer a further obstacle. This time from believers arriving from Jerusalem, Chapter 15, who preached to the believers that in order to become Christians they must first be circumcised and accept Jewish Law. Paul and Barnabas refuted this strongly, but the point was so controversial that it was decided that Paul, Barnabas and some other believers from Antioch should go to Jerusalem and decide the matter once and for all in council, backed by the authority which clearly, at this time, was centred in Jerusalem.

Welcomed by the believers in Jerusalem, who rejoiced at what they heard of the power of God and the growth of the 'church' in overseas territory, they were however bitterly opposed by a group of former Pharisees, who insisted on circumcision and obedience to Jewish Law as conditions of faith. Peter sided with Paul. Citing his own experience in the house of the Roman Cornelius, saying that God had given his approval to the conversion of Gentiles by giving the Holy Spirit to them, as he had to the Jews (verse 7,8). And tellingly, verse 11, "We believe and are saved by the grace of the Lord Jesus." Which was to become the keynote for the Church, salvation by faith, not by human effort in attempting to keep the Law.

The assembled believers then listened in silence as Paul and Barnabas told of their remarkable experiences, in which God had blessed Gentiles as well as

Jews. Then James stood, saying that all the prophets agreed with this, adding, "That we should not trouble the Gentiles who are turning to God." This was accepted by the believers, the apostles and the elders, who then sent a letter confirming this decision to Antioch by the hands of Paul and Barnabas, supported by two elders, Silas and Judas Barsabbas. Paul stayed there in Antioch for some time before feeling led by the Holy Spirit to travel again. However, this time, following a sharp argument with Barnabas over whether or not to take John Mark with them again, Paul chose Silas as companion and left. A deep division had occurred over the role of John Mark who was related to Barnabas and whose mother, Mary Mark and her house seem to have had a role in the work of the early church in Jerusalem. Remember that Peter went there on his release from prison, and where people were clearly gathered for prayer. Was this an early crisis of authority? We cannot know.

Paul, with Silas, now travelled back through Syria overland to Derbe and Lystra, where on the first journey, he had travelled by sea to Pisidia. In Lystra, he selects a young man Timothy to join them. His mother and grandmother were both devout Jews, and although his father was Greek, the young man would have been well grounded in scripture. At this stage in the Gospel message, a thorough knowledge of the Jewish Old Testament was quite crucial in convincing people of the authenticity of Jesus. He was the long-promised 'deliverer', the son of David, who was the son of God. The basis of their message was quite simply, this is the Messiah, the one whom God had promised to send, but whom you killed just as your ancestors killed the prophets. Except that this Jesus is now alive and will soon come back to establish his kingdom. In order to save yourself from judgement, you must believe in him.

The missionaries were forbidden by the Spirit to preach in Asia, so they travelled on to Troas, where Paul had a vision of a Macedonian man begging for them to come, which they did, taking ship to travel to Neapolis and from there inland to Philippi, the chief city of the province, where a devout and prosperous businesswoman became a believer. However, when Paul cast out an evil spirit from a young girl who was earning money for her owners by fortune telling, they created serious trouble, which ended in Paul and Silas being severely beaten and imprisoned. However, once again, the Holy Spirit intervened, and as they were singing and praising God that night, there was an earthquake, which caused the prison doors to open. Fearing an escape, the jailor prepared to kill himself, but on hearing Paul, he came and cried out, trembling. Paul preached the good news to him and he and his household were baptised. In gratitude, full of joy, he washed their wounds and fed them. Then, when in the morning the officials came to release them, on being told that they were Roman citizens, the officials were obliged to apologise for their treatment of them.

Travelling on to Thessalonica, they again preached in the synagogue, with a similar result. Many were converted, but unbelievers caused trouble. Moving onto Berea they were better received until more Jewish troublemakers arrived. Paul, taking advice, went on to Athens alone where he waited for Silas and Timothy to join him (Chapter 17). Here in Athens, Paul was able to minister to devout Jewish and Gentile communities and engage with some of the great philosophers who daily disputed there. They brought Paul before the Council, wanting to hear more about his 'theories' of resurrection. Struck by the fact that the Greeks had idols to so many gods, including, in case they had missed one out 'to the unknown god', Paul took that as his theme, preaching about Jesus and his resurrection. The response? Some believed and some did not.

So passing on, he went to Corinth where he met Jews, Aquila and Priscilla, and because they also were tentmakers, Paul worked with them, earning his living, until Timothy and Silas joined him, after which he then gave his full time to preaching the word of God. Disturbed by the antagonism of the Jews, Paul left that community and went to live amongst the Gentiles, where he was next door to a synagogue whose leader became a believer, as did many others. Encouraged by a vision in which the Lord told him not to be afraid but to continue, Paul stayed for eighteen months and many were converted. However, a change of governor over the province encouraged some Jews to seize Paul and take him to court. The governor, Gallio, refused to listen to "arguments about words and names" (18:15) and dismissed the charges.

Paul stayed on there for a short time, then sailed for Ephesus with Aquila and Priscilla, where he left them to continue the work and travelled to Jerusalem via Caesarea and from there on to Antioch where he stayed some time before heading off again, back to Ephesus on what would be his third journey. There, Chapter 19, he met some believers and asked them, verse 2, "Did you receive the Holy Spirit when you became believers?" They had been baptised only with John's baptism, of repentance, because they had not heard of what happened in Jerusalem on the Day of Pentecost. So Paul laid his hands on them and they too received the Holy Spirit. Paul stayed on for three months, preaching and teaching and seeing miracles of healing. All was relatively well; the more the persecution, the more the power of the word of God was demonstrated, until there was a riot in Ephesus.

In Ephesus was a large temple dedicated to the local god Artemis (Diana). Silversmiths were earning much money by making silver copies and selling them. Fearful that they were losing trade, Demetrius called his fellows to a meeting and a great riot of shouting and anger filled the amphitheatre as they shouted, "Great is Artemis of Ephesus," for over two hours, and the riot was only quelled when the town clerk warned them of the legal consequences of a riot.

When all was quiet again, Paul left, having encouraged the believers to hold fast to their faith. Travelling on through Macedonia to Achaia where he stayed three months, he then, hearing of a plot against his life in Syria, returned to go through Macedonia, accompanied by a number of believers, including Timothy. They were sent on ahead to wait in Troas. Luke having now joined Paul, they sailed from Philippi to meet the others in Troas, from there to Miletus. The group then travelled by sea to Assos, where Paul, having travelled overland, met them and took ship with them, sailing past Ephesus to reach Miletus, where elders from Ephesus came to meet them and Paul bid them farewell, conscious that they would not meet again (20:25). A very sad parting.

Paul is now intending to reach Jerusalem in time for Pentecost, if that were possible, leaving by sea to Cos, Rhodes and on to Patara, where they changed ship, and on to Cyprus before heading South to Tyre in Syria, where they had fellowship with the believers who warned Paul not to go to Jerusalem. From there to Ptolemais and a day with the believers there, before going on to Caesarea where they stayed in the house of Philip the evangelist whose four daughters, prophets, warned Paul that if he went to Jerusalem, he would fall foul of the Jews there who would arrest him. Paul's companions urged him not to go, but Paul was determined and so they set off for Jerusalem.

Arriving in Jerusalem, Paul was warmly welcomed by the Church and James their leader, believed to be his own brother who was now a believer. Here the old controversy is raised. They tell Paul that many thousands of believers are devoted also to the Law. And they advise Paul to perform a vow as an act of appeasement. He did so, but at the end of the seven days, some Jews from Asia saw him and roused the crowd who seized him, claiming that he was teaching everyone against the Law and accusing him of taking a Gentile, Trophimus, into the temple. Such was the riot that the Roman governor sent troops who took Paul into their fort, to save him from the crowd. There, learning that Paul was educated, and a Greek-speaking Roman citizen, the Governor allowed Paul to address the crowd, which he did in Hebrew, telling of his former status as a persecutor, of his conversion and then of his call to preach the Gospel to the Gentiles, at which they began to riot again.

The Commander of the troops, hearing that Paul was a Roman citizen and, therefore, above Jewish law, determined to get to the bottom of it and called for a meeting of the Jewish Council. Now events are moving very rapidly. At the Council, Paul speaks in his defence as a former member of the strict sect of Pharisees, and then splits the opposition by speaking of the resurrection of the dead, which put the Sadducees in a spin because they did not believe it. Another riot in the Council followed, from which Paul was again rescued by the Roman soldiers.

Paul that night has another vision from the Lord, who tells him that, having given his witness in Jerusalem, he must witness also in Rome (23:11). Then Paul's sister's son hears that the Jews are plotting to kill Paul. He tells the Commander of the troops who decides to send Paul away under a heavily armed escort, two hundred soldiers, seventy horsemen and two hundred spearmen, to take him to the Governor Felix at Caesarea, where Paul will make his defence again. The High Priest takes a lawyer, Tertullus, with him and they accuse Paul of being a dangerous nuisance, who is perverting the Law of Moses, causing riots 'all over the world' and that he is guilty of trying to defile their Temple.

Felix, who we are told was very familiar with the Way, simply said that he would wait until the Roman commander, Lysias arrived. Felix and his wife came again to listen to Paul talking about Jesus Christ and the coming judgement. Felix was afraid at that and left Paul in prison for two years, fearing the Jews, but allowing him some freedom. Then when Festus succeeded Felix as governor and went to Jerusalem, the Jewish leaders there appealed to him to bring Paul back to Jerusalem. They had a plot to kill him on the way. Trying to placate the Jews, Festus asks Paul if he would be willing to return to Jerusalem to face his accusers there. Faced with this ultimatum, Paul takes his final option – as a Roman citizen, he has the right to appeal to the Emperor, and so he does.

Sometime later, King Agrippa and Bernice pay a visit to Festus, and (25:22) Agrippa says that he would like to hear Paul. Festus states clearly that the Jews are thirsting for Paul's death, verse 25, "But I could not find that he had done anything for which he deserved the death penalty." However, this gives Paul a great opportunity to testify to his faith before Agrippa and Bernice, which he does so successfully that Agrippa is forced to say, 26:28, "In this short time, do you think that you will make me a Christian?" The result, they all agree that Paul had done nothing worthy of prison, let alone death, and that had he not appealed to the Emperor, he could be released – which would obviously have meant releasing him to the enmity of the Jewish Authorities. So Paul will go to Rome under guard.

Paul is taken on board ship under the care of a Roman soldier, an officer in the Emperor's Regiment, Aristarchus from Macedonia being with him. And what a journey that was. They sailed to Sidon, then under the island of Cyprus, to Myra where they changed to a ship bound for Italy. Stormy weather made the journey slow and dangerous as they passed Cnidus to sail down the sheltered side of Crete to reach a place called Safe Harbours near the town of Lasea where they were weather bound for a long time, it being too dangerous to proceed. Finally, refusing to listen to Paul, the Officer took the advice of the ship's captain, which was to try to reach a safer harbour for the winter, at Phoenix. Once at sea, they were hit by a violent North East gale and were driven by the violence of the storm for fourteen days, throwing everything they could overboard to lighten the ship. Paul rebukes the sailors for ignoring his advice but comforts them with the assurance that, because God is in charge, their lives will be spared.

Finally, after much terror, they were shipwrecked on the rocky coast of Malta, where all on board managed to get ashore. Chapter 28, here they stayed for three months until the weather improved and they could finally take ship again for Rome. During those months, however, Paul was able to proclaim his faith, and meeting Publius the Chief official of the island who gave them hospitality, Paul was able to bring healing to his father and this led to others being healed also.

Travelling on now, they reached Syracuse where they spent three days. From there they sailed to Rhegium and then to Puteoli where they spent a week with some believers and then on to Rome, where they were met on the Appian Way by some believers from Rome who had come as far as the towns of Market of Appius to meet them, and Paul was greatly encouraged by them.

In Rome, Paul was allowed to live in a house, guarded by a soldier, and here, as we shall see, he was able to write a number of his letters to the churches he had visited. Paul then was also able to meet some of the Jewish leaders and explain exactly why he was there, having been forced to appeal to the Emperor to save his life. They had heard nothing against him from Jerusalem, but they had heard that people were speaking against the followers of the Way, and so they set a date for Paul to speak to them, and from, "morning till night he explained to them his message about the Kingdom of God and he tried to convince them about Jesus by quoting from the Law of Moses and the writings of the prophets" (verse 23). They were rather sceptical, and Paul remonstrated by quoting to them Isaiah's prediction about the Jews, that they would listen but not hear (Isaiah 6:9).

Paul then lived for at least a further two years in a place which he rented, and from there, he preached the word of God to all who would listen and wrote many of his epistles. We do not know what happened after this, but we do know from his epistles, that he had many visitors and that many stayed with him there. The only further news we have is what we read in his letters to the churches.

Romans

Paul was writing this letter to the embryonic church of believers established in Rome, with the expectation that he would visit them and then with their help travel to one of the remotest corners of the empire, Spain. We now know that he would get there but, as we have seen at the end of The Acts of the Apostles, as a prisoner.

This group of converts were most probably expatriates, fleeing from the persecution which was now beginning in Israel, together with devout Gentiles who had become believers. They would no doubt have heard of Paul but not met him personally, so ahead of his visit, Paul, 'sets out his stall' as it were with a comprehensive statement of what he believed. In fact, as a summary of the development of what would become the basis of Christian theology, it explores in greater detail what Paul had been saying elsewhere; namely two things, that Jesus was the Messiah promised through the prophets and that all of the Old Testament was a foreshadowing of what Jesus Christ would accomplish by his life, his death and his resurrection. Jesus, therefore, was in himself the full revelation of God, made accessible to believers through the Holy Spirit who was God's gift as promised by the prophet Joel.

Paul begins by introducing himself, Chapter 1, as "chosen and called by God to preach his Good News." He then continues to clarify that this Good News is nothing new, not a new message at all, but something which God had promised long ago, concerning His Son Jesus Christ, who was "shown with great power to be the Son of God." Then he commends the believers for their faith which "the whole world is hearing about" (verse 8), even Paul, who wants to share with them his experience of God so that together they may benefit. Because this Gospel is so powerful, even to the point of being able to reconcile people with God, through their faith (verse 12).

Paul now gets to the heart of his message to them, which is, the power of the Gospel to bring both Jew and Gentile to a state of holiness before God, which was not possible under the Law – which will be summed up in Chapter 8. But first, it is necessary to understand that the whole world is subject to the power of evil which corrupts human nature, as is clearly exemplified by what people do. Result, God has given them over to these passions (1:26). And the consequence, "They know that God's law says that people who live in this way deserve death. Yet not only do they continue to do these things, but they even approve of others who do them" (verse 32).

Therefore, Chapter 2, even though, "God is kind because he is trying to lead you to repent." Yet, "you have a hard and stubborn heart, and so you are making your punishment even greater on the day when God's anger and righteous judgements will be revealed" (verse 5). Now Paul comes to what is a burning issue. The different values which attach to Jew and Gentile. The Jews have the Law and depend on it, verse 23, "You boast about having God's law, but do you bring shame on God by breaking his law? The scripture says, 'Because of you, Jews, the Gentiles speak evil of God.'" The fact is that if the Gentile obeys God's law, he is justified far more in the sight of God than a circumcised Jew who breaks the law. But, and here Paul introduces the 'new' teaching, verse 29, "the real Jew is the person who is a Jew on the inside, that is, whose heart has been circumcised, and this is the work of God's Spirit not of the written law."

What advantage then has the Jew over the Gentiles? (Chapter 3) Much, says Paul, in that God first trusted his message to the Jews. Verse 9, "Well, then are we Jews in any better condition than the Gentiles? Not at all. I have already shown that the Jews and Gentiles alike are under the power of sin. As the scripture says, 'There is no one who is righteous'" And verse 28, "For we conclude that a person is put right with God only through faith, and not by doing what the law commands." However, this does not mean that we ignore the law; no, we uphold it.

Now, Paul will demonstrate from scripture exactly how this was applied by quoting the example of Abraham, the father of their faith. Chapter 4, "What was his experience? If he was put right with God by the things he did, he would have something to boast about – but not in God's sight. The scripture says, 'Abraham believed God, and because of his faith, God accepted him as righteous.'" (Genesis 15:6). Even the promises which God gave him were received by faith, verse 16, "And so the promise was based on faith, in order that the promise should be guaranteed as God's free gift to all of Abraham's descendants – not just to those who obey the law." Even more significant is the fact that all of

Abraham's experience occurred more than five hundred years before the Law was given under Moses. All Abraham had was the voice of God and his own conscience, illuminated by faith.

The result of having this faith is, 5:1, "We have peace with God through our Lord Jesus Christ." Further, verse 3, "We boast of our troubles because we know that trouble produces endurance, endurance brings God's approval, and his approval creates hope." The hope we have in God is evidenced by the fact that God loved us even while we were still sinners, enough to send Jesus to die for us. So what we are now reminded of is that we are delivered from death by the death of Christ.

Paul points out that one man, Adam, brought sin into the world by his disobedience and his exercise of free will, and the consequence was death. As a result, the whole of humanity became guilty, even before the Law was given, even if they had not sinned by disobedience in the same way. Symbolically then, Jesus Christ became the second Adam, and in him, God redeemed the human race because Jesus, having been made human like us, became "obedient unto death, even the death on the Cross." So in Christ, humankind can be forgiven and also redeemed, that is, made right in the sight of God, 5:18, "So then, as the one sin condemned all people, in the same way, one righteous act (of self-sacrificial obedience), sets all people free and gives them life." The Law then becomes our schoolmaster to teach us what obedience is.

In Chapter 6, Paul answers a criticism made of his teaching, namely that if through sin the grace of God was revealed, why not sin more so that God's grace might be seen to be even greater. Not so, says Paul, for by being identified with Christ, as in baptism, we share in his death to sin, in order that we might in turn be raised to life through his resurrection. Verse 5, "For since we have become one with him in dying as he did, in the same way, we shall be one with him by being raised to life as he was." We have to be "crucified with Christ" if we are to share in the glory of his resurrection. Because verse 7, "When people die, they are set free from the power of sin. Since we have died with Christ, we believe that we will also live with him." But verse 12, "Sin must no longer rule in your mortal bodies so that you obey the desire of your natural self." In other words, as Jesus said, "We must take up our Cross daily, and follow him." Remembering that we are no longer under the power of sin. We are set free by dying with Christ.

In Chapter 7, Paul illustrates this theme by reference to the laws of marriage. A married woman is bound to her husband as long as he lives, but when he dies, she is free. If she cohabits with another man while her husband lives, she is an adulteress, but once he dies, she is free. Being dead to sin, we are no longer slaves to its passions. Is then the Law sinful? No. Without the Law, we would not know sin. Without the rebuke, we would not know the error. However, this does mean that at times there is a conflict in us, between our human desires and our Godly aspirations, verse 21, "So I find that this law is at work: when I want to do what is good, what is evil is the only choice I have." Verse 24, "Who will rescue me from this body that is taking me to death? Thanks be to God, who does this through our Lord Jesus Christ." In other words, in Christ, it is possible to become dead to sin.

Now, in Chapter 8, Paul comes to the very heart of the matter, as he develops this theme in greater detail. We are no longer condemned because, verse 3, "What the law could not do, because human nature was weak, God did. He condemned sin in human nature by sending his own Son, who came with a nature like sinful human nature, to do away with sin. God did this so that the righteous demands of the Law might be fully satisfied in us, who live according to the Spirit and not according to human nature." Further, verse 5, "Those who live as their human nature tells them to, have their minds controlled by what human nature wants. Those who live as the Spirit tells them to, have their minds controlled by what the Spirit wants." And he enlarges on this, verse 14, "Those who are led by God's Spirit are God's children." Verse 16, "God's spirit joins himself to our spirits, to declare that we are God's children." Verse 17, "For if we share Christ's suffering, we will also share his glory."

And then, Paul goes on to tell what that future glory will be, when creation itself, which "waits with eager longing for God to reveal his children. That creation itself would one day be set free from its slavery to decay and should share the glorious freedom of the children of God" (verse 21). And it is not just creation which groans, "we who have the Spirit as the first of God's gifts also groan within ourselves, as we wait for God to make us his children and set our whole being free." And verse 26, "The Spirit himself pleads with God for us in groans which words cannot express," which emphasises the fact that for the Christian, the focus is on the future.

This is followed by such incomparable words as verse 31, "If God is for us, who can be against us?" Verse 35, "Who can separate us from the love of Christ? Can trouble do it or hardship, or persecution or hunger, or poverty or death?" Verse 37, "No, in all these things we have complete victory through him who loved us." "There is nothing in all creation that will ever be able to separate us from the love of God which is ours through Christ Jesus our Lord."

Paul now, Chapter 9, reverts to one of the burning issues of his day. The question of the status of the Jewish nation in the all-embracing kingdom of God. "They are God's people... they are descended from the famous Hebrew ancestors; and Christ, as a human being, belongs to their race" (verse 4,5). Now two important points, "not all the people of Israel are the people of God." Paul points out that of the children born naturally to Abraham, and there were several apart from Ishmael, only the children of promise, that is, Isaac and his children, were God's children. It was the same with Rebecca. She had two sons, Esau and Jacob, but only Jacob was chosen. Injustice with God? No! Verse 5, "For he said to Moses, 'I will have mercy on anyone I wish.'" So then, everything depends, not on what human beings want or do, but only on God's mercy."

Paul here cites the potter in whose hands the clay is subject to his will. It is the same with the Gentiles and the Jews, and here Paul quotes Hosea 1:10, "The people who were not mine I will call 'my people'. The nation that I did not love, I will call 'My beloved'." And Isaiah 10:22, "Even if the people of Israel are as many as the grains of sand by the sea, yet only a few of them will be saved." He concludes this issue with verse 30. The Gentiles, who were not trying to put themselves right with God, were put right with him by faith, while God's people who were seeking a law that would put them right with God, did not find it. And why not? Because they did not depend on faith but on what they did." Conclusion, of all people born, there are two kinds. Those who by faith in God, through the life and death of Jesus will live, and those who do not. Jesus to Nicodemus, "That which is born of the flesh is flesh, that which is born of the Spirit of God is spirit."

Now in Chapter 10, Paul utters his lament, "How I wish with all my heart that my own people might be saved." Verse 2, "They are deeply devoted to God, but their devotion is not based on true knowledge. They have not known the way in which God puts people right with himself, and instead, they have set up their own way; and so they do not submit themselves to God's way of putting people right." Verse 8, "God's message is near you... that is the message of faith that we preach. If you confess that Jesus is Lord and believe that God raised him from death, you will be saved. For it is by our faith that we are put right with God." "There is no difference between Jews and Gentiles... Everyone who calls out to the Lord for help will be saved." Verse 16, "But not all have accepted the good news." Verse 21, "Concerning Israel he says, 'All day long I held out my hands to welcome a disobedient and rebellious people.'"

However, all is not lost for now Paul reveals what he is convinced is to happen in the future (Chapter 11). Basically it is this, verse 2, "God has not rejected his people, whom he chose from the beginning." No, when they became disobedient, God chose to use them as a means of bringing the Gentiles into the fold, and by doing that to make Israel jealous. So if the time of the Jews ended with their rejection of Jesus which led to his death, then verse 25, "There is a secret truth, my brothers and sisters, which I want you to know, for it will keep you from thinking how wise you are. It is that the stubbornness of the people of Israel is not permanent but will last only until the complete number of Gentiles comes to God. And this is how all Israel will be saved. 'The Saviour will come from Zion and remove all wickedness from the descendants of Jacob. I will make this covenant with them when I take away their sins." (Jeremiah 31:33–34). Verse 28, "Because they reject the good news, the Jews are God's enemies for the sake of you Gentiles." Verse 33, "How great are God's riches! How deep are his wisdom and knowledge! Who can explain his decisions? Who can understand his ways?" Verse 36, "For all things were created by him, and all things exist through him and for him. To God be the glory forever."

So having completed his main thesis, Paul now turns to some practical advice in Chapter 12, beginning, "Because of God's great mercy to us, I appeal to you: offer yourselves as a living sacrifice to God, dedicated to his service and pleasing to him." He then goes on to speak of humility and the use of their various gifts in God's service. To love one another, not to seek revenge or go to law and to "conquer evil with good."

In Chapter 13, he discusses responsibility towards those on authority and towards one another, verse 9, "Love your neighbour as you love yourself," because the time of Christ's return is getting closer (verse 11), and therefore, we must behave as befits the children of God. Chapter 14 continues, we should not quarrel with others over debatable issues, or personal prejudice. "Everyone of us, then, will have to give account of ourselves to God" (verse 12). Stop judging one another. "Never do anything that would make another stumble or fall into sin." "And anything that is not based on faith, is sin" (verse 23).

Nearing the end of his discourse, Chapter 15, Paul emphasises the value and importance of scripture (verse 4), which for them was the Old Testament, and he emphasises that the life of Christ was God's way of confirming the promises made to their ancestors, yes, but also to bring the Gentiles within the fold, the "other sheep" mentioned by Jesus (verse 7). Paul then states his reasons for writing so emphatically, even though, as he acknowledges, they are already believers (verse 14), and he repeats his intention to visit them, explaining that first he has to take the charitable funds raised by the Asian churches for the relief of hardship in Jerusalem. We also hear of his proposal to travel on to Spain after visiting them in Rome (verse 28), but a further comment (verse 31) indicates that he was well aware of the dangers, which had been prophesied, inherent in his proposed visit to Jerusalem. And we are only too well aware of what actually happened, from our reading of the final chapters of the Acts of the Apostles.

Chapter 16 then concludes with a list of greetings to his fellow workers, showing his deep concern for the work of God, with a caution against divisive influences (verse 17), then there are greetings from his fellow workers, Timothy, Lucius, Jason and Sosipater and a personal greeting from the writer of the letter, Tertius. Then the concluding prayer of thanksgiving and praise.

1 Corinthians

This letter is unique and extremely relevant to us in our modern society. It was written to a church, which Paul had established in a city which was known as a cosmopolitan, commercial centre. One might even call it a Pagan community, rather than the basically religious communities in which he had previously preached. Therefore, its social and moral roots were somewhat different.

This letter is not a doctrinal appeal to those who were familiar with the Jewish Scriptures, introducing Christ as the prophetic heir to the scriptural promises with which they were familiar. This letter faces the dramatic collision of the new Christian morality and values, both social and spiritual, with those prevalent in a pagan society. Therefore, what Paul is doing is to show where and how it is necessary for those new ethical and spiritual values to replace what might be acceptable in a modern pagan society with those values which were incumbent on all true Christians, if they were to become spiritually alive and responsive to, God.

Paul sent this letter to the Church at Corinth which he had founded, possibly written to also tell them that he hopes to visit them again shortly. However, the main burden of the letter is that he has had reports of misconduct amongst the believers. He begins by praising them for their faith. However, this is seen as a way to emphasise that becoming a believer in Jesus Christ and accepting his authority means that their lives need to reflect the holiness and righteousness of Christ. The very idea that there are divisions among them is totally contrary to the idea of the unity which is theirs in Christ Jesus. He also reminds them that they owe their faith to the life and death of Jesus, not to any one of the messengers. Therefore, there was no place for pride in human achievement.

He also makes quite clear that the Gospel is not a matter of human wisdom. It is not possible to know God through the exercise of human wisdom. The word and the work of God are given by human messengers, who deliver a message about Jesus Christ who alone is the wisdom and power of God. So that what appears to some to be foolish or weak is, in fact, a power and strength beyond anything humans can comprehend. Even more, God has not chosen as messengers the clever or wise in worldly terms so that there would be no confusion and no grounds for boasting. Verse 27, "God purposely chose what the world considers nonsense in order to shame the wise, and He chose what the world considers weak in order to shame the powerful. He chose what the world looks down on and despises and thinks is nothing, in order to destroy what the world thinks is important." So if anyone wants to boast, they must boast only of what the Lord has done. Christ has brought us into union with God, and he alone is our wisdom.

To back up this message, Paul states (Chapter 2) that when he came to preach "God's secret truth" to them, he did not use big words or great learning. He decided simply to preach the word of God, which is Christ and his death on the cross, "with convincing proof of the power of God's Spirit." And he did that in all humility, deliberately, so that their faith should not rest on human wisdom "but on God's power" (verse 5). However, he states that he did preach "wisdom" to the spiritually mature, in telling them that God's wisdom predates the origins of the created world, and this is something that, had they known it, their rulers would not have crucified the Son of God. The truth simply is this, that God's truth is revealed through his Spirit alone. By rejecting worldly wisdom, we open ourselves to the superior wisdom of God, who knows everything and has made it clear through His word, but only to those who have His Spirit not the spirit of the world. In words which reflect what Christ had said to his disciples (John 16:12), Paul states, verse 13, "In words taught by the Spirit, we explain spiritual truths to those who have the Spirit. Whoever does not have the Spirit cannot receive the gifts that come from God's Spirit. Such people do not really understand them."

Now, having begun by praising the Corinthian believers, Paul becomes highly critical of their spiritual condition, Chapter 3, "I had to speak to you as though you belong to this world, as children in the Christian faith." Verse 3, "Because you still live as the people of this world live." In other words, your jealousy, your pride, your emphasis on human personality, all indicate your lack of God's Spirit. And he adds that our faith is built solely upon Jesus Christ, the one foundation, not on human personalities and values. Therefore, do not judge by human values; wait until the true Judge comes, the one who understands motive." (4:10) And in human terms they were, for subjecting themselves to criticism and violence.

The criticism Paul is making now becomes very specific. He condemns gross sexual immorality which they are condoning, and he warns that by tolerating such behaviour and not condemning it, they are allowing evil to permeate their society (Chapter 5).

Further, in Chapter 6, he is critical of their practice of allowing church fellowship members to bring their grievances to heathen judges. "How dare you!" (verse 1). "Shame on you. Surely there is at least one wise person in your fellowship who can settle a dispute between fellow Christians?" (verse 5). "The very fact that you have legal disputes among yourselves shows that you have failed completely" (verse 7). And then he thunders, no immoral adulterers or homosexual perverts will possess God's kingdom (verse 9–10).

Fearlessly, Paul now goes on to discuss marital relations (Chapter 7). Because of prevalent immorality, better to marry. But marriage entails personal responsibility to one's partner. To abstain from normal relations is to encourage infidelity. However, he does recommend chastity, not as a divine command but speaking personally. Elsewhere, he defends his bachelor status, whilst remarking on the fact that Peter was married and took his wife with him on his travels (9:5). Effectively, he is saying that, in these perilous times, when we expect our Lord to return, if single, stay single; if married stay married; if circumcised, stay circumcised; if uncircumcised, stay as you are, for all these things are external to one's spiritual state. "I am not trying to put restrictions on you. Instead I want you to do what is right and proper and to give yourselves completely to the Lord's service without reservation" (verse 35).

Paul now deals with a number of issues which seem unimportant to us but were potentially problematic for them. Whether or not to eat food which had been offered to idols. The answer lies in the effect that may have on those who are insecure in their faith. To the true Christian, these gods do not exist, but if someone is still 'superstitious', the food would be contaminated. Answer, 8:9, "Be careful however, not to let your freedom of action make those who are weak in the faith fall into sin."

It is the same with the position of an Apostle (Chapter 9). Paul has been criticised for many things. Not being married, not being a true apostle, because he was not one of the original disciples (born late). And he did not take payment for preaching; he supported himself. Yet that does not alter the principle that apostles can marry and those that preach the gospel should live by the gospel. Verse 9, "We read in the Law of Moses, 'Do not muzzle an ox when you are using it to thresh corn.' Now, is God concerned about oxen?" Verse 10, "Didn't he really mean us when he said that? Of course, that was written for us. The one who ploughs and the one who reaps should do their work in the hope of getting a share of the crop." Verse 14, "In the same way, the Lord has ordered that those who preach the gospel should get their living from it." He also adds, verse 19, "I am a free man, nobody's slave; but I make myself everybody's slave in order to win as many people as possible." When working with Jews I live as a Jew, when working with Gentiles I live as a Gentile (verse 22). "So I become all things to all people, that I may save some of them by whatever means are possible."

In Chapter 10, Paul takes as an example, the sin of the Israelites in that they were all under the protection of the cloud and baptised in the sea. They ate and drank manna and water provided supernaturally, the water having come from the rock, which was symbolically Christ himself. Yet they still sinned. Verse 11, "All these things happened to them as examples for others, and they were written down as a warning for us." The 'us' in this case implying the Corinthian Christians. "Those who think they are standing firm had better be careful that they do not fall" (verse 12).

However, Paul follows this immediately with words of consolation, verse 13, "Every test that you have experienced is the kind that normally come to people. But God keeps His promise, and He will not allow you to be tested beyond your power to remain firm; at the same time you are put to the test, he will give you the strength to endure it and so provide you with a way out." And then he reminds us that the Lord's table is not a sacrifice to idols but a sharing in the life-giving body and blood of Christ, whose body and blood became the offering on the Cross, through which we have redemption.

In Chapter 11, Paul deals first with the Jewish custom for women to cover their head in worship, but today we would challenge his theory that this illustrates woman's position as being under her husband's authority. But we forgive him because he admits that this is purely a personal opinion (verse 16). However, Paul now returns to heavy criticism, especially in their conduct of worship. Divisions in the prayer meeting? Eating and drinking in their fellowship meals, at which there is inequality, drunkenness and disorder? Eat at home!

No, says Paul, when I passed on to you the institution of the 'supper on the night of his betrayal' I clearly stated (verse 23) that Jesus took bread, gave thanks for it and said, "This is my body which is for you. Do this in memory of me." Verse 25, "In the same way, after the supper, he took the cup and said, 'This cup is God's new covenant, sealed with my blood. Whenever you drink it, do so in memory of me.' Therefore, be extremely careful, examine yourselves before you do this, for if you do not recognise the meaning of this, you may bring judgement on yourselves (verse 29). "If we would examine ourselves first, we would not come under God's judgement" (verse 31).

Now follow a number of practical instructions on how to conduct their services of worship. First in the matter of the practice of the gifts of the Holy Spirit. The first principle is that no one can truly say "Jesus is Lord" except under the guidance of the Holy Spirit. Having established that fact, he discusses how the correct use of the various gifts, of speaking in other languages, of knowledge, of the working of miracles, of faith or the gift of preaching – all of these diverse gifts, when combined, create a single body in which no one can claim precedence. All contribute equally to the corporate identity.

This is followed in turn by the best known of all Paul's statements here. The chapter on love, Chapter 13. Faith, hope and love are all defined but, "The greatest of these is love" (verse 13).

Still discussing the conduct of their meetings for worship and instruction, Paul, in Chapter 14, begins by mentioning the primacy of love, which must inform all their actions and words. Preaching is very important and must take precedence over the more personal gifts, like speaking in inspired language which, unless interpreted, benefits only the one inspired. Encourage and develop the 'gifts of the Holy Spirit' yes, but with an eye to what is most beneficial to those present. Verse 18–19, "I thank God that I speak in strange tongues much more than any of you. But in church worship, I would rather speak five words that can be understood in order to teach others, than speak thousands of words in strange tongues." The distinction here is clear between worship in private and public worship, and between what is personal and what is beneficial to the whole community of believers. That is why he concludes this chapter by emphasising that all must be done in order and for the benefit of all.

Now follows what in some ways is the most important message for us today, the discussion of immortality, first demonstrated by the resurrection of Christ. And so important is this that Paul states, 15:3, "I passed on to you what I received, which is of the greatest importance: that Christ died for our sins, as written in the scriptures; that he was buried and that he was raised to life three days later, as written in the scriptures; that he appeared to Peter and then to all twelve apostles. Then he appeared to more than 500 of his followers at once." Verse 8, "Last of all he appeared to me."

This is the basis of the Gospel, and Paul continues by emphasising just how important it is. Verse 12, "Now, since our message is that Christ has been raised from death, how can some of you say that the dead will not be raised to life?" Verse 14, "And if Christ has not been raised from death, then we have nothing to preach and you have nothing to believe!" Verse 17, "If Christ has not been raised, then your faith is a delusion and you are still lost in your sins." Verse 19, "If our hope in Christ is good for this life only and no more, then we deserve more pity than anyone else in all the world." Verse 20, "But the truth is that Christ has been raised from death, as the guarantee that those who sleep in death will also be raised."

And Paul states the order, Christ first, then at the time of his coming those that belong to him. Then the end will come, and Christ will take authority and rule until all his enemies are destroyed, the last enemy being death itself. Then, when all things are under the control of Christ, he will place himself under the authority of God and God will rule over all.

All right, there are still questions, such as what kind of body will we have, etc.? The answer, a heavenly, immortal body. "What is made of flesh and blood cannot share in God's kingdom" (verse 50). "And what is mortal cannot possess immortality." "For what is mortal must be changed into what is immortal; what can die will be changed into what cannot die" (verse 53). Then the scripture will come true "Death is destroyed, victory is complete" (verse 54). "Death gets its power to hurt from sin, and sin gets its power from the Law. But thanks be to God who gives us the victory through our Lord Jesus Christ" (verse 57).

The final chapter concerns, first, the gift of money to help the church in Jerusalem, then Paul's plans to visit them in Corinth. He will stay where he is in Ephesus until Pentecost because "there is a great opportunity here" in spite of opposition. Timothy, who is travelling independently, is commended to their care, but he is still very young. Then come the usual greetings and mention of his companions who are with him; Stephanus, Fortunatus, Achaicus, Aquila and Priscilla, and then, written with his own hand, the words, "Greetings from Paul… *Marana tha* – Our Lord, come. The grace of the Lord Jesus be with you."

2 Corinthians

It is quite clear that, although this letter was addressed to the fellowship in Corinth, it was intended that it should be passed round the other churches in that area (verse 1). Consequently, what Paul had said in his first letter was not simply a rebuke to that church group; he was making statements about conduct which were applicable to all of the new churches. He appeals to them to be understanding and to assist each other when troubles arise, just as Christ helps us. He also raises an issue which Peter will take up in greater detail, in his letters, namely that through suffering, we can experience the grace and love of Christ, which when shared can encourage others also (verse 6). Paul then goes on to elaborate on the suffering and trouble which he had endured in Asia, in Ephesus for example, to which Paul refers in his first letter 1 Cor 15:32. "But this happened so that we should rely, not on ourselves, but only on God who raises the dead." He then goes on to say why he had written to them so frankly and sincerely, by the grace of God, and his hope is that they will understand and thank God for it.

He then refers to his proposed plans to visit the area, which had apparently been altered. But as he says, the only thing certain is that God in Christ never changes. He is our certainty; our security is in him. His decision not to visit Corinth was because he trusted them, was working with them, not trying to dictate to them. Another visit might have stirred trouble. 2:1, "So I made up my mind not to come to you again to make you sad." And Paul now offers forgiveness to the person who had caused so much trouble by his actions, verse 10, "For when I forgive, I do it in Christ's presence because of you, in order to keep Satan from getting the upper hand of us; for we know what his plans are."

Now follows what appears to be a little self-justification. "Do we need letters from you or to you?" he asks. "No, you yourselves are our recommendation. And what we do, we do in the power of Christ." 2:5, "The capacity we have comes from God." Because the New Covenant is so much greater than the old one

231

which, written in stone, was the harbinger of death. Whereas the New Covenant, given by the Spirit of God, brings life. If the Law, which brings death, was so honoured, how much more honour is attached to the work of the Holy Spirit who works in our hearts to transform us and to bring us immortality? If Moses had to veil his face, the people to whom he gave the Law were also blind as they read the Law. That veil, lack of understanding, is only removed by the Spirit of Christ working in us.

Continuing the theme of human frailty, he says that we have this treasure in earthen pots, so that the glory might be seen, not in the vessel itself but in the glory which is contained in it. "In order to show that the supreme power belongs to God and not to us" (4:7). Even though our physical being may decay, our spiritual being is renewed daily (verse 16). For we know that when this mortal body perishes, we shall have a spiritual body. Chapter 5, when the house of clay dissolves, we shall have a heavenly house resplendent in glory. Therefore, Paul says, "We are full of courage and would much prefer to leave our home in the body and be at home with the Lord" (verse 8). Further, because we are now the friends of God, we have no fear in his presence. "Christ was without sin, but for our sake, God made him share our sin, in order that in union with him, we might share the righteousness of God" (verse 21).

Chapter 6, "In our work together with God then, we beg you who have received God's grace not to let it be wasted." Returning to his personal suffering for their sake, he says, "Dear friends in Corinth! It is not we who have closed our hearts to you; it is you who have closed your hearts to us." He pleads with them for reconciliation in Christ's name. Then, in a more serious warning, he urges them not to be unequally yoked with unbelievers, for it cannot be done (verse 14).

Chapter 7 returns to his concern that there might be some estrangement, "Make room for us in your hearts. We have wronged no one; we have ruined no one, nor tried to take advantage of anyone." "For even if that letter of mine made you sad, I am not sorry I wrote it… because your sadness made you change your ways" (verse 9). "I wrote it to make plain to you, in God's sight, how deep your devotion to us really is. That is why we were encouraged" (verse 13). Their help to Titus being an example of their true feelings.

Chapter 8 continues his appeal for help for the churches in Judea, citing the blessings which followed those in Macedonia, who in spite of their poverty had helped. "They begged and pleaded for the privilege of having a part in helping

God's people in Judea. (verse 4)" "You know the grace of our Lord Jesus Christ; rich as he was, he made himself poor for your sake, in order to make you rich by his poverty" (verse 9). We are then told that Titus will be visiting them, together with an unnamed brother, in order to receive their gift for the churches. Paul praises the work being done by Titus, "They represent the churches and bring glory to Christ."

And in Chapter 9, he thanks the Corinthians in advance for the response which he is assured they will make. But he says that he will be following after them, in time to receive the gift, which Paul says is an outpouring of their gratitude to God, as he prays that the churches in Judea will receive the gifts in the spirit in which they were sent, without feeling humiliated by them.

The letter then ends with Paul defending his ministry among them, Chapter 10, but in humility he claims that his authority is from God, and that if he is seen to boast, it is only his pride in what God has done. Chapter 11 begins, "I wish you would tolerate me, even when I am a bit foolish." But you are to me like a pure virgin promised in marriage to Christ. I am concerned that you will be chaste and pure when he comes to claim you, not like Eve who was deceived by the serpent.

He then, at some length, defends his apostleship, even if, as some say, his appearance and his speaking are inferior to the false apostles.

Galatians

This letter is extremely important and needs to be considered very carefully because it explains the reasons why Paul preached as he did. It explains why he was so persecuted by the Jews, and it picks up on ideas formulated first elsewhere, as in his letter to the Romans, and it answers many questions about the life of our Lord which are not dealt with anywhere else. Further, it helps us to understand how and why there was so much division in the early teaching of the Church, between the three leaders in Jerusalem and Paul, and which is reflected here and elsewhere, especially as we read in The Acts of the Apostles.

This letter was written because the churches in Galatia were being misled. Other teachers were insisting that the new Gentile converts should be circumcised, that is, become obedient to the Law. Paul insists that this completely undermines the whole essence of the work of Christ. First, we need to see why this view that non-Jewish converts should be circumcised became an issue.

During his life on earth, our Lord, born a Jew, lived as a Jew. He was circumcised and kept the Festivals, worshipped in the Synagogue and would have been seen in his early life simply as a devout Jewish person. His conflict with the religious leaders of his day was not with the Law. It was their interpretation of the Law of Moses which was at fault. Their insistence was on a strict observance, which actually frustrated its purpose, such as their refusal to sanction the healing of a sick person on the Sabbath, even though they would rescue a trapped animal. Their insistence that by claiming to fulfil one part of the Law, they could avoid something else, as in saying that if a gift was dedicated to God, the giver could evade responsibility to parents (Mark 7:11). "They teach human rules as though they were my rules" (Matt 15:9 Mark 7:7,13.). But of far greater importance was that they had added to the Law their traditions, until Jesus was driven to comment, "You have made the word of God nonsense by your traditions." The reason, as Paul comments in his letter to the Romans, is that our

Lord's intention was to illustrate the weakness of the Law, but yet in his life and death to fulfil the Covenant of the Law and thereby replace the Law with a New Covenant based on God's original Covenant, 430 years earlier, the Covenant which he made with Abraham, which was by Faith. As in Paul's illustration of the two sons, Ishmael, who was born naturally and Isaac, born supernaturally by faith, but only Isaac became one of God's chosen.

Now, the early disciples, as recorded in Acts, kept the Jewish Law. They worshipped in the Temple at the hour of prayer, simply because they were following the example of Jesus prior to his death. What Paul realised, and he was a very strict Jew, a Pharisee, was that the death of Jesus on the Cross had freed believers from the Law, enabling the introduction of a New Covenant. And this was the underlying fact behind the Last Supper, his body and blood 'given for them' which granted forgiveness by a person's belief in who Jesus was and what his death meant; something which required what Abraham had had all those years ago, namely Faith.

In his opening words, Paul expresses his surprise that the new converts should so easily be deflected from the truth. He then reasserts, verse 11, the source of his authority. Explaining that he was a Jewish Jew, devoted to the Jewish religion to the extent that he persecuted the 'followers of the Way', he then outlines his conversion and how his knowledge of the facts of the Gospel were not learnt from others but directly inspired by the Holy Spirit (verse 15). We then hear of his first visit to Jerusalem, meeting only Peter and James very briefly.

It was only fourteen years later, Chapter 2, that he returned to the church in Jerusalem, with Barnabas and Titus, to explain to them his teaching to the Gentiles and try to obtain their approval of his message to the Gentiles, on the basis of what God had done in giving the Holy Spirit to the Gentiles as confirmation of their belief in Jesus, just as Peter had found with Cornelius. And verse 8, the leaders, James, Peter and John agreed that whilst Peter was called to preach to Jews, Paul was called to take the message to Gentiles. However, Paul does accuse Peter of being inconsistent during his visit to Antioch, living like a Gentile while there, until James arrived (verse 11–14). "You are a Jew living like a Gentile, not like a Jew. How then can you try to force Gentiles to live like Jews?"

However, what was established through all this was a certain fact, verse 16, "Yet we know that a person is put right with God only through faith in Jesus

Christ, never by doing what the Law requires." Paul then enlarges on this in verse 19, "So far as the Law is concerned, I am dead – killed by the Law itself – in order that I might live for God. I have been put to death with Christ on his cross." Verse 20, "So it is no longer I who live, but it is Christ who lives in me. This life that I live now, I live by faith in the Son of God who loved me and gave his life for me."

Chapter 3, "You foolish Galatians, who put a spell on you?" Paul then continues by reminding them that the true descendants of Abraham are those who (Isaac) live by faith. Verse 11–12, "Only the person who is put right with God through faith shall live. But the Law had nothing to do with faith." However, to keep the Law, one had to keep all of the Law. To break one part was to fall foul of the Law. As Paul had previously stated in Romans 8. "What the Law could not do because human nature was weak, God did. He condemned sin in human nature by sending his own Son, who came with a nature like sinful human nature to do away with sin." Therefore, in God's plan, the main purpose of the Law was to show what sin was (verse 19). This does not negate the law, but before faith came, humanity was trapped, until Faith should be revealed (verse 23). Further, by doing this, Jesus opened the way for non-Jews also to believe. They also could become God's sons through the Faith which Abraham had long ago, nearly 500 years, before the Law was given under Moses.

Now in Chapter 4, Paul directs his comments to the Galatian people. Explaining that, when the right time came, God sent his own Son. "He came as the son of a human mother and lived under the Jewish Law, to redeem those who were under the Law so that we might become God's sons and daughters" (verse 4). However, the Gentiles in the past were slaves of gods because you did not know God (verse 8). How then is it that knowing God, or rather being known by God, do you want to return to become subject to the evil forces of your past? Effectively, these strange preachers are wanting you to turn your backs on the glorious freedom of the children of God and become subject to a Law which has so horrendously failed. It is at this point that Paul introduces his illustration of Abraham's two sons, Ishmael, born naturally and Isaac, born supernaturally by faith. Read what happened to them! (See verse 29).

In Chapter 5, Paul then urges the Galatians, having been set free by Jesus Christ, to preserve their freedom. For if they return to the Law via circumcision then Christ is no longer of use to them, indeed were that possible, the death of Christ would be in vain. They would be bound to obey the whole Law, being outside of the grace of God and his redeeming forgiveness. Further, they would no longer be joint heirs with Christ of the future glorious kingdom of God, reserved, as Paul says, in heaven for us. Further, verse 19, what human nature does is plainly seen in the conduct of those who are outside the Christian faith. It reveals itself in immorality, and the worship of idols. A reminder that as believers, the Spirit of God must control our lives (verse 25).

The final part of this letter, Chapter 6, encourages them to "bear one another's burdens and so fulfil the law of Christ." Don't be fooled, we reap what we sow (verse 7). So then do not tire of good works because the time will come when we will "reap the harvest." In conclusion, he warns of the motives of those who want to bring them under Jewish Law; it is only so that they will be able to boast of what they have achieved and enhance their own authority. We must also remember that almost all of Paul's problems, during his time of Christian ministry, came from those very people – people who were annoyed and angry at what they believed undermined the fundamental idea of scriptural Law, rejecting what had been proclaimed by the prophets. Like their forebears, they could not see from the scriptures, what was in fact the revelation of the work of the coming Messiah, in which God's plan was to redeem and transform the whole of the human race. Like the Pharisees, they saw only someone who challenged their status and undermined their interpretation of the Law – as can so easily happen today.

Ephesians

This letter of Paul to the Church at Ephesus introduces some quite remarkable new ideas. He is clearly writing to believers, whom he regards as quite mature. There are no rebukes here, just thanksgiving for their faith, and his exploration of fundamental issues all centre on the idea of unity. This must have been a predominantly Gentiles Church because Paul's main focus is on the fact that in Christ, there is no Jew or Gentile, no Hebrew or Greek. God's ultimate plan, which he had determined from before he created the world, was not just to deliver the Jewish people, but to use them as a stage in the further development of offering union with himself to all, through the salvation which became possible through the sacrifice of his Son, Christ Jesus.

In other words, we have confirmation that God's plan, originally declared in Genesis, was in two parts. First by using the faith of Abraham to create a unique people governed by Law, who would be a means of demonstrating to the rest of humanity, the power, the love, the generosity of God. But also, to serve as a warning of what failure would involve. And also, through the Jews, to bring his offer to all humanity. However, the known weakness lay in the inability of human nature to obey fully the demands of the Law, as Paul quotes in Romans 8:3, "For what the Law could not do because human nature was weak, God did." The answer was Jesus, a Jew, who became human, as we see in Galatians, and became the fulfilment of the Law.

In other words, God knew from the beginning what would happen, 1:4, "Even before the world was made, God had already chosen us to be his through our union with Christ." Which meant, for the Gentiles, that God had already planned to include them, as so many prophets had foretold. This 'secret plan', spoken of by the prophets, was made known through Christ but appears to be far greater than Paul envisaged, verse 10 "This plan, which God will accomplish when the time is right, is to bring all creation together, everything in heaven and on earth, with Christ as head."

To the Apostle, as to the most learned of his day, the heavens were limited – the earth being the centre of the solar system, with the sun, moon and the planets revolving round it. We say how naïve, but it is only now, with the benefit of science, that we have any idea just how vast the whole thing is, vast beyond anything one could imagine. So for the Christian, the question will be, what does "everything in heaven and on earth" mean? All we can say is that, according to scripture, everything is under God the creator's control. Creation itself was created at God's command and for a purpose, and that purpose includes us!!! Wow!

Paul now enlarges on his first premise, verse 11, "All things are done according to God's plan and decision; and God chose us to be his own people in union with Christ because of his own purpose, based on what he had decided from the very beginning." Gentiles, you were included from day one! Verse 13, "And you also became God's people when you heard the true message, the good news that brought you salvation." (Please tell that to the Galatians.)

Therefore, Paul rejoices over their faith, verse 15, and prays that God will bless them with wisdom and understanding. And speaking of the glory of God, of his rich blessings, he speaks of the power which raised Christ from death, working in them, but he goes on to talk of the authority given by God to Jesus, "in this world and the next" (verse 21), when Christ, who is the head of the Church, which is his body, will become supreme ruler under God.

The next chapter, 2, develops two themes. First that although we were spiritually dead in sin through disobedience, the mercy of God is so great that through salvation God has raised us up to rule with Christ in "the heavenly world." Not through our own efforts – therefore, nothing to boast about – but only through our union with Christ. Then the second theme, that you, Gentiles, who previously had nothing, who had no part in God's covenant, and were without hope, have now been brought together by the blood of Christ. By doing away with the Law, replacing it by the sacrifice, on our behalf, of Jesus Christ, thus, uniting the whole world, now the Gentiles are no longer strangers but "fellow citizens with God's people and members of the family of God" (verse 19).

Which leads Paul, Chapter 3, to speak of his specific commission, which was to bring God's message to the Gentiles also. And for this reason, he was being persecuted and suffering at the hands of the Jews, who hated him for it. But once again, he enlarges on the issue of the Church being the combined body of Christ and God's purpose through the Church, which is, "In order that, at the present time, by means of the Church, the angelic rulers and powers of the heavenly world might learn of his wisdom in all its different forms" (verse 10). Because this is so important, Paul begs God, through the power of his Spirit, to enable the believers, the Church, to know and understand, verse 18, "how broad and long, how high and deep, is Christ's love."

On to Chapter 4 where Paul speaks of the fact that in unity, the body must measure up to the standard set by God. Each person having received from Jesus at his ascension, specific gifts, "When he went up to the heights... he gave gifts to people." Some to be Pastors, or teachers and evangelists, in order to prepare all for their Christian service, which is to proclaim the Gospel and to build up the Church to maturity in love, to the fullness of Christ. He then goes on to state what the new life in Christ should mean in practical terms of daily living. "And do not make God's Holy Spirit sad; for the Spirit is God's mark of ownership on you, a guarantee that the Day will come when God will set you free." (See Romans 8).

Chapter 5 gives further meaning to what the phrase 'living in the light' means to us, including verse 16, "Make good use of every opportunity you have because these are evil days. Don't be fools then, but try to find out what the Lord wants you to do." And a repeat of his previous instructions on the behaviour of wives to husbands, and conversely of husbands to their wives, because marriage is a symbolic picture of the relationship of Christ to his Church. Verse 32, "There is a deep secret truth revealed in the scripture, which I understand as applying to Christ and his Church. But it also applies to you."

Chapter 6 speaks of the Christian relationship between children and their parents, reminding us that "respect your father and mother" is the first commandment which has a promise added. Parents discipline your children in love. Slaves obey your master in Christ. Masters treat your servants with respect, knowing that they belong to the one master in heaven whose judgement is upon all.

Paul ends his letter with a moving description of the elements of our faith, illustrated by the armour of the soldier who was guarding him. The sword of the Spirit is the word of God, our shield is our faith, our salvation is as a helmet, truth as a belt. Put on, therefore, the whole Armour of God so that when the enemy attacks, you will be able to overcome. And finally as usual, the greetings, and the news that he is sending Tychicus to them and that he will update them with all the latest news.

Philippians

On their first visit here, Paul together with Timothy, who had joined them at Lystra, found there was no synagogue, so they went to the riverside where a group of Jews were in the habit of meeting for prayer, and there they would meet Lydia, a businesswoman who was from Thyatira.

Once again, this letter opens on a note of thanksgiving and hope, thankful for their faith and their relationship of love towards him, as evidenced from their help from the first time he met them. Again, there is this emphasis on 'union', their union with Christ which in turn put them in fellowship with him and with all believers, and verse 9, "I pray that your love will keep on growing more and more, together with true knowledge and perfect judgement." This, because Paul was only too aware of the false teachers, who were trying to drag the believers back into the prison of reliance on the human ordinances of the Law and not enjoy the freedom which Faith offers, a faith which brings with it, responsibility.

In verse 12, Paul enlarges on the fact that his sufferings had actually furthered the Gospel, to the extent that he was able to bear witness to the power of God here in Rome, and his victorious life was actually an encouragement to other believers (verse 12–13). Then he just touches on the problem. Yes, believers were encouraged to preach the Gospel, even though some might be acting from selfish motives (verse 15). The power of God is such that when Christ is preached, God's Holy Spirit can make the word live. And he believes that he will ultimately be set free. However, he says, "For me to live is Christ," therefore, whether I live or die it is all to the glory of God. So much so that I am actually torn between wishing to die, which is to be with the Lord, or continuing to serve, which be beneficial to you. For your sakes, I believe that I shall live to continue and you will have even more reason to be proud of my service for you. However, what is most important is that whether we live or die, our lives should be in union with the life of Christ. Don't give up; don't be afraid, of suffering or of death.

To serve God is a privilege and by your faith you demonstrate to all, the power of God. You will then share with me in the battle which you have seen I fight.

In Chapter 2, Paul commends to them the utter humility of Christ. Don't do anything from pride or selfish ambition (verse 3). Remember Jesus who, though he was rich, yet for our sakes he became poor so that through his poverty we might be made rich. "Of his own free will, he gave up all he had, and took the nature of a servant... He was humble and walked the path of obedience all the way to death – his death on the cross" (verse 6–8). He took upon himself the form of human flesh. But for this reason, God has raised him to the highest place, given him a name above all other names and honoured him so that, in turn, all glory might be to God, in heaven and on earth (verse 9–11). Follow the life of Jesus! Now, it is more important, whilst I am absent from you, for you to work, with fear and trembling, to complete your salvation (verse 12).

Paul then refers to his desire to send Timothy to them. Interestingly, he says that of all his companions, Timothy has great love for them, a love which had been demonstrated when he and Paul were last with them. Paul admits that many of the 'preachers' were activated by selfish motives not by the true love of God. Timothy was anxious to also act as a communicator, bringing to them the latest news of Paul, and in return giving Paul an update on their progress. Epaphroditus was also planning to visit them, not least because they had heard of his illness, indeed he had risked his life for the furtherance of the Gospel.

Paul then concludes his letter with a warning against those who required them to be circumcised (3:2). These external ceremonies denied the essential value of faith. He then admits to personal details of his previous actions whilst a Pharisee, stating that as far as the Jewish faith was concerned, he, Paul, exceeded all of them in his zeal. But all to no effect once he encountered Christ and found freedom through faith in the power of God in Christ. As he says, verse 8, "I reckon everything as complete loss, for the sake of what is more valuable, the knowledge of Christ Jesus my Lord. For his sake I have thrown everything away." And verse 9, "I no longer have a righteousness of my own, the kind that is gained by obeying the Law. I now have the righteousness that is given through faith in Christ." And verse 10, "All I want is to know Christ and to experience the power of his resurrection, to share in his sufferings and become like him in his death." Paul then uses the symbolic image of an athlete who, to secure the prize, is prepared to go to extraordinary effort. That I may win Christ who will "change our weak mortal bodies and make them like his own glorious body" (verse 21) when he comes.

Then, Chapter 4, the personal notes to two sisters Euodia and Syntyche to stop their arguments. Help them, for their ministry is useful in enlarging the Gospel. In all things, remember that the Lord is coming soon (verse 5). And then Paul thanks the church for their gift, which meant so much to him. He reminds them of their past generosity when he first visited them, bringing the good news. He states that his needs are simple; he is used to hardship, but now, since Epaphroditus has brought him their gift, he is well supplied. He is also certain that as they give to other servants of God, God will supply all their need also (verse 19).

Paul ends with, "Greetings to all believers from all of us here, especially those who are in the Emperor's palace."

Colossians

This letter is different from most of the others, in that Paul had not personally established this church, but yet he still felt a personal concern for them as part of the church of believers, and because they were also being troubled by visiting 'preachers' who were undermining their faith, by insisting on the practice of circumcision and other external practices of Jewish Law. These 'false preachers' also were in danger of bringing the church under the influence of other 'evil spiritual powers', rather than the power of the Holy Spirit. This was a warning to all, as Paul elsewhere comments, "For we wrestle not against flesh and blood but against spiritual forces and powers, the rulers, authorities, and cosmic powers of this dark age" (Ephesians 6:12). All of these letters share in common Paul's faith, his love and his confidence in the power of the risen Christ to overcome all obstacles, as we live 'in union' with Christ. For this reason, in most cases, as he does here, he begins by celebrating the faith of the believers, of which he had heard. "We always give thanks to God, the father of our Lord Jesus Christ, when we pray for you, for we have heard of your faith in Christ Jesus."

Paul's real reason for writing, however, was to challenge the evil influences of these troublesome people who were undermining their faith, and he does this in two ways. First he commends the believers' knowledge of the power of that truth, verse 6, "… just as it has among you ever since the day you heard about the grace of God and came to know it as it really is."

But then Paul, immediately, verse 15–20, declares emphatically and in no uncertain terms, what the truth about Christ really is, "Christ is the visible likeness of the invisible God… For through him God created everything… God created the whole universe through him and for him… Christ existed before all things… He is the firstborn Son… For it was by God's own decision that the Son has in himself the full nature of God. Through the Son, then God decided to bring the whole universe back to himself. God made peace through his Son's blood, and so brought back to himself all things, both on earth and in heaven."

No room for any other powers, for they must either be subject to God through Christ, or at odds with God and, therefore, his enemies!

Paul then replaces the negative by some very positive statements. First, again, he states his mission, verse 24, "By means of my physical sufferings, I am helping to complete what still remains of Christ's sufferings on behalf of his church." "It is the task of fully proclaiming his message" (verse 25). "God's plan is to make known his secret to his people, this rich and glorious secret which he has for all peoples. And the secret is that Christ is in you, which means that you will share in the glory of God" (verse 27). And to this end, we preach Christ... in order to bring each one into God's presence, as a mature individual."

Now in Chapter 2, Paul speaks of his hard work in the Gospel, both for those who have heard him personally and for others, like them, whom he has never met. And at that point, he issues a specific warning, verse 4, "Do not let anyone deceive you with false arguments." And then, verse 8 "See to it, then, that no one enslaves you by means of the worthless deceit of human wisdom, which comes from the teachings handed down by human beings and from the ruling spirits of the universe, and not from Christ." Verse 11, "You were circumcised, not with the circumcision that is made by human beings but by the circumcision made by Christ, which consists of being freed from the power of the sinful self." And again, verse 20, "You have died with Christ and are set free from the ruling spirits of the universe. Why then do you live as though you belonged to this world?" By obeying all these human regulations. In fact, "Such rules appear to be based on human wisdom in their forced worship of angels and false humility and severe treatment of the body, but they have no real value in controlling physical passions" (verse 23).

Then in Chapter 3, Paul adds to this the fact that we are dead to sin in Christ but raised to new life in him. Therefore, he says, live the life of Christ. Put aside all earthly passions and unworthy ambition. You are united with Christ, Jews and Gentiles, so, therefore, seek to show his love and his power. Teach one another; sing psalms, hymns and sacred songs with thanksgiving. And yet again, we have instruction for wives, husbands, children, parents, servants, masters, to behave as Christ would.

And finally, in Chapter 4, he gives instructions to pray and give thanks to God, to act correctly towards each member of the fellowship. As he then commends to them Tychicus who will bring them all the news together with Onesimus, the former slave, who is a faithful and dear brother. Paul sends greetings from Aristarchus, who is in prison with him, together with Mark, cousin to Barnabas, Joshua and Epaphras. Significantly, Luke and Demas send their greetings, so the doctor was still with Paul. It ends with the request that the letter be shared with others in Laodicea, who will share his letter to them in return, and he asks them to tell Archippus to finish his task in the Gospel. "With my own hand I write this: greetings from Paul. Do not forget my chains. May God's grace be with you."

1 Thessalonians

Once again Paul begins his letter to them by thanking God for their faith, and for the very practical examples of their faith in their attitude towards him and his companions, which all proved that his ministry had not been a result of human wisdom but a demonstration of the power of God. In fact, so great was the effect that the news of their conversion had spread not only locally in Macedonia and Achaia but, verse 8, "The news about your faith in God has gone everywhere." No doubt it was this success which stirred up some Jews to attack Paul out of jealousy. Whilst there, Paul and his companions had been badly attacked by these Jews who opposed his teaching, and they had had to leave in a hurry. However, the fact that the fellowship still existed was a tribute to the success of his ministry, 2:1, "You yourselves know that our visit to you was not a failure. You know how we had already been ill-treated and insulted in Philippi before we came to you... And even though there was much opposition, our God gave us courage to tell you the Good News."

But there was another reason for Paul to be glad, verse 13, "When we brought you God's message, you heard it and accepted it, not as a message from human beings but as God's message." And in fact, he continues, "What happened to you was exactly what happened in Judea. You suffered the same persecutions from your own people that they suffered from the Jews, who killed the Lord Jesus and the prophets" (verse 12). Paul now expresses a desire to visit them again, having failed on a previous occasion when, whilst staying in Athens, he had commissioned his companion Timothy to visit and encourage them (Chapter 3). Now Timothy had returned and Paul was much encouraged by their news.

Paul then adds much advice regarding personal holiness in Chapter 4, before coming to what appears to be the main reason for writing to them at this time. There was much confusion about what would happen when our Lord returns. Would those who had died before his return be able to take part in the glorious advent? To which Paul simply states that just as we believe that Jesus died and rose again, so when he comes, those are dead in him will also rise with him (verse 14). So that those who are alive at his coming will not precede those who have died, but all together will meet the Lord in the air. "And so, we will always be with the Lord" (verse 17).

In the light of this, in Chapter 5, he says, that because we know that the Lord will come suddenly, unannounced, and "like a thief at night" (verse 2), we must always live in a state of readiness, "awake and sober."

He then ends his brief letter with instructions, "Pay proper respect to those who work with you… Pray at all times, be thankful in all circumstances… Do not restrain the Holy Spirit, but put all things to the test," as he had instructed the Corinthian church in much greater detail.

Finally, as always, he ends with his greetings, verse 23, "May the God who gives us peace make you holy in every way," "Pray also for us," and verse 27, "I urge you by the authority of the Lord to read this letter to all believers. The grace of our Lord Jesus Christ be with you."

2 Thessalonians

This second letter to the church in Thessalonica was occasioned by the fact that Paul had heard news that there was still confused teaching about the coming of Christ. Remember that the early church had believed that our Lord's return was imminent. The letter is written on behalf of the three fellow workers, Paul, Silas and Timothy.

As usual, Paul begins by praising their continued and developing Christian faith, "Our brothers and sisters, we must thank God at all times for you. It is right for us to do so because your faith is growing so much." "We boast about the way you continue to endure and believe through all the persecutions and sufferings that you are experiencing" (verse 4). He also encourages them by saying that when Christ comes he will judge those who are now persecuting them and reminds them, verse 10, that when our Lord comes to receive honour and glory from those who believe, they, the believers, will be among them.

However, in Chapter 2, he now comes to the point at issue, his real reason for writing. This time, it is the report that some people are teaching that Christ has already returned! At great length, Paul explains that before Christ comes many things will have to happen. Rebellion, the appearance of the Wicked One who will oppose God and the believers and set himself up in The Holy Place, God's Temple, and claim to be God. This is now being prevented by something or someone. Apparently, Paul believes that they know who he is talking about, but he dare not mention it publicly, verse 7, "The 'Mysterious Wickedness' is already at work, but what is going to happen will not happen until the one who holds it back is taken out of the way. Then the Wicked One will be revealed. But when the Lord Jesus comes, he will kill him with the breath from his mouth and destroy him with his dazzling presence."

This wicked one will come with all the power of Satan and perform false miracles and wonders and use wicked deceit on those who will perish (verse 9).

And his role will be to test those who say they believe, but are not genuine in their faith (verse 11).

Here again, Paul comforts these believers in that, because their faith is genuine, they will be saved from wrath at the coming of our Lord. "So stand firm" (verse 13).

In Chapter 3, Paul asks for their continued prayers that the Lord's message may spread and be received, just as they, having believed are continuing in the faith. He then concludes by adjuring the believers to avoid lazy and ignorant people who are not following the way of faith. He reminds them, that he did not look to them for financial support whilst he was with them, but he has heard that some amongst their number are lazy and gossipers, whose meddling is dangerous, but you… "must not get tired of doing good."

And then he ends with a cheerful greeting and his own signature.

1 Timothy

The interest in this letter lies as much in the person addressed as what the letter itself is saying. Timothy, a young man from Lystra/Derbe, was of mixed race. On the maternal side, he was a Jew, but on this father's side, Greek. And he was educated in the Jewish tradition, that is in the Jewish scriptures. He joins Paul and Silas on their missionary journeys, clearly learning of this new Way that Paul was expounding, as we see from The Acts of the Apostles, and later, he also travels for Paul as an ambassador. He stayed in Beria with Silas, when Paul, persecuted by Jews from Thessalonica, was sent off to Athens, later travelling to Athens to join Paul (Acts 16 and 17). In 1 Corinthians 16:10, we find that Paul, in Ephesus, writing to the Corinthian Church, tells them to expect Timothy to visit them on his way back to him. And in his second letter to Corinth, Paul sends greetings from Timothy, referring to him as a brother and reminds them that the message had been preached to them by himself, together with Silas and Timothy (2 Cor 1:19). And in Phil 2:19, he says that he hopes to send Timothy to them. In 1 Thess 3:1, whilst in Athens, Paul sends Timothy to the Church in Thessalonica; and in Hebrews 13:23, Paul comments that Timothy had been 'let out of prison'. Where we are not sure, but Paul wants him to continue to travel with him. It is clear that for some time, Timothy was left in charge of the Church in Ephesus, where Paul was now persona non grata, following the riots created in the community by the silversmiths.

So the letter begins, "I want you to stay in Ephesus," because there were false teachers in the church there, introducing legends and lists of their ancestors, all of which, like circumcision, were distractions from the life of faith. Timothy was well suited to challenge these teachers who were so confident but ignorant (verse 7). Yes, the Law had had a purpose but it was now superseded by the New Covenant based on faith, not on the keeping of the Law. Paul was only too well aware of this danger, having been a strict Pharisee before he learnt the truth from

Jesus through the Holy Spirit. And Timothy is urged here, as later, to use the scriptures to provide evidence for this gospel.

Chapters 2 and 3 then deal with matters of conduct in worship and the role of leaders. Paul expresses the hope that he will be able to visit them, but failing that, Timothy should follow the advice given in this letter, 3:14. In Chapter 4, Timothy is reminded that the scripture says that some people will abandon their faith in later times (verse 1), and that totally unnecessary and useless ideas will be introduced. This is followed by some very personal advice to Timothy on spiritual and physical health. Verse 13–14, "Until I come, give your time to the public reading of the scriptures and to preaching and teaching. But do not neglect the spiritual gift given you by the laying on of hands." Verse 15, "Practice these things and devote yourself to them, in order that your progress may be seen by all."

Chapter 5 deals with the best way to maintain respect and discipline, remembering that Timothy was a very young man, teaching older men. Here are rules with regard to the care of widows, rewards for service and, because Timothy was inclined to sickness, "Do not drink water only, but take a little wine to help your digestion, since you are ill so often" (verse 23).

The letter ends, Chapter 6, with further warnings about false doctrine and some personal instruction about his own spiritual life in the light of the expected return of our Lord (verse 14). And "Avoid the profane talk and foolish arguments of what some people wrongly call 'Knowledge'".

2 Timothy

This second letter to Timothy is full of personal advice, presumably because Paul cannot see himself being able to revisit Ephesus. Having a great regard for the man he affectionately calls 'his dear son' and knowing both how young he is and how quite problematic the church there in Ephesus could be, he wants to reassure Timothy. As a result, Paul both compliments the young man and gives him some further spiritual counsel, as one older and more experienced to one placed in a highly responsible position. However, we can also detect a sense of his own declining years.

His opening greeting is both a personal testimony to his own faith, verse 3, "I give thanks to God whom I serve with a clear conscience, as my ancestors did," which echoes Timothy's own background, verse 5, and is an encouragement for him to persevere in the faith, verse 8, and not to be ashamed of his, Paul's, imprisonment.

Immediately, he then plunges into a doctrinal justification of suffering, and the fact that our position in Christ is a result of the suffering of our Lord, through whom God has revealed the miracle of his grace, which had been decided before time began, but had now been revealed to us through His Son Jesus Christ, whose coming has ended the power of death and brought immortality to God's creation; for which purpose he has chosen Paul, as an apostle and teacher, which is the cause of his present suffering. But Paul states, verse 12, he is totally confident in his faith. And now tells Timothy also, verse 14, "Through the power of the Holy Spirit, who lives in us, keep the good things that have been entrusted to you."

For the first time here, in this very personal epistle, Paul does express some sense of isolation in verse 15, "You know that everyone in in the province of Asia has deserted me." And he compliments the actions of Onesiphorus, who so diligently sought him out in prison.

He then entreats Timothy to be prepared to suffer but also, so important now that Paul is coming to the end of his public ministry, 2:2, "Take the teachings that you have heard me proclaim in the presence of many witnesses and entrust them to reliable people who will be able to teach others also." "Think about what I am saying because the Lord will enable you to understand it all" (verse 7). And "because I preach the Good News, I suffer and am even chained like a criminal. But the word of God is not in chains, and so I endure everything for the sake of God's chosen people."

Remind your people of this. "Do your best to win full approval in God's sight as a worker who is not ashamed of his work, one who correctly teaches the message of God's truth" (verse 15).

And he repeats his warning of false teachers, who will reap their own reward from God. But "The solid foundation which God has laid, cannot be shaken". As again Timothy is cautioned to "keep away from foolish and ignorant arguments."

In Chapter 3, Paul returns to the importance of the Second Coming of Christ, warning that in the 'last days', people's behaviour will deteriorate. And in a very powerful accusation, verse 4, "They will be treacherous, reckless and swollen with pride; they will love pleasure rather than God; they will hold to the outward form of our religion but reject its real power."

Then Paul returns to the fact that he, Timothy, has been a witness, of his, Paul's, teaching and of the troubles which arose from false teachers, reminding him that he, Timothy, has known the Holy Scriptures from his childhood and, verse 16, that, "All Scripture is inspired by God and is useful for teaching the truth, rebuking error, correcting faults and giving instruction for right living."

And so finally, in Chapter 4, he solemnly charges his 'dear son', "in the presence of God and of Christ Jesus... to preach the message, to insist upon proclaiming it (whether the time is right or not), to convince, reproach and encourage" (verse 2) "For the time will come when people will not listen to sound doctrine but will follow their own desires and will collect for themselves more and more teachers who will tell them what they are itching to hear" (verse 3).

Now the note of sadness can be seen in Paul's parting words to his 'dear son', verse 6, "As for me, the hour has come for me to be sacrificed; the time is here for me to leave this life. I have done my best in the race, I have run the full distance, and I have kept the faith. And now there is waiting for me the victory prize of being put right with God, which the Lord, the righteous Judge will give me on that day – and not only to me." "Do your best to come to me soon." Verse 11–13, "Only Luke is with me. Get Mark and bring him with you because he can help me in the work. I sent Tychicus to Ephesus. When you come, bring my coat that I left in Troas (winter is setting in) with Carpus; bring the books too, especially the ones made of parchment."

Then the greetings, to Priscilla and Aquila and to the family of Onesiphorus. Erastus was in Corinth, Trophimus in Miletus. "Do your best to come before winter." Greetings from those who were with Paul – Eubulus, Pudens, Linus and Claudia. "The Lord be with your spirit. God's grace be with you all."

Titus

This very short letter was written to Titus who had been left in charge of the work in Crete. He too was a young man, a Gentile convert so, therefore, appropriate for the oversight of the probably Greek-speaking church there.

The real significance of this letter is that here we have Paul, an elderly but very experienced apostle of Jesus Christ, passing on from his own experience and from scripture, just what was required in a church leader. More especially so as the inhabitants of Crete had a somewhat bad reputation.

Beginning with an introduction, which would, no doubt, be read by the Church, Paul establishes himself as an apostle, chosen by Christ with the specific task of establishing and confirming in faith those who have recently become believers. And he reminds Titus that this is no new message, but one which was foretold in scripture, verse 2, "God, who does not lie, promised us this life before the beginning of time, and at the right time, he revealed it in his message." So there can be no doubt, it was God-given.

Now he confirms the authority given to Titus, "I left you in Crete so that you could put in order things that still needed doing and appoint church elders in every town" (verse 5). And he then goes on to describe the nature and character of men who would become leaders, men of high standing and good reputation who would set an example to the other believers. But this comes with a serious warning, again, about those Jewish converts who were causing unnecessary trouble by insisting on keeping to the old Jewish traditions and doing so for profit (verse 10). "Rebuke them," says Paul, because they will undermine the true faith. Verse 16, "They claim that they know God, but their actions deny it."

Then to the positives, Chapter 2, "But you must teach what agrees with sound doctrine." And that, for Paul, inevitably included right behaviour towards each other. Here, again, he emphasises the right human relationships in family and in society. Because "We wait for the blessed day we hope for, when the glory of our great God and Saviour, Jesus Christ, will appear" (verse 13) – which was, for all believers, the true test.

Finally, in the last chapter, Paul once again lays emphasis on the need to alter their social behaviour to conform with the life and teachings of Jesus. Bearing always in mind that our salvation does not come from what we do but is the result of the mercy and grace of Jesus Christ, given to us through the Holy Spirit who gives us new life. "I want you to give special emphasis to these matters, so that those who believe in God may be concerned with giving their time to doing good deeds, which are good and useful for everyone." And he repeats what he said to Timothy, "Avoid stupid arguments," about the Law, etc.

Paul's final instructions are that Titus should visit him in Nicopolis when he is relieved by Artemis or Tychicus, because he intended to winter there. "Help Zenas the lawyer and Apollos to start on their journey," give them anything which they need. And here a little dig about living useful lives. Then, greetings from all of us to all of you. "God's grace be with you all." Simple but direct and to the point.

Philemon

This letter is unusual for Paul because it is a personal appeal to a well-to-do believer in Colossae. Apparently, one of his slaves had run away and had actually travelled so far that he reached Rome, where he had sought out Paul who was in prison and had been a great help and blessing to him, as well as becoming a believer – which tells us quite a lot about this slave, named Onesimus. Paul has clearly told him that it is his duty, now that he has become a believer, to return to his master, BUT the penalty for a runaway slave could be very severe, even death.

Therefore, Paul writes a letter appealing to his owner, Philemon, to receive the slave back without penalty. And he advances several reasons for this. First, that Onesimus had been a great blessing to him, Paul, in prison, and then that because the slave was now a believer, he was also a Christian brother. Further, Paul claims that, as his partner in the gospel, Philemon has a duty towards him and he asks that any debt or liabilities might be charged by Philemon to his, Paul's, own account of love. As a brother in Christ, I could order you. But because I love you, I make a request instead. "I do this even though I am Paul, the ambassador of Christ Jesus and, at present, also a prisoner for his sake."

The whole letter speaks of love and fellowship. His opening greeting, "From Paul, a prisoner for the sake of Christ Jesus… to our friend and fellow worker… Every time I pray, I mention you and give thanks to my God. For I hear of your love for all God's people." Who could resist that? He then prays that their fellowship will bring a deeper understanding of our blessings in Christ, adding, "You have cheered the hearts of all God's people."

Then he gets down to the real issue, Onesimus the runaway slave. He claims that, by his standing, as a brother in Christ, he could order Philemon to act, but out of love, he makes a request on behalf of his 'son' in the faith, Onesimus. "At one time, he was no use to you," and I would like to keep him here with me so that he could help me in your place! To his request, that he receive the slave back, he adds, "I would like you to do this of your own free will. So I will not do anything unless you agree."

Paul even suggests that, perhaps all this has happened in order that Onesimus might become a believer, and that Philemon might have not a slave but a brother. "So if you think of me as your partner, welcome him back just as you would me." And he repeats, if he owes you anything, "I Paul will pay you back," written in his own hand!

Finally, assured that Philemon will respond graciously, Paul asks that they prepare a room for him, hoping that God would answer their prayers and allow him his freedom. And as usual, the greetings, from Epaphras in prison with him and his fellow workers, not in prison but with him, Mark, Aristarchus, Demas and Luke. "May the grace of our Lord Jesus Christ be with you all."

Hebrews

This letter was written by Paul with the express purpose of strengthening the faith of Jewish Christians who were being persecuted for their faith. Its purpose is to declare the whole truth of the Gospel, by reference back to their known understanding of the Jewish faith, showing decisively that Jesus was no interloper but the Messiah, whose coming had been foretold by their prophets in scripture – with which scripture Paul, as a Pharisee, would have been very familiar, having studied it in depth, and he would have believed it to be the revealed word of God. Paul, under the inspiration of the Holy Spirit, was by this means able to demonstrate convincingly, to Jews, that the new Way of Christ was not new but was, in fact, the fulfilment of the faith of Abraham, as foretold by the prophets. It was the New Covenant, foretold by Jeremiah (Jeremiah 31). For non-Jewish readers, like ourselves, yes, it is sometimes difficult because we are not always familiar with the complexities of the Jewish faith. However, it does serve to show, to us also, that our faith is part of a progressive revelation of God, which was first indicated right back in the time of Adam and Eve. Our Lord is the "seed of the woman" who will crush the head of the serpent, but in doing so will himself be wounded (Isaiah 53). As God had told the serpent, Genesis 3:15, "Her offspring will crush your head, and you will bite her offspring's heel."

Very carefully and systematically, in this letter, Paul develops this theme, showing that every aspect of the Law was fulfilled in Christ, the details of the old Law being seen as symbols, of what was now shown to be the reality, of what was ultimately required in order to deliver mankind from the power of sin and death – namely, that the forgiveness for man's sin and the deliverance of humanity from its power, could only be achieved through the death of the Son of God on the Cross and not through the sacrifice of animals. There was no other way. The old Law, like the old Covenant, were good, but they had failed because they were dependent upon human effort as well. As Paul had already declared in his letter to Romans 8:3, "What the Law could not do because human nature was weak, God did. He condemned sin in human nature by sending his own Son, who came with a nature like human sinful nature, to do away with sin." The book also shows how scripture is a unity from beginning to end, and that the Jewish nation had a vital role to play in achieving God's ultimate purpose for creation. The death of Christ and the conversion of souls were ordained by God, "before the world was created." A theme constantly repeated in the other epistles by Paul and Peter.

In fact, what we have here, taken in conjunction with his letter to Romans, is Paul's summary of Christian belief, which has become the cornerstone of our faith today, as defined in the Creed. Some may wish to disregard parts of it, but it remains the word of God. Jesus being the "word revealed in human flesh," as John so powerfully expresses it in his Gospel. "In the beginning, the Word already existed." "The Word became a human being, and lived among us." "God gave the Law through Moses, but grace and truth came through Jesus Christ."

So Paul now begins at the beginning, by stating that what was previously promised by the prophets in the scriptures was now being declared to us by God's own Son; going back to Romans 8:3, who had, in his life and death, completed God's work, and was now back seated in Heaven, work accomplished (verse 1– 3), using words very similar to John 1:1–4.

Paul then enlarges on the status of Christ, as being greater than the angels (verse 6), and in support of this, he quotes from the Psalms, notably 45:6–7; 102:25–7; 110:1; 8:4–6. Paul also emphasises the future role of us, mere mortals now, as having authority greater than the angels, but not yet; in the meantime, it is Christ, who by his obedience and death has been raised to life, who has all authority which he will later share with us. Chapter 2:16 gives greater details, that it is not the angels whom Christ helps, but the descendants of Abraham, mortals in other words. His suffering, during his period as a human on earth, has given Jesus personal experience of our suffering, therefore, he understands us (verse 18).

Moses was regarded by Jews as the Great Law Giver, but Jesus is greater (3:3), therefore, we must avoid treating Jesus in the way that the nation of Israel treated Moses when, in rebelling against him, they were actually rebelling against God who appointed him (verse 8–10). Verse 16, "Who were the people who heard God's voice and rebelled against him? All those who were led out of Egypt by Moses." Paul is not mincing his words. Further, God had promised a rest to Israel, but they could not receive it because they did not believe and, powerfully, Paul declares that God's work was actually arranged to be completed, 4:3, "from the time He created the world," which has been stated repeatedly by both Paul and Peter in their letters. Paul concludes this argument by urging the Jews, to whom he is writing, to see in Jesus the true High Priest, who has entered heaven for us, not entering an earthly Temple, and verse 15, because he has been tempted like us, as our High Priest, he can have every sympathy for our weakness, whilst as God he is the sacrifice.

Now, in Chapter 5, Paul deals with the issue of the priesthood of Christ, who was born to a royal dynasty, that of David, but not a priestly one. First, he stresses that Christ did not choose the role (verse 5), but he became a high priest in the manner of Melchizedek (Exodus 28:1) whose existence predated the Law, and this ancestry is enlarged on in 7:3. He also reminds us that "even though he was God's Son, Jesus had to learn, through his sufferings, to be obedient" (5:8), in order to overcome the disobedience of the first man, Adam.

Meanwhile, in Chapter 6, he encourages his readers to move forward in faith, not allowing them to be dragged back into the bondage of the Law. Rather, to become the true descendants of Abraham, they needed to seize upon the promises made to Abraham, those which had been promising what Israel had not yet received, but were now available to all through Jesus Christ, in accordance with his promise which was unchangeable (verse 17).

In Chapter 7, Paul enlarges on what he had said about the priesthood of Christ (verse 7–10), but more importantly, just as the Law had failed through the frailty of humanity and had to be changed, as foretold by Jeremiah 31, so the priesthood had also failed. The priests themselves, being sinful, had first to be sanctified before they could act on behalf of others (verse 11). Now with a change of priesthood and law, a new High Priest is required. Jesus fulfilled this role because, like Melchizedek, verse 16, "He was made a priest, not by human rules and regulations but through the power of a life which has no end." "The old rule was set aside because it was weak and useless (verse 18), for the Law of Moses could not make anything perfect. And now a better hope has been provided" (verse 19). Jesus, as God's Son, was holy and without sin, unlike the old priesthood in which the priests first had to be made pure, by the sacrifice, before they could offer it for others.

In Chapter 8, Paul develops the theme of the weakness of the old Law and the first Covenant, verse 7, "If there had been nothing wrong with the first covenant, there would have been no need for a second one." And then, back to

Jeremiah 31:31–34, "The time is coming when I will make a new covenant with the people of Israel and Judah... I will put my law within them and write it on their hearts." So this weakness had been foreseen by God and preparation to cope with it had already been put in place. (Before creation.)

In Chapter 9, Paul raises the issue of worship, and says that the very construction of the Temple, with its inner sanctuary, which could only be entered by the High priest once a year and then only because he is carrying the blood of the sacrifice, indicated that the way into the Holy presence of God was not open. "As long as the outer Tent still stands" (verse 8). Interesting, therefore, that after the death of Jesus, the Temple was destroyed, as we know, in AD 70 and has never been rebuilt! As indeed, Jesus foretold in the Gospels. Verse 10, "These are all outward rules, which apply only until the time when God will establish the new order. But Christ has already come... the tent in which he serves is not a tent made by human hands." Christ, bearing his own blood, entered onto the most Holy Place of all, into heaven itself, there to appear in the presence of God for us. And then, verse 26, "Now, when all ages of time are nearing the end, he has appeared, once and for all, to remove sin through the sacrifice of himself." And most gloriously, Paul tells us verse 28, "He will appear a second time, not to deal with sin but to save those who are waiting for him."

Chapter 10 begins with the simple statement, "The Jewish Law is not a full and faithful model of the real things; it is only a faint outline of the good things to come." More importantly, the new covenant is better than the old one. Verse 5–7, "When Christ was about to come into the world, he said to God: 'You do not want sacrifices and offerings, but you have prepared a body for me. You are not pleased with animals burnt whole on the altar or with sacrifices to take away sins.' Then I said, 'Here I am O God, just as it is written of me in the book of the Law.'" Further, in verse 9–10, "So God does away with all the old sacrifices and puts the sacrifice of Christ in their place. Because Jesus Christ did what God wanted him to do, we are all purified from sin by the offering that he made of his own body once and for all." And verse 18, "So when these sins have been forgiven, an offering to take away sins is no longer needed." Therefore, because we have peace with God, through Jesus Christ, we have freedom to enter the Holy Place, through His death. (verse 19-20) So let us draw near to God, (verse 22) Let us hold firmly to our faith (verse 23) and do not neglect our fellowship with God and with one another. (verse 25) Remember also that to fail to keep the faith is to incur the judgement of God. Verse 26-27 , "You have shared in the sufferings of Christ, and you did this gladly. "Do not lose your courage then, because it brings with it a great reward." (verse 35) , Be patient then in order to do the will of God." (verse 36)"for, "Just a little longer, and he who is coming will come; he will not delay." (verse 37) My righteous people, however, will believe and live; but if any of them turns back, I will not be pleased with him."

Chapter 11. Here Paul, very powerfully, tells us that what is required above all else is faith. Without faith, it is impossible to please God, for only by faith can we know God. So to support this, Paul defines faith as, "To be sure of the things we hope for, to be certain of the things we cannot see." For, "It was by their faith that people of ancient times won God's approval." And this faith concerns both our understanding of creation, that it was created by God ex nihilo, literally out of nothing that can be seen, and also the actions of those people who had faith. Here Paul names many whose actions brought them into a living relationship with God. Abel, as opposed to Cain. Enoch and Noah who built an ark on dry land. But especially Abraham, whose faith made him acceptable to God and, through his faith, God gave him a son, supernaturally, and made him the ancestor of the Jewish race, with the promise also of an eternal, everlasting inheritance. However, that faith required an obedience which was won at great cost, in Abraham's case, by his willingness to sacrifice all his hopes in being prepared to kill his son as a sacrifice. What Adam lost by disobedience can only be regained by strict obedience – Abraham and Isaac, and then God's Son, Jesus.

Paul quotes Moses, who by faith chose, verse 25, "To suffer with God's people, rather than to enjoy sin for a little while." Obviously, the pleasures of an Egyptian prince were great, but sinful. But this first test of his faith, having proved true, would ultimately enable Moses to carry out the enormous task, under God, of bringing a whole nation out of Egypt and right up to the borders of their new home, in spite of all the problems. Yet for all their faith and their remarkable achievements, verse 40, "Yet they did not receive what God had promised because God had decided on an even better plan for us. His purpose was that only in company with us would they be made perfect." And that was throwing out a challenge to these Jews. If we fail, they fail too. So if you wish to be a blessing to your race and nation, obey the promise of God, now.

Enough is enough. Now in the two closing chapters, Paul deals with more mundane matters. In our relationship with God, he treats us as sons, 12: 5, which means punishment and reward, discipline. He also adds, verse 14, "Try to live a holy life because no one will see the Lord without it." And he quotes the example of Esau, who lost his birth right to Jacob "for a mess of pottage." And afterwards, he wept when he found that he could not regain it. On the bright side, look at the advantages. We can come freely into God's presence. No longer separated from God, by Law, by flaming mountains and the threat of death. No "you have come to Mount Zion, and to the city of the living God." Verse 23, "You have come to the joyful gathering of God's firstborn, whose names are written in heaven." "You have come to Jesus who arranged the new covenant."

Then the greetings, Chapter 13. Keep on loving one another; remember to welcome strangers in your homes. There were some that did that and welcomed angels, without knowing it. Marriage is good and honourable in all. Keep your lives free from the love of money and be satisfied with what you have. Remember your former leaders. Jesus Christ is the same yesterday, today and forever. Be prepared to suffer shame with Christ, who died outside the city, for there is no permanent city for us here, but we seek one to come. Then the closing prayer, "May the God of peace provide you with good things you need in order to do his will."

"Listen patiently to the message of encouragement, for this letter is not very long." Timothy has been let out of prison. If he comes soon enough, he will join me when I come to see you. (So apparently, he was not in prison in Rome with Paul.) Greet all and, "May God's grace be with you all."

James

This short letter was most likely written by our Lord's brother; the other James, brother to John, having been beheaded by Herod earlier. It is an intensely practical approach to the Christian faith, encouraging new believers to express their faith through the way they live.

In beginning he faces the fact that all Christians must expect to experience problems, but "when your faith succeeds in facing such trials, the result is the ability to endure," which in turn is a good thing. However, seek wisdom, because God is generous and will give graciously to all. He appeals for equality, the poor to be thankful when God "lifts them up," and the rich to be careful lest they fall.

James is very encouraging to those who suffer yet remain faithful, because God will reward them, but reminds them that temptations do not come from God but from the weakness of our own humanity. On the other hand, all good things come from God, who created us to have a privileged position in creation.

He then delivers some very practical advice, verse 20, "Human anger does not achieve God's righteous purpose." "Whoever listens to the word but does not put it into practice is like a man who looks in a mirror," sees his image, then immediately forgets it. If you think you are a Christian, control your tongue.

Chapter 2. True Christianity is shown in your actions. Always treat people as equals; never judge by outward appearance. Love one another, for if you break one commandment, you break all. Then some serious comments on 'faith', verse 14, "What good is it for people to say they have faith if their actions do not prove it?" Verse 18, "Show me how anyone can have faith without actions. I will show you my faith by my actions." "Do you believe that there is only one God? Good! The demons also believe – and tremble with fear."

James then makes an important statement, simply that Abraham, father of the nation and race, was put right with God by faith, when he was prepared to offer his son on the altar. "Can't you see? His faith and his actions worked together; his faith was made perfect through his actions!" Followed, of course, by, "Abraham believed God, and because of his faith, God accepted him as righteous." So we see then, "that it is by people's actions that they are put right with God, and not by their faith alone" (verse 24), which really reinforces the issue.

Chapter 3 begins with a warning to teachers, of whom he is one, because they will be judged more severely. Yet, verse 2, he admits that we all make mistakes, especially in what we say. The tongue is dangerous and difficult to control. "All of us often make mistakes. But if a person never makes a mistake in what he says, he is perfect and is also able to control his whole being." And he then enlarges on this by using as metaphors, ships and forest fires. Both can be controlled or begun by very small things, just as, "No one has been able to tame the tongue." He also adds that the same mouth can produce words which bless or curse.

He concludes this chapter with a warning that those who profess wisdom or understanding should demonstrate that by the way they live and speak. For envy, jealousy and selfishness are evidence of disorder, whereas compassion, friendship and peace are evidence of goodness and are free from hypocrisy.

Chapter 4 speaks against friendship with an evil world, warns that God looks at our motives. "You do not have what you want because you do not ask God for it. And when you ask, you do not receive it because your motives are bad" (verse 2–3). To which he adds, verse 7, "Submit to God. Resist the devil, and he will run away from you. Come near to God, and he will come near to you." Avoid criticism of others. Equally be humble and do not boast of what you propose to do (verse 13). And finally, verse 17, "So then, those who do not do the good they know they should do are guilty of sin."

James ends his discourse, Chapter 5, with a caution to the rich and an appeal for patience as we wait for the Lord's coming. Take the prophets as "examples of patient endurance under suffering." If in trouble, pray; if happy, sing. If ill, send for the elders to pray for you and anoint you with oil.

Of prayer, he comments, verse16–18, "The prayer of a good person has a powerful effect." Elijah was such a person, and he prayed earnestly that there should be no rain, and no rain fell for three and a half years. Then he prayed again, and the sky poured.

His final comments concern repentance, "He that turns a sinner from his ways will save that sinner's soul from death and bring about the forgiveness of many sins."

1 Peter

This brief letter from Peter is of great value to us. It was written to the then scattered believers in Northern Asia, where many groups of believers had been established as Christian communities, sharing fellowship and meeting together for worship. But through much persecution and trouble, many of these new 'converts' were experiencing problems of faith, and we need to recognise that this new 'Way' was all very new to them. They had only the old Jewish scriptures to read, and word of mouth for reference. Therefore, letters like these would be passed around and serve as a common reference point for their faith. We need to see these letters also, today, as being a witness to the early faith of these new Christians; especially now, at a time when our faith is under scrutiny, in a modern, sceptical and scientific age.

Here their faith was frequently evidenced by events. People were physically healed, set free from prison, as was Peter, but above all things, their belief depended on a vital, living faith in the almighty power of God. And that is what Peter tries to convey here.

As he begins, he refers to these believers as, "God's chosen people, who live as refugees scattered throughout the provinces." In other words, they are part of the 'family', but chosen for a purpose, verse 2, "to obey Jesus Christ and be purified by his blood." However, Peter says, the resurrection of Christ fills us with a 'living hope', which means that we look forward to receiving God's rich blessing which is reserved, incorruptible in heaven for those who in turn are, through their 'living faith', also protected, kept and saved, waiting for the coming day – which is the return of Jesus Christ to earth. So even though now you are experiencing problems, be glad not sad, he says, for it means that your faith is being tested to see if it works, just as gold needs to be refined by fire. And although this is in the future, your present experience is the evidence that you are included in and receiving 'the salvation of your souls', which is what it is all about (verse 9).

Further, you are more privileged than the old prophets because although they received the promises, they did not actually experience them. We now, through the Holy Spirit, are experiencing what they could only picture, through the death and resurrection of God's Son, Jesus Christ. Therefore, cherish the moment, live in a state of spiritual alertness, but also of holiness before God, and set your hopes on what is to come (verse 13). And at this point, Peter reminds them of the enormous price which was paid to set them free from the, "worthless manner of life handed down by their ancestors" (verse 18). The costly sacrifice of Christ, "who was like a lamb without defect or flaw," who had been chosen by God, verse 20, "before the creation of the world and was revealed in these last days for your sake. Through him you believe in God." And to this you are joined, verse 23, "For through the living and eternal word of God you have been born again as the children of a parent who is immortal, not mortal." And he quotes Isaiah 40:6–8, "The word of the Lord remains forever," and that word is the Good News that was preached to you! Mighty stuff.

Now, in Chapter 2, Peter develops further what is the very concise statement of the basis of their faith. Christ, he says, is the "living stone," rejected by men but seen by God as part of the "spiritual temple" in which they, as holy priests, can worship God, "In spirit and in truth," as Jesus put it to the woman at the well of Sychar. Then, changing his metaphor, he calls Christ the stone that, and here he quotes Isaiah 8:14–15, will make people stumble because they did not believe God's word for them, (verse 8). In other words, here Peter is relating what he says to the words of their own (OT) scripture, which had been their basis of faith in the past. For, he says, they are a chosen race, "chosen to proclaim the wonderful acts of God" (verse 9). Therefore, submit yourselves to God as his 'slaves' but, for the Lord's sake, also submit yourselves to the authority of the Emperor because that is right, as they represent justice. But do it also to silence any foolish criticism of your conduct by ignorant people – which had, as we know, caused major problems for Paul as well. Christ himself submitted to the severity of Roman authority, being insulted and blamed, even though he was totally innocent. But he did it for your sakes.

Chapter 3 repeats, yet again, the necessity of maintaining the right relationship in marriage, and we remember here that unlike Paul, Peter was himself married. But the relationship has to be a two-way exercise, with responsibility on both parties to maintain their true relationship as partners. Be prepared to suffer for doing what is right, do not suffer from your own wrongdoing (verse 8–18). In verse 19, Peter reminds us that Christ was resurrected as a spiritual being, and as such went to preach to the 'disobedient' spirits who had died. For Christ is now in heaven, "ruling over all angels and heavenly authorities and powers" (verse 22).

Chapter 4. Using the example of Christ's earthly life, Peter exhorts the believers to live as Christ lived, "controlled by God's will and not by human desires" (verse 2). The unbelievers may be surprised at you not joining them in their way of living, but they do not realise that God will judge them (verse 4). They will have to give an account of themselves, which is why the Good News was preached also to those who had died (verse 6). "If you suffer as Christ's followers, rejoice" (verse 14), but never as evildoers because, "The time has come for judgement to begin, and God's own people are the first to be judged" (verse 17). However, if you suffer for the sake of Christ, trust God (verse 19).

In Chapter 5, Peter appeals to them, from his own experience of suffering, to serve God, not for financial gain but out of love. Be humble, be alert (verse 8).

Then the final greetings. Peter has written this letter with help from Silas. Greetings from the sister church in Babylon, and from Mark, whom he calls 'my son' but is probably John Mark, cousin to Barnabas, whom we have already met.

2 Peter

This, Peter's second letter, is also written in answer to some major issues which were becoming prevalent in some of the new churches. This issue of false teaching was an ever-present problem, caused in part by two things. First the lack of any written statements of their belief which could be circulated and which would bring some coherence of thought. And to that was added the fact that there were a number of 'preachers' travelling around, many claiming to be 'inspired', who were visiting the churches or coming from within their ranks. Some were clearly either simply misguided or misinformed, but some were also seeking to win the affection of these people for their own personal enhancement. In our Lord's day, the same had been true, and provided they acknowledged his authority as the Son of God, Jesus was tolerant; if not, they were told where to go.

As before, Peter begins with some areas of fact which are indisputable – their faith and their recognition of the power of God in their lives, which is able to deliver them from the 'destructive lust' of the world and enable them to share in the divine nature, which is in Christ Jesus. He then lists the qualities which need to be part of our faith, stating that if we exhibit goodness, faith, knowledge, self-control, endurance, godliness, Christian affection and love, then our relationship with Christ is shown. But if these qualities are not in evidence in people, the question remains as to whether they have been 'born again' in the likeness of Christ. Peter says that these things are common knowledge, but (verse 14) aware that soon he will leave them, he is concerned that these things shall be always kept in mind.

He then reminds them that his own authority for the teachings, which he brought them, were not fairy tales but, "With our own eyes, we saw his greatness. We were there when he was given honour and glory by God the Father" (verse 18). "We ourselves heard this voice coming from heaven, when we were with him on the holy mountain." This was a first-hand experience. We saw Jesus with

272

our own eyes; we heard his teaching; we ourselves heard the witness of God to his Son. Irrefutable, personal, powerful and life changing, as were our Lord's miracles and teachings.

So we are even more confident about the words spoken by the prophets, remembering, above all, that "no one can explain by himself or herself a prophecy in the scriptures. For no prophetic message ever came just from human will, but people were under the control of the Holy Spirit as they spoke the message that came from God" (verse 20).

Peter then, Chapter 2, speaks of the false prophets of the past, who deny the truth about Jesus Christ and who, for profit, will fabricate stories. In past time, God did not spare the angels that sinned but threw them into hell. If God condemned Sodom and Gomorrah, how shall the wicked of this day escape eternal punishment? These false teachers are bold, arrogant, having no respect even for the heavenly beings but, "They will be destroyed like wild animals, (verse 13) and they will be paid with suffering for the suffering they have caused." "It would have been much better for them never to have known the way of righteousness than to know it and then turn away from the sacred command that was given them" (verse 23).

Then, finally, Peter names specifically one element of these pernicious false messages. He comments that, in both of these letters, his sole purpose has been to instruct, teach and encourage them in their faith – which faith is witnessed both by the prophets of old and, most particularly, by the words spoken by Jesus himself. In those, we have the promise that our Lord will himself return, yes, but that before his coming there will be those who mock, deny or suggest that because he has not come yet, he will never come. They will say, "He promised to come, didn't he? Where is he? Our ancestors have already died, but everything is the same as it was since the creation of the world." In this, "They purposely ignore the fact that long ago God gave a command and the heavens and the earth were created" (verse 5). "But the heavens and the earth that now exist are being preserved by the same command of God, on order to be destroyed by fire" (verse 7). In God's eyes, time does not exist. There is no difference between one day and a thousand years. What we call delay is, in fact, God's mercy, because he does not want anyone to be destroyed. But verse 10, "the Day of the Lord will come like a thief. On that Day, the heavens will disappear, the heavenly bodies will burn up, and the earth with everything in it will vanish."

Therefore, your lives should be holy and dedicated to God, as we wait for the Day of God. "Look on our Lord's patience as the opportunity he is giving you to be saved, just as our dear brother Paul wrote to you." And he ends with the salutation, "But continue to grow in the grace and knowledge of our Lord and Saviour Jesus Christ. To him be the glory, now and forever. Amen."

1 John

The writer here, John, who also wrote the Gospel, is for us an interesting character. His Gospel stands out from the other three as written by someone with a more intimate experience of Jesus, and it breathes with the sense of God's Holy Spirit. This letter, focusing as it does on the power of love, exemplifies that impression. In the Gospel, he is referred to as 'the disciple whom Jesus loved', and we know that John was, apparently, the only disciple who was there at the cross and to whom, in his dying moments, Jesus commended his mother. But there is more to it than that. We were told that when Jesus was taken into the High Priest's house after his arrest, John had access 'because he was known to the High Priest', a fact which is only mentioned in John's Gospel, and it was he who enabled Peter also to go in to the outer courtyard.

Further, it was the mother of James and John who asked Jesus, when he came into his kingdom, to promote her two sons to the two most important positions, one at the right and one at the left, of Jesus, which implied that she thought that her two sons were better qualified for such high positions. So it might be that socially, and in terms of education, the family were regarded or regarded themselves as 'different'. We do know that Jesus saw no social differences in his followers, having been accused of 'eating with publicans and sinners'. But we do know that when it came to extending the Gospel beyond the bounds of Israel, he chose Saul of Tarsus, later named Paul, who was highly educated. When arraigned before Festus and Agrippa (Acts 26:24), Festus shouted at him, "You are mad, Paul! Your great learning is driving you mad!" And it was Paul's status as a Greek and Hebrew-speaking Roman citizen that enabled him to gain access to the Gentiles.

Anyway, we are only concerned here with what John has to say, although the 'false teaching' to which he refers was most probably Greek in origin, namely that the physical world was evil, and therefore, Jesus could not have been both

God and human. But the 'false teachers' took this further by saying that social morality and human relationships were also valueless.

In his introduction, John echoes the theme of his Gospel, John Chapter 1, "In the beginning, the Word already existed, and the Word was with God and the Word was God." He then goes on to echo Peter's words in his Epistle, "We have heard it, and we have seen it with our own eyes; yes, we have seen it and our hands have touched it." And to that he adds, what we speak of is what we have physically witnessed. This is not some philosophical argument; this is hard fact, and that is the subject of our message (verse 1–3).

In fact, verse 5, "The message we preach is what we heard from his lips, and in him is light." By 'light' John means understanding, knowledge. So if we live in the truth, that becomes the basis of our fellowship with each other, and through this truth, we have received eternal life. And one of the first 'truths' we receive is that we are ALL sinners (verse 8), but able to be delivered through the life and death of Christ.

Chapter 2 then discusses our relationship with God, which is only possible through the work done by Christ on his cross. The proof of our knowing God is that we obey him. To say we know him but do not obey him is to make that person a liar. Further, our obedience leads us to love God, and perfect knowledge is shown in perfect love, which in turn leads to our being in union with Christ and living as he lived. So that love becomes the evidence of our new relationship with God, through Jesus Christ.

In verse 7–8, John now shares the message put forward by Peter. This commandment I give you is not new. It is exactly what your ancestors have believed. What is new about it, is that this message has actually been revealed, evidenced, in the life and teachings of Christ and is now seen in you who believe. The chief evidence being your love for each other. To say you have understanding and yet hate your brothers and sisters means that you are living in 'darkness'. In other words, how can you say that you love God, who is love, and not love those whom he loves? At this point, John becomes very passionate, "I am writing to you, my children, to you fathers, to you, young people, because your sins are forgiven, by God through His love for Jesus (verse 12).

Now John gets to the point of this false teaching, verse 15, "Do not love the world or anything that belongs to the world. If you love the world, you do not love the Father." For not only is the world bad, but it is also transient; it will disappear with all who love it, but those who obey God, will live forever (verse

17). In actual fact, it is more than that; the appearance of evil, the Enemy, is evidence that Christ is coming, for he foretold this would happen first. And the fact that some have left the fellowship, demonstrates that they were never really at one with us. But you, having received the Holy Spirit, have been led into 'all truth' (John 14:17). Liars are those who say that Jesus is not the Messiah, who in doing so actually reject God as well, for whoever denies the Son, also denies the Father (verse 22). Further, verse 27, as you now have the Holy Spirit in you, you do not need other teachers. (John 16:13–15). Such as the false teachers.

Chapter 3 takes John back to his main subject, the love of God for us, which is so great that he now calls us "his children". Our future is unknown to us, except that, "when Christ appears, we shall be like him, for we shall see him as he really is" (verse 2). And John then exhorts all believers to live as Christ lived, to love him and not to sin, because as God's children, we have the nature of Christ in us. The Devil's children are those who don't do what is right and don't love others (verse 10).

From that point, John enlarges on the need for us to love, illustrating this from scripture. As with the account of Cain and Abel, where Cain's jealousy and lack of love led him to kill his brother, so, says John, expect the world also to hate you because you are doing what is right in the sight of God. God's love for us is evidenced by the fact that, even while we were sinners, Christ died for us (verse 16). In this, our courage is increased, by the fact that God answers our prayers, through our obedience and our belief that Jesus Christ is His Son, and by our love for each other (verse 22).

In Chapter 5, John emphasises the central core of our faith. "Whoever believes that Jesus is the Messiah is a child of God, and whoever loves a father loves his child also" (verse 1). He then repeats the message. We know that we love God when we also love His children and obey His commands, which are not arduous; and because we are God's children, we have the means to overcome the world, by our faith. For it is only those who believe that Jesus is the Son of God can do this. When Jesus came, his relationship with the Father was confirmed by God, and by baptism, and by the Holy Spirit and, ultimately, in his death. God's approval of His Son is confirmed in that, through his death, we have life. "Whoever has the Son, has this life; whoever does not have the Son does not have life" (verse 12). God's relationship with His Son and our relationship with Jesus are both interwoven and cannot be separated. To love God is to love

Jesus, and to believe in him, and that results in us having love for all of God's children. It is a chain reaction, a causal link.

Now, says John, we gain courage in God's presence because he hears and answers our prayers. Therefore, the answered prayer is in itself evidence of God's love for us (verse 14).

In the matter of discipline, verse 16, "If you see your brother or sister committing a sin that does not lead to death, you should pray to God who will give them life." "All wrongdoing is sin, but there is sin which does not lead to death." "We know that none of God's children keep on sinning, for the Son of God keeps them safe, and the Evil One cannot harm them" (verse 18).

And he ends his letter by repeating his main theme, verse 20, "We know that the Son of God has come and has given us understanding, so that we know the true God. We live in union with the true God and in union with His Son Jesus Christ. This is the true God, and this is eternal life."

"My children, keep yourselves safe from false gods."

2 and 3 John

These two epistles from John are both very brief and to the point, so I am linking them together.

The second letter of John was written by one describing himself as the 'Elder', which is simply a position of authority in the Church, but which enabled comments to be made without their being taken as personal criticism. It was most probably written to a specific local church. However, it is included in scripture because the contents are applicable to all believers, and in fact, it replicates some of what he says in his previous letter, but without the need to warn against the specific false teachers who were corrupting the church. This is much more general, verse 7, "Many deceivers have gone out all over the world, people who do not acknowledge that Jesus Christ came as a human being." In other words, if God was not in Christ Jesus, then his death could not deliver us from sin, he is not the Messiah spoken of by the prophets, and the testimony of 'Jesus' was false, and the witness of the Apostles was lies. Verse 8, "Be on your guard then, so that you will not lose what we have worked for but will receive your reward in full."

And a further warning, this time about teachers who would take Christian belief into areas which were not sanctioned by Jesus himself, verse 9, "Anyone who does not stay with the teaching of Christ, but goes beyond it, does not have God." Plain words, no doubts! So then, if someone comes into your fellowship bringing these 'strange' ideas, do not welcome them, do not extend hospitality to them, and do not even greet them in peace.

John here greeted the church with loving words and he ends with: 'so much more to say' but it must wait until I can visit you. Greetings from your 'sister' church.

The third letter of John was again headed from, "The Elder," but this one is addressed to a specific individual, Gaius, probably a church leader. It rejoices in Gaius' good health and in the excellent news which he has received from fellow

279

believers who had visited him. The real point of the letter is to appeal to Gaius, as a good Christian brother noted for his generosity to believers, to give help, money, to these visitors to enable them to continue with their "journey in the service of Christ," in a way which will be pleasing to God. In this case, they had clearly refused financial help from non-Christians. Whereas we Christians, in order to show the love of Jesus, should help them, for by doing so, we share with them in their good work.

John then warns against a man named Diotrephes who, "likes to be their leader," but who refused to pay any attention to the letter which he had written to him. Obviously, a very bad person because John says that when he comes, he will deal with these matters which have arisen, for example, the terrible lies he has spoken about him, and the fact that he refuses to receive fellow believers when they come – possibly because they would expose his lies. He even tries to prevent those who do want to receive these visitors. On the other hand, everyone speaks well of Demetrius.

John ends this letter, like the previous one, by saying that there are many more things he needs to discuss with them, but which he does not want to put into writing; which implies that the letter needed to be private. He ends with a salutation, "Peace be with you. All your friends send greetings. Greet all our friends personally."

Jude

Yet another letter, this time written by Jude who says that he is the brother of James. Therefore, he is possibly another of our Lord's brothers. It would be lovely to think that this was the case because, clearly, he is here a devout believer. However, this letter, like that of 2 Peter and 2 and 3 John, was written to warn about the very serious dangers to their faith, resulting from false teachers amongst their fellowship and from those who had "slipped in unnoticed" and who were perverting the faith in order to justify their own immorality.

Jude begins by complimenting the believers on their faith and encourages them to fight on for the faith which, "once and for all, God has given to his people." These others are "godless" people who "distort the message about the grace of our God in order to excuse their immoral ways."

To do this, they also reject the basis of our faith by rejecting Jesus Christ, who is our only Lord and Master. Jude reinforces his condemnation by reminding his readers of the punishment meted out in the Old Testament scriptures to those who sinned. And he goes on to quote a number of outstanding examples, such as the Israelites, whom God had delivered so miraculously from their slavery in Egypt but were wiped out as a nation because of their sin; only their children were allowed into the promised Land.

In the same way, before creation, the angels who sinned by exceeding their authority and leaving their proper place, are now bound in eternal chains, being "kept in the darkness below," awaiting God's Day of Judgement. Remember also Sodom and Gomorrah and their neighbouring towns, whose inhabitants acted, as those angels did, in sexual immorality and perversion, and were destroyed by fire.

In the same way, he says, these people sin against their own bodies, they despise God's authority, and they insult the "glorious beings above," when not even the chief angel Michael would do that when disputing with the Devil over the body of Moses. These people attack what they do not understand; they behave like wild animals, and they sin for money, like Balaam.

And then follows a very dramatic description of their evil behaviour, ending with, "They are like wandering stars, for whom God has reserved a place forever in the deepest darkness."

Jude's denunciation of them is extremely dramatic, violent but scriptural. He does not 'mince his words'. He goes on to quote the prophecy of Enoch (which was a part of their scriptures but which we do not have), "The Lord will come with many thousands of his holy angels to bring judgement on all, to condemn them for the godless deeds they have performed and for all the terrible words that godless sinners have spoken against him."

Not content with this damning condemnation, Jude goes on to say, "Remember what was spoken in the past by the apostles of our Lord who said, 'When the last days come, people will appear who will mock you, people who follow their own godless desires.' But you my friends… pray in the power of the Holy Spirit, and keep yourselves in the love of God as you wait for our Lord Jesus Christ, in his mercy, to give you eternal life."

And he ends with the very powerful prayer, verse 24, "To him who is able to keep you from falling and to bring you faultless and joyful before his glorious presence – to the only God our Saviour, through Jesus Christ our Lord, be glory, majesty, might and authority, from all ages past, and now and forever and ever! Amen."

Revelation

It is easy to be put off from reading this book because it is very difficult for us to understand what it is saying. And the reason for that is simply because it uses symbolism to express truths which were to be understood by those to whom the symbols were familiar. For example, it echoes some of the symbolism already seen in the Old Testament, in the prophecies of Ezekiel and Daniel, and which, to a lesser extent are recorded in the dream visions of Pharaoh, king of Egypt, and his butler and baker, which were interpreted by Joseph, who himself had dreamt dreams of the future. It is the same with Belshazzar, the Babylonian Emperor, who is frightened by the words which a 'moving hand' writes on the wall.

So read this book, try not to figure out what all the symbolism means, and see instead a projection given to a persecuted and discouraged Christian church which was in its infancy. See in it the promise of a glorious future, a future in which the coming years would see the church involved, but ending in the final victory of our Saviour, the Lord Jesus Christ, over all his enemies. And, if you want a more graphic and detailed picture without the symbolism, read Milton's *Paradise Lost*. One of the most, if not the most, remarkable surveys of God's purpose for humanity which, written in the seventeenth century, by a man who had gone blind, must have been inspired.

This book opens with a third-party explanation of what the book contains, that John has been given a revelation of future events by Jesus Christ, through the visit of an angel. The reader is told to be glad because the events will happen soon.

Then the first-person account begins as John sends greetings to seven churches in the province of Asia. He greets them with love and affection from the Eternal God and His Son, the Lord Jesus Christ, who is our Redeemer, the first raised from death, and who is the ruler of the world which he created –

whose love for them was revealed through his suffering and death, and who will soon return.

Then, speaking to the churches, John states that he is their brother in Christ and a fellow sufferer in the cause of the Gospel, who had been exiled on the Isle of Patmos for preaching the Gospel. Whilst there, on the Sabbath, he had had a vision, given by the Holy Spirit, in which he was told to send messages to the seven churches, verse 11, "Write down what you see and send the book to the churches in these seven cities."

In his vision, he 'saw' the speaker, standing among seven golden lampstands, looking like a spectacular human being, so awesome that John fell at his feet as one dead. And his voice was like a roaring waterfall, as he held seven stars in his right hand. The lampstands which John saw were the seven churches, and the seven stars, the angels of those churches.

John then addresses each of the seven churches in succession, (Chapter 2) delivering God's message to them. To Ephesus, that in spite of their good work, they had lost their 'first love'. To Smyrna, that they were being put to the test by false prophets claiming to be believers. To Pergamum, encouragement, even though their city was the seat of Satan. To Thyatira, the warning that they were tolerating a Jezebel who was misleading believers. To Sardis, that they were fast asleep, therefore, they must awake before they die completely. To Philadelphia, a warning against the 'group that belongs to Satan', though they themselves were endeavouring to be faithful. And to Laodicea, that they were neither hot nor cold, that Jesus was standing at the door, knocking, and waiting for them to open the door. (See Holman Hunt's famous picture 'Behold I stand at the door and knock' in which the handle is on the inside.)

At this point, John has a second vision of (Chapter 4), an open door, and he hears a voice which bids him, "Come up here, and I will show you what must happen after this" (4:1). This vision revealed a throne, on it a glorious person, surrounded by twenty-four other persons also on thrones. Around the central throne were four 'living creatures' each having a different face and six wings, who sang "Holy, holy, holy, is the Lord God Almighty, who was, who is, and who is to come." Then he saw, Chapter 5, that on the central throne was, "One who held a scroll, written on both sides and sealed with seven seals, which no one could open." Then he saw a Lamb, standing in the centre of the throne and the living creatures, who appeared to have been killed. He took the scroll and, as he did so, all the voices cried out that he, the Lamb, was worthy to open the scroll because by his sacrificial death, he had redeemed to God, people from throughout the world.

Now, Chapter 6, the Lamb begins to open the seals, one by one. And as he does so, from the first, a rider on a white horse appears, holding a conqueror's bow. From the second, a red horse whose rider held a sword. From the third, a black horse, in its rider's hand a pair of scales. From the fourth, a pale-coloured horse whose rider was Death and Hades. These were given power to kill over a quarter of the whole earth. Then the fifth seal was opened, and under the throne were the souls of those who had been killed for witnessing and declaring the word of God, all crying "How long?" Then the sixth seal was opened, and there was a violent earthquake, the sun was darkened, and the moon turned red like blood. The stars fell, the sky disappeared, and the mountains and islands moved out of place. At this, all the people on earth hid themselves in fear, at the anger of the Lord.

The angels were warned not to harm all those who had the seal of God. One hundred and forty-four thousand Jews, and then also a vast multitude, beyond number, from every race and language. John was told that these were the believers who had suffered, and whose robes had been cleansed, "in the blood of the Lamb" (7:14). Then the Lamb opened the seventh seal, Chapter 8, and there was silence in heaven for half an hour, then seven angels were each given a trumpet. As the first six blew a blast, one by one, all manner of dreadful things happened on earth. But through all the disasters and plagues which were happening, the unbelievers who had not been killed by the plagues, refused to stop their sinful, idolatrous practices (9:20).

Then, Chapter 10, another even more mighty angel appeared, carrying a small scroll. He placed one foot on the sea and the other on dry land and called out with a loud voice, to be answered by seven thunders. At this point, John, about to write it down, was told to stop, verse 4, "Keep secret what the seven thunders have said; do not write it down." The mighty angel then declared, "There will be no more delay! But when the seventh angel blows his trumpet, then God will accomplish his secret plan, as he announced to his servants, the prophets."

Now John is given a measuring stick, Chapter 11, and told to go and measure the Temple of God, but not the outer court which had been given over to the heathen, who "will trample on the Holy City for forty-two months." Two witnesses will be sent out, and they will proclaim their message, having authority to, "shut up the sky," so that there will be no rain. When they have completed their mission, a beast from the abyss will kill them and their bodies will lie in the streets of "the great city where their Lord was crucified." Three and a half days later, God will give them life again and take them back to heaven. Then the seventh angel blew his trumpet and loud voices were heard in heaven, saying, 11:15, "The power to rule over the world belongs now to our Lord and his Messiah, and he will rule forever and ever." At this, the four and twenty elders on their thrones worshipped God, God's temple in heaven was opened and the Covenant Box was seen there. Then, Chapter 12, a great and mysterious sight appeared in the sky. A woman, whose dress was the sun, who had the moon under her feet, and a crown of twelve stars on her head. She was about to give birth.

Another mysterious sight also appeared in the sky, this time a huge red dragon with seven heads and ten horns, each of which held a crown. The woman gave birth to a son, "who will rule all the nations with a rod of iron," who was then taken up to heaven to avoid the dragon, and the woman fled to a desert place, prepared for her by God, where she will be taken care of for 1,260 days.

Then war broke out in heaven. Michael and his angels fought against the dragon and his angels, the dragon being defeated and cast out down to earth with all his angels. He is the Devil, Satan, who had deceived the whole world (verse 9). Then a loud voice in heaven declared that God has shown his power and His Messiah has shown his authority, for the accuser of the believers who had overcome by "the blood of the Lamb," has been sent to earth. "But (verse 12) how terrible for the earth and the sea! For the Devil has come down to you, and he is filled with rage because he knows that he has only a little time left." Here the Devil pursues the woman who was given the wings of an eagle to fly to refuge in the desert, where she will be safe for three and a half years. Furious, the dragon goes off to fight with the rest of her descendants, those who have been faithful to God and to the truth revealed by Jesus. "And the dragon stood on the seashore."

In Chapter 13, we are introduced to a number of beasts. First, one coming from the sea with ten horns and seven crowned heads, each with a name which was insulting to God. Everyone worshipped the dragon because it had given immense authority to the beast. The beast made claims which were insulting to God, but it was allowed to fight against God's people and had power for forty-two months. All people, except those whose names were recorded before creation, worshipped it. Then another beast came out of the earth, having two horns, and having also the authority of the beast. It deceived all people by means of its miraculous powers, and it forced all people to receive a mark, on hand or forehead, without which no one could buy or sell. The mark was the beast's name or number, 666.

Then, Chapter 14, John looked and saw a Lamb standing on Mt Zion, together with 144,000 people bearing the Father's name. These are faultless, redeemed ones, who worship the Father and are the first to be offered to God. Then he saw another angel flying through the air, bearing an eternal message of Good News and saying, "Honour God and praise his greatness, for the time of judgement is come." He was followed by a second angel who said that the city, 'Great Babylon' had fallen, followed in turn by yet a third angel who warned that all who worshipped the beast, its image, or who receives the 'mark of the beast' will suffer the fury of God's anger. Verse 12, "This calls for endurance on the part of God's people, those who obey God's commandments and are faithful to Jesus." Then John heard a voice from heaven saying, "Write this: happy are those who from now on die in the service of the Lord!" "They will enjoy rest from their hard work."

John now looked and saw a white cloud with a crowned human-looking figure, and an angel who came out from the temple to tell the figure on the cloud to use his sickle because the time for harvest has come. He was followed by a further angel, also with a sickle, and a third with fire, who told the first angel to use his sickle to harvest the grapes which were then cast into the winepress of God's furious anger, and the result was an enormous flood of blood, 300 kilometres long and nearly two metres deep.

In Chapter 15, John sees yet another 'mysterious' sight. Seven angels with seven plagues, which are the final expressions of God's anger, together with a sea of fire, like glass. But then also he saw those who had been victorious over the beast, his image, and the one whose name is a number. They were holding harps and singing the victorious song of Moses, the servant of God, and the song of the Lamb, "Lord God Almighty, how great and wonderful are your deeds!" John then saw the temple in heaven. Seven angels with plagues came out from it and one of the four 'living creatures' gave to the angels bowls full of the anger of God. No one could enter the temple, which was filled with the glory of God, until the seven plagues brought by the angels had come to an end. These angels were told to, "Go and pour out the seven bowls of God's anger on the earth"

(16:1). These plagues which followed resemble the plagues in Egypt, except that they were indescribably more terrible and were visited on those who had the mark of the beast, on the sea, on the rivers, on the sun, and on the throne of the beast; also on the river Euphrates, from which had appeared unclean spirits from out of the mouths of the dragon, the beast and the false prophet. These are the demons who will bring all the kings of the earth together, "for battle on the great Day of Almighty God" verse 14, at the place called in Hebrew Armageddon.

Then the seventh angel poured out his bowl in the air, at which a Great voice cried out, "It is done." And there were peals of thunder, lightning and a massive earthquake, greater than at any time, which split the great city into three parts and affected the cities of all countries, which were then destroyed. All the mountains vanished and the islands disappeared. All this was followed by massive hailstones which fell on the people, who cursed God because of them.

In Chapter 17, John was introduced, by one of the seven angels, to the "famous prostitute, the great city built near many rivers, with whom the kings of the earth had committed sexual immorality," to see how she was to be punished. He is then (verse 3) taken by The Spirit to the desert, to see a woman dressed in purple and scarlet, sitting on a red beast that had names insulting to God written all over it. She held in her hand a gold cup containing the sins of her immorality, and on her forehead a secret name, meaning, "Great Babylon, the mother of all the prostitutes and perverts in the world," for she was drunk with the blood of the martyrs.

John, on seeing her, was amazed, but was told, verse 8, "That beast was once alive but lives no longer; it is about to come up out of the abyss and will go off to be destroyed." The people living on earth, not having their names recorded in the book of the living, will be amazed at this. The seven heads are seven hills on which the woman sits. They are also seven kings, and the beast that once was alive is the eighth king, who is going off to be destroyed. The ten horns are ten kings who have not yet begun to rule but will rule with the beast for one hour. They and the beast will fight against the Lamb and his faithful ones, but will be defeated by them, because he is the Lord of lords, and King of kings. The waters on which the prostitute sits are nations. The ten horns will destroy the prostitute on God's authority, when God's word comes true. The woman is the great city which rules over the kings of the earth.

Now the picture becomes more complex in Chapter 18, as John then saw another angel, coming with great authority and splendour, who cried with a loud voice, "She has fallen! Great Babylon has fallen! She is haunted by demons and unclean spirits." Another voice in heaven then cried out, calling to God's people to come out from her to avoid being caught in her punishment, whilst the kings of the earth mourn her loss, because she had been the source of their revenue. The cause of the overriding punishment was, verse 24, "Because the blood of prophets and of God's people was found in the city; yes, the blood of all those who have been killed on earth."

Following this, Chapter 19, John heard, "what sounded like the roar of a large crowd of people in heaven, saying 'Praise God! Salvation, glory and power belong to our God!' Because the 'prostitute' had received her just reward." Which is followed by what is described as, "The Wedding Feast of the Lamb," in which Jesus is the bridegroom and the purified church, his bride. The bride's apparel is her good deeds and, presumably, the guests are the heavenly host, who rejoice. At this, John falls to his knees to worship the angel who brought the news, only to be told that he, the angel, is simply also a fellow servant.

Then John sees heaven open, and what he sees there is a white horse, whose rider is called, "Faithful and True." He brings justice and truth, the truth being, "The Word of God," and he is followed by an army of riders, also mounted on white horses. He, the rider, is named "King of kings and Lord of lords" (verse 16). And out of his mouth comes a sharp sword, which is the word of God. Then an angel calls together the forces of good and evil to a final conflict. The beast and the kings of the earth, are to fight the rider on the white horse armed with the Word of God, and in the battle, the evil forces are overthrown, defeated by the sword, the Word of God.

Now, Chapter 20, comes a period of one thousand years, during which the Devil, or Satan, is chained and thrown into the abyss. During this one-thousand-year period, the dead believers were brought to life to rule over the nations as kings, with Christ. The rest of the dead were not raised until after that period was over, at which time, the Devil is set free to go out to attempt to deceive the nations again. He will gather them to a final battle, before he is overthrown.

Then comes the Final Judgement, verse 11, as John sees a great white throne and the one who sits on it. He sees the dead, great and small, standing before the throne. Books were opened, and then another book was opened, the book of the living. The dead are then judged according to what they had done, from the records in the books. At this time, the sea gave up its dead, and death and the world of the dead give up their occupants. "And all were judged according to what they had done" (verse 13). Those whose names were not in the book of life were thrown into the "Lake of Fire, which is the second death."

Now, Chapter 21, John is shown the new heaven and the new earth, and the Holy City coming down out of heaven, adorned to meet her husband, the old heaven and earth having disappeared. The bride is the new Jerusalem, and the groom, Jesus Christ. We are then told that, verse 3, "God's home is with human beings! He will live with them, and they shall be his people." Here there will be no sorrow, no pain or grief, because the old things have passed away. Here there will be no place for evil, and there will be no death, verse 5, "Then the one who sits on the throne said, 'And now I make all things new!'" Then follows a vivid picture of the Bride, the wife of the Lamb, described as a holy city, glorious in dimensions and beauty, whose light is Jesus himself. Here, Chapter 22, are the life-giving waters, and the tree of life whose leaves are for the healing of the nations. Here is the throne of God and of the Lamb and the inhabitants, his people who serve him day and night because there is no darkness anymore.

The book and its vision conclude, verse 6, "These words are true and can be trusted. And the Lord God, who gives his Spirit to the prophets, has sent his angel to show his servants what must happen very soon." "'Listen!' says Jesus, 'I am coming soon! Happy are those who obey the prophetic words in this book' I, John, have seen and heard all these things!" He is then told not to keep these things secret.

And the book ends with solemn warnings to keep the faith, and the promise that Jesus will soon come. "The time is near when all this will happen." John also warns against adding to or detracting from these words. Anyone who does will incur the wrath of God. "So be it. Come, Lord Jesus."

9 781398 419438